Contemporary Scottish Poetry and the Natural World

Rodzicom

Contemporary Scottish Poetry and the Natural World

Burnside, Jamie, Robertson and White

Monika Szuba

EDINBURGH
University Press

Edinburgh University Press is one of the leading university presses in the UK. We publish academic books and journals in our selected subject areas across the humanities and social sciences, combining cutting-edge scholarship with high editorial and production values to produce academic works of lasting importance. For more information visit our website: edinburghuniversitypress.com

© Monika Szuba, 2019, 2021

Edinburgh University Press Ltd
The Tun – Holyrood Road, 12(2f) Jackson's Entry, Edinburgh EH8 8PJ

First published in hardback by Edinburgh University Press 2019

Typeset in 10.5/13 Adobe Sabon by
Servis Filmsetting Ltd, Stockport, Cheshire

A CIP record for this book is available from the British Library

ISBN 978 1 4744 5060 7 (hardback)
ISBN 978 1 4744 5061 4 (paperback)
ISBN 978 1 4744 5062 1 (webready PDF)
ISBN 978 1 4744 5063 8 (epub)

The right of Monika Szuba to be identified as the author of this work has been asserted in accordance with the Copyright, Designs and Patents Act 1988, and the Copyright and Related Rights Regulations 2003 (SI No. 2498).

Contents

Acknowledgements		vi
	Introduction	1
1.	Wandering in the Open World: Kenneth White's Poetics	25
2.	'Buried in the flesh': Home, Embodiment and Interanimality in John Burnside's Work	58
3.	'Gifts of the Wild': Dwelling, Temporality and Landscape in Kathleen Jamie's Writing	91
4.	'A word will set the seed / of life and death': Robin Robertson's Protean Lyric	122
Bibliography		159
Index		173

Acknowledgements

My deepest gratitude to Jean Ward, who provided me with valuable help and positive encouragement. I would also like to extend my gratitude to David Malcolm for his kind support over the years. My warm thanks to my colleagues at the Institute of English and American Studies, particularly Tomasz Wiśniewski, Mirosława Modrzewska, Maria Fengler, Arkadiusz Misztal and Magdalena Wawrzyniak-Śliwska.

I also wish to thank Tomasz Swoboda and Maciej Michalski, Deans of the Faculty of Languages at the University of Gdańsk, for funding that allowed me to finish this book.

My heartfelt thanks to Mary and Nigel Dower, who looked after me when I was a Bednarowski Trust fellow in Aberdeen in autumn 2015 and spring 2016.

Special thanks to Robin MacKenzie for inviting me to speak at 'Scotland in Translation', organised at St Andrews University (7 April 2017). I thank Nicole Anderson and Lynn Turner, the organisers of the 5th Derrida Today Conference hosted by Goldsmiths, University of London (8–11 June 2016), where I presented my views on interanimality in John Burnside's poetry. I am also grateful to the organisers of the biennial Association for the Study of Literature and Environment (UK & Ireland) (ASLE-UKI) conference 'Green Knowledge', which took place at the University of Cambridge (2–4 September 2015), and the 'Landscaping Change' conference at Bath Spa University (29–31 March 2016), during which I presented early versions of the chapter on Kathleen Jamie.

I am grateful to Michelle Houston of Edinburgh University Press for thinking that this would be a publishable book and for her enthusiasm and support, and to Ersev Ersoy, James Dale, Wendy Lee and Rebecca Mackenzie for their kind assistance.

I take this opportunity to thank Marta Salvesen for letting me use *Wind from Wind'ard* by Jon Schueler on the cover.

To my parents, Wanda and Jan Szuba, to whom this book is dedicated, I am deeply indebted.

Finally, I thank Julian Wolfreys, my first reader, who patiently looked through the many versions of the manuscript, and whose sensitive and thoughtful readings and insightful comments contributed so much to the book. For his profound belief in my work, invaluable advice, unwavering support and so much more – *bardzo dziękuję*.

Introduction

Poetry and the World

Poïesis – production, creation, making – transforms and continues the world where thought, matter and time are mediated and attuned in and for the human subject. Following a certain phenomenological discourse, about which there is more to be said in this Introduction, what I will be calling throughout this study the body–subject becomes integrated with the world. Thus, through making, *poïesis* connects the world of creation to the poetic human-made world, which is the rendering of the natural in form. Neither technical production nor creation in the Romantic sense, poetic work reconciles thought with matter and time, and self with the world. The process of *poïesis* consists in making visible without offering an abstract representation. It is making things manifest, or clearly revealed – from *manifestus*, plainly apprehensible, apparent – bringing them to view.

Poetry in general, and nature poetry in particular, is one mode of bearing witness to, and affirming, that immanence, overcoming the divergence between self and the natural world, or subject and object. *Contemporary Scottish Poetry and the Natural World* aims to offer an examination of human intertwining with the world as represented in the work of four contemporary Scottish authors: John Burnside, Kathleen Jamie, Robin Robertson and Kenneth White. It aims to explore the ways in which those poets engage with the natural world through artistic means, examining how the poetic imagination conspires with nature. Seeking to bring theoretical and philosophical insights to the close reading of poetry and, in turn, to make visible the philosophical work within the poetic meditation, it provides a phenomenological perspective, with a particular interest in Maurice Merleau-Ponty's writings on the subject's relation to the world, understood as a chiasmic human–non-human intertwining. Reading that particular aspect of nature poetry defined as ecopoetry will serve to deepen our understanding of the human subject as a non-dualistic Being, the locus of an intertwining between language and thought, self and the world, inside and outside, most prominently expressed in poetic form. Our understanding is deepened as poetry gives access to the truth of the world in a revelatory manner, poetry concerning self and world being an alethic modality of truth-telling and truth-making. It is through poetry that we feel the truth of the world, and it is this experience that Merleau-Ponty helps articulate so clearly. The main premises of Merleau-Pontyan phenomenology, including such concepts as flesh, the intertwining, chiasm, dehiscence and reversibility, are expounded in the section devoted to phenomenology in this Introduction. While acknowledging the work of other phenomenologists, chiefly Husserl and Heidegger, I focus here on Merleau-Ponty for two reasons. First, his philosophy of embodiment helps to illuminate poetic envisionings of the natural world. Second, in the last two decades at least in the field of ecocriticism, the work of Merleau-Ponty, not least his lectures on Nature, has had a profound impact, Louise Westling's sustained intervention with Merleau-Ponty in *The Logos of the Living World: Merleau-Ponty, Animals, and Language* (2013) being by no means the only reorientation, but amongst the most significant, along with the work of David Abram. Abram was the first to employ the philosophy of Merleau-Ponty, in a wide-ranging study that highlights the significance of the interdependence of humans with the natural world in various systems of thought. Both Heidegger and Merleau-Ponty tried to express 'a more immediate modality of awareness, a more primordial dimension' (1996: 206–7) that would allow for the non-dualistic inhabitation. Particularly relevant in this age of the Anthropocene, Westling's study illuminates semiotic links between human and non-human animals, highlighting the phenomenological participation in Being, originating in a pre-reflective experience and expressed in language. Approaching human relations with the natural world through the ontology of intertwining, *The Logos of the Living World* calls for a non-anthropocentric view of the world, foregrounding 'the proliferation of languages we are relearning to hear' (2013: 99). Westling, importantly, situates Merleau-Ponty's philosophy in current ecocritical considerations, arguing that it precedes some debates in animal studies and 'understands literature and the other human arts as part of a continuum of meaningful communications and aesthetic behaviours throughout the living world' (2013: 3).

I will be addressing other critics and philosophers throughout the readings of Scottish authors in the various chapters but, given that this study is primarily about literature, the subject and the landscape, I have chosen to focus on presenting the main threads in ecocritical thought, particularly its Romantic roots, as well as expounding phenomenological philosophy in order to frame and ground the readings that follow. Through an introduction to phenomenology in general and Merleau-Ponty's thought in particular, I will direct the reader toward a renewed as well as possibly a new appreciation of poetic language. I am not a Romanticist; nor do I wish to propose a study of post-Romantic poetry. As this is a book concerned with ecopoetry, however, I recognise the necessity to introduce Romantic ideas on nature, as, generally speaking, it can be suggested that modern thinking on the natural world starts with Romanticism and a lot of ecocritical thought is steeped in it. It is important to note here that the four poets on whom I focus very often challenge Romantic visions, largely offering a departure from such representations of nature where the descriptions of the natural world are the vehicle for the poet's ego.

The four Scottish poets on whom I have chosen to focus in this study embody this ability to unfold the self-world, intertwining in particularly powerful and intimate ways. I have selected poetic voices whose major preoccupations concern the phenomenological relation between the self and the environment. Phenomenally immersed in the immediate world, perceiving acutely and sensing other creatures, Kenneth White, John Burnside, Kathleen Jamie and Robin Robertson explore new ways of Being: a meaningful existence, transcending the limited and limiting separation between culture and nature. The manifold implications of such a dualistic distinction have been explored at length in environmental studies considering the nature/culture divide. The false divide strengthens the anthropocentric hierarchy whereby Man is 'the apex of creation' and is at the heart of anthropocentric thinking (that which might be said to render nature as the unthought of the Anthropocene). Such thinking has resulted in the strict post-Enlightenment separation between human cultural formations and the non-human world of beings and things. Seeking to transcend the dichotomy, the poets in question in this study move away from bardic, ego-based pretences, separating humans from the more-than-human world, to use David Abram's term (1996: 7). The world does not exist *for* these poets; they exist *with* and *in* it, their poetry a making and mediation, a *poïesis* and alethic figuring of the truth between the self and world. Aware that they form an inextricable part of it, they do not seek to lift themselves above the world in an egoistic gesture. They propose a renewed way of being in the world whereby humans co-exist with the environment, being organically intertwined. Widely understood, this poetry is concerned with how we interact with the world, which today seems more important than ever.

While the estrangement from the natural world seems to be ongoing, certain poets continue to focus on the importance of the sense of wonder and enchantment at being immersed in things, which is significant inasmuch as it introduces the reader to a renewal of perception. As John Burnside argues, 'It is to nature that they owe their first allegiance, it is to nature they belong, and to the "wild etiquette" proposed by Gary Snyder as a way, not only of living well with other creatures but also of preserving *our own* connection, wherever we are, with the earth's music' (Burnside 2003: 5). In *The Practice of the Wild*, Gary Snyder writes about 'tawny grammar', a term he takes from Henry David Thoreau's essay 'Walking' (1861), 'this wild and dusky knowledge, *Gramatica parda*, tawny grammar'. Snyder adds, 'The grammar not only of language, but of culture and civilization itself, is of the same order as this mossy little forest creek, this desert cobble' (1990: 83). Demonstrated in the work of the four poets in this study, such an understanding of the world, foregrounding the relation of the self with the landscape and other beings, points to many directions: American transcendentalism, Zen Buddhism, a post-Romantic sensibility, phenomenology and environmental literary criticism. In recognition of the significance of these influences, in the further sections of the Introduction I will explore some of these strands: namely, the Romantic heritage, ecocritical contexts and phenomenological philosophy, turning to the other dimensions in subsequent chapters as their significance surfaces.

Some readers might be forgiven for thinking that I spend too much time, giving too much detail to the close reading of the poetry in this volume. The reasons for this, however, are two-fold. On the one hand, there is not, as yet, a sufficient body of critical work on the poets in question, particularly from philosophical perspectives – which close reading can aid and serve to illuminate, as well as being illuminated by – and on the other hand, given the close involvement of the poets with landscape, environment and the natural world, it is important to take one's time in reading the poetry and to unpack formal elements and various epistemological connections in order to show how such poetry not only represents or depicts the world, as if it stood outside it, but is a material expression, an enactment of that world, and the subject's apprehension of and enfolding within that, through language.

This study is not concerned with a revision of Western literary representations of external reality but it is perhaps necessary at this point to take a stance in the discussion concerning the 'idea of nature'. Needless to say, 'nature' (or 'Nature') is a fraught and much-debated term, and so all its implications cannot be discussed here. After all, what is it if not 'a twelve-thousand-year structure, a structure that seems so real we call it Nature' (Morton 2016: 5), 'a concept of a something, a thing of some kind, "over yonder"' (Morton 2010: 3). Being a construct of society, politics, science and technology, as Bruno Latour suggests (1993: 144), 'Nature' is composed of hybrids, or that locus where 'every hybrid is a mixture of two pure forms' (Latour 1993: 76). Latour proposes a synthesis whereby there occurs 'a preliminary purification, a divided separation, and a progressive reblending' (Latour 1993: 76). Such a reblending, leading to a phenomenological fusion of the self with the world, occurs in the work of the four poets at the centre of this study and thus the term will be employed in this manner here.

Related to the problematic term is another question: namely, that of naming the movement in poetry that deals with the relation between the self and the natural world. This poses a problem. All proposed labels – landscape poetry, nature poetry, nature writing, new nature writing, green poetry, ecopoetry, ecological poetry, environmental poetry – create a sense of discomfort. For Gary Snyder, being called 'a nature poet' is 'the kiss of death'. As he says, 'Being called a nature poet is like being called a woman poet, as if it were a lower grade of writing, and one based in romanticism. I am a poet who has preferred not to distinguish in poetry between nature and humanity' (Goodyear 2008: n.p.). What he says might apply to all four poets here. For Kenneth White, poetry is about openness to the world where narrow categories do not apply. John Burnside and Kathleen Jamie have expressed their disagreement at being categorised as nature poets. There are 'many labels that critics like to hang on Burnside – green poet, nature poet, mystical poet, Scottish poet, religious poet – but he refuses to be identified as any of these' (Dósa 2009a: 113), and Burnside himself agrees to just three labels: 'I'm happy to call myself a green poet or an environmental poet or an ecological poet, but not a nature poet. I'm not a Scottish poet and I'm not a religious poet. These are not useful labels for me' (Dósa 2009a: 126). A name that Burnside suggests is 'ecological poet' and an 'ecologically-*mindful* poet' (Crawford 2006: 99). Jonathan Bate offers a term, 'ecopoem', which he understands as a 'post-phenomenological inflection of high Romantic poetics' (2000: 262). The problem with Bate's reading is that it fails to account for difference in his attempted recuperation of certain later poets, such as those discussed in the present volume, within an epoch that ignores the fact that Romanticism might have little or nothing to do with their work – indeed, that phenomenology might have little or nothing to do with Romanticism as conceived in such historical–literary constructs as Bate's.

Tom Bristow's 'the poetry of the *oikos*' foregrounds the importance of place, embeddedness in the land and rootedness in a location. An ancient Greek term denoting home, family and environment, *oikos* lies at the basis of *oikopoetics* – ecopoetics – concerned with learning how to dwell on earth. 'In an Anthropocene context,' Bristow argues, '*oikos* means the domicile of a planet, or planetary house (2015: 127). 'The proper dwelling plight', as Heidegger puts it, is a preoccupation that pervades the work of the four poets at the centre of this book. In the process of *poïesis*, *oikos* becomes intertwined with *logos*, the language employed by poets. Marked with 'green consciousness', to use Buell's term (1995: 31), their poetry of the *oikos* recognises the necessity to renegotiate our place in the natural world through acts of representation that are also acts of making. As this concern became particularly pronounced in Romanticism and was further developed by modern environmental studies, in the next part of the Introduction I will offer a brief overview of both fields.

Romanticism and Ecocriticism

As ecological writing in the twentieth and twenty-first centuries is inevitably immersed in a post-Romantic thought, and the poets discussed in this study continue in many significant ways to challenge the Romantic tradition, it is necessary to present a brief overview of the movement, particularly attitudes to the natural world, before exploring their work. Understood broadly, the relationship between humankind and environment has been explored in literature since 'primeval days', as Francis T. Palgrave puts it in the Introduction to *Landscape and Poetry: From Homer to Tennyson* (1897: 1). In Western literature, the Homeric model provided in *The Odyssey* offers the earliest representation of this relation in the form of a man's struggle with the sea and the elements. Throughout the ages, the relationship has taken various forms but it was not until the end of the eighteenth century that it was reconsidered in depth when the *topos* of nature and the phenomenon of environmentalism in literature became prominent: 'Nature' came to the fore. The relationship between nature and imagination was at the centre of Romantic poetry, accompanying political and social upheaval. As Nicholas Roe argues, 'in the early 1790s nature and political revolution were two mutually sustaining ideals, to be fulfilled – depending on one's viewpoint – in a universal democracy, or at the millennium which would lead to Christ's rule on earth' (1992: 2). He argues that, in Romanticism, politics, nature and the imagination were inextricably combined, foregrounding 'the historical force of nature in politics and poetry of the revolutionary period' (1992: 3). Their political engagement meant that Romantic poets could be conceived as proto-environmentalists, demonstrating an emerging awareness of the importance and, at the same time, the gradual loss of a coherent sense of place. The poetics of sensibility ushered in by Romanticism continues to have a bearing on poetry concerned with the relation of the self and the world. Romantic conceptions of nature, freedom, beauty and wilderness continue to be present in ecopoetry and environmental studies, offering reflections on the engaged response to the natural world. Concerned with the connection between Romantic literatures and the environment, the critical movement is variously named: 'Romantic ecology', 'environmental Romanticism' or 'green Romanticism'. British Romanticism proves to be a 'fertile and varied ground for ecocritical revisionism' (Buell 2005: 3). In his pioneering study *Romantic Ecology: Wordsworth and the Environmental Tradition*, published in 1991, Jonathan Bate established the association between British Romanticism and ecocriticism, clearing the path for discussions of poetry concerned with the correspondence between the self and the natural world. As Lawrence Buell puts it, Bate's book on Wordsworth 'inaugurated British ecocriticism' (2005: 3). It opened the field to many discussions on the subject of environmental Romanticism, provoking numerous critical discussions and debates. It is necessary to note that links between ecology and British Romanticism were suggested much earlier by Karl Kroeber, in his essay '"Home at Grasmere": Ecological Holiness' (1974: 132–41). Highlighting the significance of dwelling in the creation of a sense of wholeness that he recognises in Wordsworth's writing, Kroeber thus makes a highly valuable point in the development of environmental literary criticism. He develops the argument in his study *Ecological Literary Criticism: Romantic Imagining and the Biology of Mind* (1995), in which he points to Romanticism as an age when ecological thinking began. Timothy Clark offers a critique of such a view, suggesting that modern ecological thinking began earlier, in the mid-eighteenth century (2011: 16). Nonetheless, it can be said that the ecological views that emerged in the Romantic age, particularly a sense of alienation from the natural world and an urge to re-establish wholeness and unity, can be perceived in green writing today. Other important contributions to environmental Romanticism include *Green Writing: Romanticism and Ecology* (2000), in which James C. McKusick examines the ways in which British Romantic poets influenced the American environmental movement. Onno Oerlemans expands the discussion on Romantic proto-ecologists, placing Wordsworth, Shelley and other Romantic poets, as well as artists and thinkers, in a material context of the physical world, arguing that 'consciousness can no more escape being "interpellated" by landscape than it can by social forces' (2002: 209).

Offering 'a "green" mode of reading' (2002: 13), Oerlemans articulately enlarges the ecocritical discourse of Romantic understandings of nature. In an excellent study grounded in continental philosophy, *Topographies of the Sacred: The Poetics of Place in European Romanticism* (2004), Kate Rigby explores the wider-ranging implications of the rediscovery of nature by Romantic poets and thinkers. Dewey W. Hall's two books, both published in 2016 and offering a transatlantic view, merit attention: *Romantic Naturalists, Early Environmentalists: An Ecocritical Study, 1789–1912*, and an edited collection of essays, *Romantic Ecocriticism: Origins and Legacies*. All the studies mentioned above foreground connections between various versions of green Romantic thought, forming bridges between the British Isles, continental Europe and America. This is in no way an exhaustive list, as the number of publications in the field of green Romanticism continues to grow exponentially, demonstrating the fertility of this strand in contemporary critical studies; Romantic understandings of nature have a bearing on contemporary environmental ethics and environmentalist activism, and thus inevitably influence ecological literary criticism.

As a study of literature and environment, several strands of ecocritical thought have evolved from Romantic scholarship. For the purposes of this study, it is particularly important to note that one of the most significant developments has been a reconsideration of a subject–object relation, as well as the emergence of a deepened understanding of the significance of place, which has had a bearing on the modern ecocritical discourse. Rigby notes that environmental criticism has looked to Romanticism for 'the new ways of view in and valuing, representing and relating to the natural world that emerged during this period' (2014: 62). As Kevin Hutchings puts it, 'One of ecocriticism's basic premises is that literature both reflects and helps to shape human responses to the natural environment' (2007: 172). Thus another vital Romantic legacy for the discussion in this study is how Romanticism re-evaluated the significance of place, affecting the ways we perceive it. Timothy Morton suggests further that environmental Romanticism recognised that a 'coherent sense of place' was being eroded by globalisation (2007: 84), and as a result our sense of place has been undermined. Similarly, Ursula K. Heise notes that 'The rhetoric of place has now been absorbed into some strains of ecocritical research' (2008: 8), urging the development of 'eco-cosmopolitanism'. As a result, an important concern of post-Romantic poetry is the idea of place: the understandings of the local and the global, the sacred and profane, the everyday and the mundane.

Similar to environmental Romanticism, ecocriticism proves to be a highly fertile field of study, producing numerous books and articles that re-examine literary texts in the light of contemporary ecological debates. It is not the aim of this study to offer an exhaustive account of its history and development. Thus what follows is a very brief overview of the most significant publications. Two early studies – Leo Marx's *The Machine in the Garden: Technology and the Pastoral Ideal in America* (1964) in America and Raymond Williams's *The Country and the City* (1975) in Britain – inaugurated debates on pastoral and post-pastoral, fuelling considerations of the rural and the urban. At the beginning, the movement developed more robustly on American soil. Several founding works of environmental ecology appeared in the 1970s: Joseph Meeker's *The Comedy of Survival: Literary Ecology and a Play Ethic* (1974) and William Rueckert's 'Literature and Ecology: An Experiment in Ecocriticism' (1978). John Elder's *Imagining the Earth: Poetry and the Vision of Nature* (1985) opened the field for the analysis of poetry in the context of literary ecology. A real boom in this area started in the early 1990s with publications by Lawrence Buell, John Elder, Karl Kroeber and Scott Slovic in America, and Jonathan Bate in Britain. Leonard M. Scigaj's *Sustainable Poetry: Four American Ecopoets* (1999) merits special attention, as it offers an early application of phenomenology in environmental criticism. Exploring ecological thought in poetry, Scigaj's phenomenological readings focus on four contemporary American ecopoets (A. R. Ammons, Wendell Berry, W. S. Merwin and Gary Snyder). As he argues, in the second half of the twentieth century there emerged poets who demonstrate a 'sustainable' approach to literature and environment, not focusing solely on language but expanding their interest to the natural world, stating that poetry that 'addresses our connection to the natural world has enjoyed a renaissance' (1999: 7). He believes that these poets explore the ways in which people relate to the natural world, where nature serves not as a background but as something that 'sustains human, as well as non-human life' (1999: 7). Published in 1996, Cheryll Glotfelty's and Harold Fromm's anthology, *The Ecocriticism Reader: Landmarks in Literary Ecology*, gathers essays on ecotheory, as well as discussions of literary texts that demonstrate the potential of this field of study. The first edited collection of essays on literature and environment, presenting a varied choice, *Writing the Environment: Ecocriticism and Literature* (1998), edited by Richard Kerridge and Neil Sammells, highlights a vast array of critical positions, including ecofeminism and deep ecology. Since then, the field has been characterised by a dynamism in Britain too, with notable publications by Timothy Clark, Greg Garrard, Terry Gifford, Kate Rigby and Kate Soper.

A leading voice in the field, Lawrence Buell prefers the term 'environmental criticism' to 'ecocriticism', which, he argues, 'better captures the interdisciplinary mix of literature-and-environment studies, which has always drawn on the human as well as the natural sciences and in recent years cross-pollinated more with cultural studies than with the sciences' (2005: viii). According to Buell, there are several criteria for 'the 'environmental text': 'the nonhuman environment is present not merely as a framing device but as a presence that begins to suggest that human history is implicated in natural history', the text does not place humans at the centre, it bears 'ethical orientation', and finally, it demonstrates an understanding of the environment as process (1995: 6–8).

Demonstrating 'an essential and virtuous *wildness*' (Burnside 2014: 38), the work of many Scottish writers challenges and transcends national and regional definitions. Thus, it is vital to contextualise Scottish literature in general, and contemporary Scottish poetry in particular, more broadly in literary and philosophical traditions in order to open it up more fully and go beyond narrow nationalistic categories. It is also vital to undertake such work in order to apprehend, and so impress upon the reader, the singularity of a Scottish ecopoetics. Hence I argue that poetry focused on the subject's relation to the world, a chiasmic human–non-human intertwining, is an expression of a philosophy grounded in phenomenological thoughts, particularly that thinking pursued in the Merleau-Pontyan concept of intertwining and the Heideggerian concept of dwelling. By widening the theoretical field, my aim is to propose a manner of discussing poetry that negotiates environmental humanities, phenomenology and the work of a number of philosophers and thinkers such as Jane Bennett, Jacques Derrida, Gilles Deleuze and Félix Guattari, Luce Irigaray, Immanuel Kant, Emmanuel Levinas, Catherine Malabou, Jeff Malpas and David Wills. While the significance of Derrida's thought to environmental humanities is now recognised, with books such as *Eco-Deconstruction: Derrida and Environmental Philosophy* (Fritsch et al. 2018), other thinkers may not seem an obvious choice. In the next section of the Introduction, I shall expound the ideas of phenomenology in order to attempt to demonstrate the significance of the ideas to the reading of contemporary poetry.

Phenomenology and the Natural World

I shall explain, in this section on phenomenology, the natural connection between philosophy and the world; also, I will direct the reader to the importance of the Scottish poetry in question. In a reading of texts concerned with dwelling, where the self and the world become intertwined, phenomenology seems to be the necessary place to turn after the brief explanation of the significance of Romantic and environmental thought. I will broaden out the discussion of phenomenology beyond Merleau-Ponty, though I wish to retain his significance, given his writings on nature, and what he calls wild Being. I will, however, acknowledge and seek support from the phenomenological tradition, through Husserl and Heidegger (the latter is particularly important to John Burnside's way of seeing the world, with the question of 'dwelling' being at the forefront), and other phenomenological thinkers, or in those areas where there is a cross-over between phenomenology, poetry and ecocriticism (as mentioned above, Louise Westling's work is particularly significant here). The field of phenomenology is not a single one; huge, diverse, and often marked by internal disagreements, arguments and contradictions, it would be misleading to present a model of phenomenology as all-inclusive. Thus, I will seek to justify why I choose particular strands in phenomenological discourse, as these are pertinent to the question of the world, and representing the landscape and natural world in the work of the poets in question.

Human experience is inextricably bound with the natural world. We define ourselves through it, and engage with it through our senses: a dialogue, an exchange – a dialogic exchange – occurs between us and our *Umwelt*,[1] wherein both elements find their place. 'Place is temporal, but it is also spatial (and so also stands in an essential relation to body),' to use Jeff Malpas's words (2006: 63). Interlaced in an intimate relationship, human beings co-exist with other living beings, as well as with inanimate ones. As a study of the appearance of things, and our experiential involvement, phenomenology explores the manner in which they come to our experience and assume meanings for us. Widely concerned with lived experience, study methods include description, hermeneutics, analysis and interpretation. Focusing on the subjective experience, phenomenology studies perception, cognition, thought, memory and imagination, among other things, all of which show the ways in which we are directed towards the world. An important aspect of phenomenological investigations, bodily awareness, including temporal and spatial awareness, self-reflexivity and embodied action, all form part of our Being in the lifeworld.

In 1913, Edmund Husserl published *Ideen zu einer reinen Phänomenologie und phänomenologischen Philosophie: Buch 1, Allgemeine Einführung in die reine Phänomenologie* (translated into English as *Ideas: General Introduction to Pure Phenomenology* and first published in 1931), which became a founding text for the phenomenological movement. Phenomenology foregrounds the relational account of experience. As Husserl posits, our experience is 'intentional' – that is, directed toward the world, filtering things through particular ideas and images, which then endow the experience with significance, different from things and their true meaning: 'It is then to this world, *the world in which I find myself and which is also my world-about-me*, that the complex forms of my manifold and shifting *spontaneities* of consciousness stand related' (2012: 53). Through 'the act of the Ego' and my reactions towards it, 'I become acquainted with the world as immediately given to me, through spontaneous tendencies to turn towards it and to grasp it' (Husserl 2012: 53). Part of this 'wakeful' living, as Husserl puts it, is self-reflexivity, as 'I am present to myself continually as someone who perceives, represents, thinks, feels, desires' (Husserl 2012: 54). There constantly occurs an exchange between myself and the world as 'the natural world, the world in the ordinary sense of the word, is constantly there for me, so long as I live naturally and look in its direction' (Husserl 2012: 54). The world remains 'present' for me to perceive and experience it. Even if it is differently apprehended by other people, there exists an intersubjective aspect to this experience.

Following Husserl, Martin Heidegger investigates everyday experience to reveal the transcendental. For Heidegger, phenomenology is hermeneutic, its role being to offer an interpretation of Being, which occurs through language through which our fundamental relation with the world takes place. According to him, philosophical language is inadequate in uncovering the world; it is only through the language of poetry that *aletheia*, or 'unconcealment', may happen, leading to 'disclosure of beings through which an openness essentially unfolds' (1993: 127). His writings, gathered in the collection *Poetry, Language, Thought* and including 'The Thinker as Poet', 'What Are Poets For?', 'Language' and 'Building Dwelling Thinking', are particularly pertinent for this study. In 'Building Dwelling Thinking', Heidegger emphasises the importance of learning how to dwell properly: we '*must ever learn to dwell*' (2013a: 159; original emphasis), he insists, because how we dwell on earth is who we are. To dwell is to be situated, to maintain a relationship with the world, as 'dwelling itself is always a staying with things. Dwelling, as preserving, keeps the fourfold in that with which mortals stay: in things' (2013a: 150–1). As he explains, '*The fundamental character of dwelling is this sparing and preserving*' (2013a: 147; original emphasis). These two words – 'preserving' and 'sparing' (as well as their grammatical forms), used by Heidegger to describe the necessary nature of human interaction with the world, point to a sustainable relationship and suggest that dwelling is a process that is constantly renewed, a becoming together with other beings and things. As he argues, 'to preserve' and 'to spare' means to 'take under our care', as the world 'must be kept safe'

(2013a: 149). We should cultivate, 'nurse and nurture the things that grow' (2013a: 149). Finally, dwelling is a manner of being on Earth, a path leading to a free, authentic Being: 'To dwell, to be set at peace, means to remain at peace within the free, the preserve, the free sphere that safeguards each thing in its nature' (2013a: 147). In order to see the world 'in its essential being, its presencing' (2013a: 149), we should approach it with a refreshed perception, unveiling its essence.

Influenced by Husserl and Heidegger, Maurice Merleau-Ponty developed his own phenomenological discourse, which he understood as the 'study of essences' (1962: i): that is, the essential meanings of phenomena, or what appears to us (1962: vii). In his late writings, particularly his unfinished work, *The Visible and the Invisible*, published posthumously, his concern with our interaction in the world offers a significant shift in the understanding and reception of phenomenology (and especially Edmund Husserl's thought) in post-war continental philosophy. *The Visible and the Invisible* opens with the philosopher challenging our seeing of the world: what it is that we see – 'We see the things themselves, the world is what we see' (1968: 1) – who are we, what this world is, and finally, what seeing is. By inaugurating his study with this unequivocal statement and its emphasis on vision and the world, Merleau-Ponty invites us to be watchful and vigilant. The question of vision returns throughout his study, its role explored and expanded in reference to his previous analyses. The world is what we see, yet what occurs during the act of seeing goes beyond this seemingly simple statement. As with time, which seems familiar to everyone but is inexplicable, so it is with the world, the philosopher argues. Replete with wonder, the world remains unknowable as a totality. It is concealed, hidden from us, covered as if by a veil. Poetry – *poïesis* – makes possible the impossible: that is, the alethic figuring of a truth through revelation, a lifting of the veil, language becoming the performative analogical apperception of the world as it is, to use Husserl's term.[2] We grasp the part that allows us to know the whole. Yet everything is 'waiting for you to notice it' (Rilke 2009: 32): the world invites us to see its things, its objects, and engage with them. We may say that we are, in a way, created in that moment as the visible constitutes the seer. The work of poetry constitutes a bringing forth of the truth of the world, a speaking of the world. This is not a static experience, for, as they appear to us, things open a dialogue. Simultaneously, our perception reveals to us a gap, what the philosopher calls an *écart*, translated as 'divergence', 'spread', 'deviation' or 'separation'.

In his revision of the phenomenological work of Edmund Husserl,[3] Maurice Merleau-Ponty developed his philosophy of Being against the philosophy of oppositions, as, according to him, contradictions are the 'ruin of philosophy' (1968: 183), undermining the supremacy of the cogito and its illusory separation from the world. In Merleau-Pontyan phenomenology, 'we are our bodies' (Carman 2014: xii), a vision that makes a detachment of mind from body, as well as subject from object, impossible. He does not separate the mental from the physical. He sees Being as a dialogic relationship of the embodied subject with the world, the former not standing outside but corporeally, sensorially entangled. Thus, through an ontology of the intertwining, or the chiasm, Merleau-Ponty's phenomenology is an exploration of an embodied intersubjectivity, an incarnate life whereby the body orients the subject in the world through an envelopment with it; our flesh and the flesh of the world, the former self-sensing and the latter sensible, intertwine.

Being and the world are at the heart of Merleau-Ponty's phenomenology. He strives to describe a *corps-sujet*, the body-subject, immersed in a *Lebenswelt*, or lifeworld, which is irreducible to any representation, because the subject of the lifeworld is the experience of being alive, or the 'lived-through-world' (1964: 71). His 'ontology of brute Being' (1968: 165), where brute or wild Being, a Husserlian term, is the originary source of the sense, is an attempt to access the infinity of *Lebenswelt*, through uncovering 'layers of wild being' (1968: 178). Merleau-Ponty associated wild or brute Being with the domain of pre-reflective experience. Thus wild Being is 'silent knowing', 'a pre-knowing' (1968: 178) occurring at the level of the human body. Being immersed in the 'environment of brute existence and essence is not something mysterious: we never quit it, we have no other environment' (1968: 117).

Bodily perception is, in effect, Merleau-Ponty's concern in a large majority of his writings. In order to expound his phenomenological ontology, he develops a set of concepts such as flesh, chiasm, dehiscence, reversibility and *logos*, which will be defined below. All these terms are important in the present study, as they constitute a foundation for understanding our corporeal intertwining with the world.

Sense is rooted in sensual experience resulting from our corporeal presence in the world, and this is most often apprehensible in the manner of poetry's foregrounding of the world through the subject's perception and linguistic proximity. Through the chiasmic intertwining of beings, humans become embodied sense-givers. Drawing repeatedly on Husserl, Merleau-Ponty assumes that Being becomes endowed with meaning only in the moment of a self's realisation of connectedness to the world (1968: 172). For Husserl, the body is fundamentally 'a bearer of sensations ... a thing "inserted" between the rest of the material world and the "subjective" sphere' (Husserl 2012: 161, qtd in Carman

1999: 212). Thought and sensation can occur only through engaging with the world in a sensual, bodily way, as our body is 'a means of communication with the world' (Reynolds 2004: 11). Sensations bridge the lacunae of alterity as the becoming subject strives to transcend the fragmentation of experience. As Merleau-Ponty writes, 'The body unites us directly with the things through its own ontogenesis [the origin and development], by welding to one another the two outlines of which it is made' (1968: 136), where the two outlines are its sensible nature and openness. Thus, the body is a thing among things, it is of things (1968: 137): we are not separate from the world, we are *of* the world. Everything – all beings – is interlaced, forming the fabric of the world.

Merleau-Ponty foregrounds how the body is part of the visible, a belonging that enables it to see and 'open forth' (1968: 154), where seeing is an act of opening. *Offenheit*, or openness, suggesting a mutual inherence of things, is a concept he borrows from Husserl, who employs it to describe our relation to the earth, the opening of our bodies to the world. For Merleau-Ponty, it is a reciprocal relationship: as we are open to the world, the world is open to us. In order to describe that movement, he employs the concept of 'dehiscence'.[4] A term employed in botany, dehiscence means the opening of flower buds or fungi when they are ready to release their content. The spilling that occurs as a result may send the seeds or spores out and into the world. Thus the body's 'coupling with the flesh of the world' (1968: 144) enriches the latter, while 'floating in Being with another life ... making itself the outside of its inside and the inside of its outside' (1968: 144), it immerses the body in intersubjectivity. Our corporeal existence consists in what Cary Wolfe calls 'our readiness to be vulnerable to other knowledges in our embodiment of our own' (2003: 5). Living creaturely lives, we are open to other beings.

In *The Visible and the Invisible*, Merleau-Ponty develops his ideas on the relationship between the consciousness and the world, which he analyses in *Phenomenology of Perception*, and introduces one of the fundamental concepts in his thought: namely, that of 'flesh'. In order to explain it, the term 'element' can be used, in the same sense that we

> speak of water, air, earth, and fire, that is, in the sense of a *general thing*, midway between the spatio-temporal individual and the idea, a sort of incarnate principle that brings a style of being wherever there is a fragment of being. The flesh is in this sense an 'element' of Being. (1968: 139)

Merleau-Ponty's phenomenological ontology finds an application in various, sometimes quite disparate areas: for example, deep ecology, biosemiotics, medical anthropology, psychoanalysis, psychiatry and the cognitive sciences. In recent years his philosophy has become influential in the burgeoning field of ecocriticism, many scholars having noted and extended its usefulness in describing the human relation with the world. Louise Westling's book, already acknowledged, which employs Merleau-Ponty's phenomenological model in the analysis of cross-species affinity, remains the most comprehensive study, but we must also mention David Abram's *The Spell of the Sensuous: Perception and Language in a More-Than-Human World* (1996), Suzanne L. Cataldi and William S. Harrick's *Merleau-Ponty and Environmental Philosophy* (2007) and Kelly Elizabeth Sultzbach's *Ecocriticism in the Modernist Imagination* (2016).

But why is Merleau-Ponty's phenomenological ontology important to understanding the Scottish poets of this study? One might ask, why Scottish poets? As I have demonstrated in this Introduction, poetry is readable as the most intimate reflexive mediation of the real that reveals in its elliptical force the connectedness to the world. Scottish poets – particularly the four poets in question – connect to the real with a seemingly unparalleled, not to say almost pre-cognitive immediacy that gives the subject and language over to a mediation, with the minimal interference of an ego. They write about human attunement with, and the becoming-enfolded in, the world, the relation between human beings and the landscape, their *Umwelt*. Even if the poetic representation of the world is a construct, poems make the world we feel. The self is intimately entwined in and mediated by place in a phenomenological relationship, and mediates it in turn. As Axel Goodbody and Kate Rigby aptly put it, 'Poetry depicts and produces atmospheres, evoking bodily responses' (2011: 9). Corporeally entwined in between the leaves of the world, the Scottish poets in question tap into its tacit language to sing its song. Through their work, they demonstrate an organic and intimate interrelation between the self and the world, foregrounding their lived relationship to the landscape, and the intertwining with the natural world, including relations with other beings.

About this Book

'Remarkably varied', Scottish literature is full of oppositions and antitheses, and comes 'under the stress of foreign influence, almost a zigzag of contradictions', as George Gregory Smith puts it in his landmark essay (1919: 4), *Scottish Literature, Character and Influence*. That is certainly one way of seeing the richness of the literature produced in Scotland. As Smith argues, 'disorderly order is order' (1919: 5): an ecosystem, an organic whole, unified in its diversity. Reflecting on these words, Burnside suggests that it is

> the more-than-human order that will sometimes seem disorderly, and even destructive to us – is the only true and organic order (an implicit, spontaneous, unplanned orderliness we have come to associate with emergence, which is to say, with a new and more generous idea of natural law). (2014: 39)

In a constant state of becoming, Scottish literature resembles a mesh, to use Timothy Morton's term. As he writes, first asking and then answering his own question,

> Yet what is this whole if not a flowing, shifting, entangled mess of ambiguous entities – entities that become even more ambiguous the closer we look? The whole . . . is a mesh, a very curious, radically open form without center or edge. (2011: 22)

This image, alluding to Darwin's 'entangled bank' and employed by Morton to describe the environment, may well serve to describe Scottish literature as a whole.[5] Indeed, it is undeniable that all literature is just this rhizomic entanglement. But, starting with a literature, with that particularity I am calling Scottish ecopoetics that immediately exceeds its national bounds in its singularity, provides the good reader with an exemplary model *par excellence* for learning how to read again, as if from the start – both literature and the world.

Given the number of Scottish poets concerned with the natural world and the ever-burgeoning but already well-established field of ecocriticism, it is surprising that there do not exist more studies devoted to environmental readings of Scottish literary texts.[6] Louisa Gairn's pioneering book, *Ecology and Modern Scottish Literature* (2008), remains the only one, to my knowledge. A broad survey of modern Scottish literature, it started an important discussion on the subject, without exhausting it. Gairn aptly notes that 'writing about the natural world is a vital component of a diverse Scottish literature' (2008: 1). Focusing on fiction, travel writing and poetry, it offers re-readings in the light of environmental criticism of such authors as Robert Louis Stevenson, Hugh MacDiarmid, Edwin Morgan and Alan Warner. It ambitiously covers a large number of topics, including farming and civilisation, the Highland Clearances, hunting, mass media and interdisciplinarity, sometimes at the cost of a deepened literary analysis. Wide-ranging, *Ecology and Modern Scottish Literature* does not exhaust the subject of the relations between the self and the natural world; in effect, as the author admits in the Introduction, the study 'is not intended to be an exhaustive survey' (2008: 3). Nevertheless, it is a very important attempt to place Scottish literature in a broader context of contemporary ecological debates.

All four poets in question here write within the Scottish tradition, yet they exceed it in fascinating ways, reaching for European, American and Asian literary and philosophical framing, thus greatly expanding the context of their writing. While there are many important poets writing in Scotland today, the four authors of my study arguably present significant bodies of work and have garnered enough critical recognition, yet they have not been given serious consideration from a sustained philosophical, and particularly an ecophenomenological perspective. The four authors selected for this volume – Burnside, Jamie, Robertson and White – present in their writing an array of relationships to landscape as each proposes a different engagement with the natural world, with the use of various means such as language, style and form, but in a manner that significantly extends beyond mere formal concerns, with which the reader must always start, and to which the reader must always return, in order to be grounded in the world, the emotional, imaginative and always real landscape of Scottish poetry.

The title of this study requires explanation as it includes words that may be considered problematic and/or controversial. The first of these words is 'Scottish'. My aim is not to make a case for Scottish exceptionalism. The exploration of the phenomenological potentiality of four contemporary Scottish poets does not depend on claims for this as a feature unique to Scottish poetry. The Scottish context of this study is not insignificant, but it does not seek to argue for a narrow national context; rather, it aims to recognise wider features in the modern Scottish literary landscape. Thus the book is not about the Scottish landscape but rather about a highly distinctive manner of responding to the world. Yet, the work of John Burnside, Kathleen Jamie, Robert Robertson and Kenneth White proves a good source for a poetic manifestation of experiencing a landscape with its organic and elemental aspects, which reveals ways of thinking the self and world.

Another highly problematic component of the title is the term 'natural world'. One of the reasons why the phrase poses problems is the fact that, being a construct, 'the natural world' is a human epistemological concept. To use it without self-reflection – indeed, to think of 'nature' without reflection – is to fall into binary thought and so that static impasse of self/other that Merleau-Ponty's thought seeks to overcome, and which the poetry discussed in this book realises. By employing the term 'natural world' in the title of this study, I do not mean to suggest that I wish thus to separate humans from the rest of the world. (Raymond Williams notices that whenever some people speak of nature, they 'often contrast it with the world of humans and their relationships' [1980: 67].) The phrase 'natural world' is provisional and so whenever it is used in this study, it is accompanied by invisible quotation marks, which flag the many concerns regarding it. At times I replace it with the 'non-human' or 'more-than-human world', or, more narrowly, 'the living world', neither of which seems to be a fully satisfactory choice.

A final clarification concerns the choice of texts. With the exception of Robin Robertson, all the authors discussed in this study combine writing poetry with prose, which I consider essential to their work, and so the discussion of poems is often accompanied by and complemented with references to their essays.

Contemporary Scottish Poetry and the Natural World: Burnside, Jamie, Robertson and White focuses on close, ecophenomenological readings of the work of the four poets, aimed at exploring the ways in which their poetry seeks to reconcile the self with the world, integrating the numinous in the landscape. The pronounced nature of the land's sway over their work contributes to a unique ecopoetics, infusing it with 'secularised reverence' (Nicholson 2009: 82); this expression, employed to describe Robertson's work, may be extended to apply to the other poets here. White, Burnside and Robertson have resided outside Scotland (White in France, Burnside in Germany, Robertson in England), yet all remain imaginatively grounded in Scotland, attached to the land in its geological form, and to light in its northern inflection. Appreciating the complexity of regional and linguistic contexts, I wish to argue that even if, in this poetry, the subject position entails the local rather than the national, all the four poets discussed in this book, even if they are in different many ways, share what Robert Louis Stevenson called 'a strong Scotch [sic] accent of the mind' (1887: 1): the accent inflected, or perhaps even spoken, by the land. They challenge the national and nationalistic, the historical and representational idea of Scotland. How do these poets transcend the containment of national identity? Demanding a constant national and territorial definition, Scottishness, for the poets discussed here, offers a possibility to move beyond a narrow sense of a national subjectivity as all of them move beyond the Scottish context. As Robertson admits, the sense of place is 'absolutely crucial', something that draws him to north-eastern part of Scotland where he grew up: 'there is something about trying to get back to that beach where I walked' (Wroe 2008: n.p.). Among the four poets, Kathleen Jamie uses Scots, the language, the most frequently, writing poems that are not limited to 'Scottish matters'. She realises the political implications of such a linguistic choice, as for her 'it seems to come with a little political baggage attached. A tartan suitcase!' It can nevertheless come in handy 'because it can do a job that standard English can't do, reach parts that language cannot reach' (Fraser 2001: 22). For White, 'more rewardingly engaged with Gaia than with Gallup' (Brown and Nicholson 2009: 136), being Scottish meant feeling 'closer to America than to England' at the beginning of his career (White 2003: xxiv). Following the statement that 'ecosystems know no national boundaries' (Hutchings and Miller 2016: 1), I wish to offer readings of Scottish poetry from complex philosophical and theoretical perspectives transcending national definitions in order to situate it in contemporary critical discourses and to demonstrate how the poets engage with modern thought.

There are many other possible areas of enquiry. I wish to avoid the implication or suggestion on the part of some readers that the poets read in this volume are, by any means, the only poets whose work is so in touch with the world. It is important to stress that these are not the only poets, or necessarily the most important ones. Yet I wish to argue that poetry as practised by them is central to an understanding of the necessity for a dialogue among poetry, ecology and philosophy, a dialogue that these poets organically embody and embrace in the manner in which they write about the world. I believe that their writing is about feeling and sensing the world, a re-enchantment of place, but also about ethical responsibility, about bearing witness. Therefore, the study aims to show how, through the way the poets engage with the world responsibly, they illuminate for the reader a shared philosophical project that can best be explained through the discourses of ecocriticism and phenomenology.

The first chapter, 'Wandering in the Open World: Kenneth White's Poetics', is devoted to the work of an author who has created a vast project, considering the relation of the self and the world. An 'intellectual nomad', White left Scotland in the 1960s and settled in France, defending a doctoral thesis in philosophy and working as Professor of Twentieth-Century Poetics at the Sorbonne from 1983 to 1996, while travelling extensively. In 1989 he founded the International Institute of Geopoetics in Paris, and six years later the Scottish Centre for Geopoetics was founded in Edinburgh. Geopoetics focuses on bringing together various literary and philosophical traditions, stressing the need for a holistic approach to the natural world. In the inaugural text for the International Institute of Geopoetics, White foregrounds connections that permeate geopoetical thought:

> In the fundamental geopoetic field come together poets and thinkers of all times and of all countries. To quote only a few examples, in the West, one can think of Heraclitus ('man is separated from what is closest to him'), Hölderlin ('man lives poetically on the earth'), or Wallace Stevens ('the poems

of heaven and hell have been written, it remains to write the poem of the earth'). In the East, there is the Taoist Tchuang-tzu, the man of the ancient pool, Matsuo Bashō, and beautiful world-meditations such as one can find in the Hwa Yen Sutra. But geopoetics is not the exclusive domain of poets and thinkers. Henry Thoreau was as much an ornithologist and a meteorologist ('inspector of storms') as he was a poet, or rather, we might say, he included the sciences in his poetics. The link with biology is just as necessary, and with an ecology (including mind-ecology) well-grounded and well-developed. In fact, geopoetics provides not only a place, and this is proving more and more necessary, where poetry, thought and science can come together, in a climate of reciprocal inspiration, but a place where all kinds of specific disciplines can converge, once they are ready to leave over-restricted frameworks and enter into global (cosmological, cosmopoetic) space. One question is paramount: how is it with life on earth, how is it with the world? (1989c: n.p.)

White draws on the traditions of ancient Greece and China, Taoism and Zen Buddhism, German Romanticism, American transcendentalism and modernism, the network of relations reaching beyond philosophy and literature to other forms of human activity. Such an interdisciplinary approach, focused on the interdependence of all living and non-living things, characteristic of modern ecology, has a deeply artistic meaning for White.

As he puts it, 'It begins with Nietzsche' (White 1989c: n.p.), whose vision of an artist White embraces. His influences are Friedrich Nietzsche, Martin Heidegger and Edmund Husserl, as well as Gary Snyder and Robinson Jeffers. His attunement to natural phenomena resulted in White's 'way-books', or psychogeography. At the margins of Scottish literature, some of his books have appeared only in French: *L'Esprit nomade* (1987), *Le Plateau de l'albatros* (1994), *Dialogue avec Deleuze* (2007) and *La Mer des lumières* (2016). The chapter aims to examine Kenneth White's œuvre, focusing on the interconnectedness and intertwining of the poetic subject with the natural world. It analyses his concept of intellectual nomadism and the open world by means of tracing the main philosophical influences informing his writing. Further, it considers the syncretism of poetic forms employed by White, ranging from haiku to 'diamond' poems, to polyphonic itinerary poems. It examines the poet's explorations of landscape and mindscape, stemming from philosophical contemplation and spiritual realisation. Covering vast areas, White's work is archipelagic, the wingspan of his cultural project unparalleled, his highly coherent poetic programme involving a cross-cultural, transdisciplinary field of study. The analysis includes an attempt to follow the poet's mapping of extensive territories of the globe in the context of the problem of proper dwelling, and how it mediates place in a phenomenological relationship.

Chapter 2, '"Buried in the flesh": Home, Embodiment, and Interanimality in John Burnside's Work', considers poetic explorations of the nature of home in the context of the Heideggerian concept of dwelling, understood as 'the proper dwelling plight'. It seeks to provide an analysis of its geographical, as well as temporal and ontological aspects. Further, it discusses how these negotiations are related to Burnside's poetic search for connection with the natural world, demonstrating a longing for unity and wholeness. It also examines the function of language in creating the sense of home, highlighting the constant construction and reconstruction of place as reflected in Burnside's poetics. Part of the chapter is devoted to the act of naming foregrounded in many of his poems, which focuses on the capacity of language to order the world, a way to create the centre of the real, the ability to name offering a possibility to dwell. Struggling with the inexpressible, Burnside's poetic language invests signs appearing in the natural world with meaning. Yet language also invents, in an attempt to define, shape and frame, but at times also ushering in imprecision and vagueness. Both thematic aspects and the technical variety of Burnside's writing are considered in the chapter.

Chapter 3, '"Gifts of the Wild": Dwelling, Temporality and Landscape in Kathleen Jamie's Writing', focuses on the poetry of Jamie's poetry, as well as looking at her nature essays. Jamie's writing is informed by her travels to the mountains of the eastern Karakoram (northern Pakistan), Tibet and China in the 1980s, where she became acquainted with the figures of Princess Wen Cheng, a sixth-century Buddhist pioneer, and Fa-hsein, a fourth-century monk. First appearing in 1992, a travel book, *The Golden Peak*, was later published as *Among Muslims: Meetings at the Frontiers of Pakistan* (2002a). More recent travels by Jamie to Greenland, Norway and the Scottish islands (St Kilda, Rona) resulted in the publication of two collections of essays, *Findings* (2005) and *Sightlines* (2012). The publication of the two latter collections following the appearance of the poetry volume *The Tree House* in 2004 revealed Jamie's keen interest in the natural world. As she admits in a *Scottish Studies* interview, 'it takes . . . much more courage that it takes to talk about being a woman poet or a Scottish poet to say, I'd like to work my way back into some idea of what is true and sanctified, or sanctifiable' (Fraser 2001: 20).

The chapter is devoted to an analysis of Jamie's poetry in the light of her argument that her verse is a 'connective tissue where [the writer] meets the world, and it rises out of that, that liminal place' (Scott 2005: n.p.). Connectivity is an important aspect of Jamie's work, indicating numerous interrelations between land and poetic form. Following the poet's statement, 'I rub up against the world' (Jamie website 2019: n.p.), the chapter thus concerns Jamie's phenomenological approach. Another point that will be explored is that of continuity. Jamie demonstrates that perception of the land – and, concomitantly, our co-existence with it – is affected by the awareness of the passage of time and how temporality is inscribed in the landscape. The analysis focuses on poems recording the experience of landscape stretched over time: how a sense of permanence is intermingled with a pervasive sense of transience. It is centred around Jamie's emphasis on redundant human intrusions into the landscape (the residue of human presence described by Jamie includes littered beaches, light pollution and settlements that 'stain' the land), juxtaposed with the brittleness of flora and fauna, their transience underlining the temporality of our dwelling. Offering a reflection on the passage of time embedded in the land, Jamie points to the necessity of negotiating our own dwelling place within a temporal framework. As temporality, represented in past, present and future considerations of change, is a major preoccupation in Jamie's writing, the main focus of the chapter is thus the interweaving of permanence and impermanence.

Chapter 4, '"A word will set the seed / of life and death": Robin Robertson's Protean Lyric', is concerned with phenomenological readings of this Scottish poet. Though born in Scone, Perthshire, in 1955, Robin Robertson has spent much of his life in London, his Scotland being significantly a place of the imaginary and memory. He made his poetic debut in 1997 with *A Painted Field*.[7] Robertson recognises the intrinsic value in the landscape, which has left a lasting impression on his work, the significance of sensory impression rather than empirical encounter. As he argues, the sense of place is 'absolutely crucial'. Images of the natural world – both beautiful and menacing – abound in his work. He writes about history, legends and stories that are forged in the Scottish landscape, combining them with classical myths and folk tales, which merge in his poetry. This chapter aims to analyse the technical and thematic variety of Robertson's poetry and attempts to address its fusion of the philosophical and the mythical, the literary and the metaphysical, the existential and the material. It discusses selected poems, demonstrating how, through his finely chiselled verse and vivid, striking imagery, Robertson foregrounds temporality, vulnerability and the fragility of Being. Finally, it analyses the poet's lived relationship to the landscape. It focuses also on his immersion in the ancient Greek world with its mythical view of things, the landscape filled with raw violence, as this has significance for his vision of his particular, largely remembered region of Scotland.

Notes

1. *Umwelt* is a term meaning 'environment', or 'surrounding world', introduced by Edmund Husserl in the second volume of *Ideas* (2012). Using the term *Umwelt*, Husserl describes the world of beings meaningful to us, which exert a motivating force, and by means of which we create a circle of objects towards which we have a personalistic attitude. The Estonian-German biologist, Jacob von Uexküll, developed the concept of *Umwelt* in relation to the world of animals. He argues that various organisms differ in the manner in which they experience their surroundings, even though they may share the same environment. He developed the concept in his study 'A Stroll Through the Worlds of Animals and Men: A Picture Book of Invisible Worlds' ([1934] 1957: 5–80), which he opens with a description of a tick's *Umwelt*. Further, he demonstrates how the experience of the oak tree differs from, for instance, that of an owl, a fox, a bark-boring beetle, an ant, an ichneumon fly and a forester. In *Nature*, Merleau-Ponty explores the ramifications of *Umwelt*, as described by Uexküll (2003: 167–78).
2. As Husserl explains, apperception is a 'peculiar type of apprehending or experiencing', which 'completes what is brought about by this so-called "linking-on", this realisation of consciousness'. Linking psychological with bodily in 'apperceptive interweavings', consciousness – or, as Husserl puts it, 'the stream of experiences' – appears through the senses to the 'corporeal Being', as it is 'given as human and animal at once, in close empirical connexion with corporeality' (2012: 105).
3. Edmund Husserl had a considerable influence on Merleau-Ponty's thought, yet it needs to be stressed that Merleau-Ponty's contribution is not only an interpretation but also an original input in phenomenology, as he brings to Husserl's idealism a necessary focus on the materiality of the world.
4. In 'Signature Event Context', Derrida writes that dehiscence 'marks emphatically that the divided opening, in the growth of a plant, is also what, in a positive sense, makes production, reproduction, development possible (1988: 59).
5. Elsewhere I develop the metaphor of the mesh in the context of Burnside's work (cf. Szuba 2016: 47–59).
6. For a condensed survey of texts that are concerned with the natural world in Scottish literature see: Christopher MacLachlan (1998: 184–90).
7. I have not included Robertson's latest book, *The Long Take* (2018), in my discussion, as it seems to offer a new departure in his work, distinctly different from his other volumes in form.

Chapter 1

Wandering in the Open World: Kenneth White's Poetics

'The simple and immediate grasp of being'

Kenneth White has published extensively over the past forty years, in French and in English, even though the critical reception of him is not widespread. His prolificacy may be exemplified in the number of publications in the first half of 2018 alone, during which White published four books: *Un Monde à part: cartes et territoires*, *Territoires chamaniques*, *Premiers temps, espaces premiers* and *Borderland*. In 1979 he defended a state doctorate thesis in France on the theme of 'intellectual nomadism', and four years later he was appointed to the chair of Twentieth-Century Poetics at the Sorbonne. In 1989 he funded the International Institute of Geopoetics in Paris and *Cahiers de géopoétique*. In the early 1960s White moved to France, which was in intellectual ferment at the time, and as a result began to produce the ideas that would later inform his geopoetics, his writing of poetry and, indeed, the entire intellectual project of his work to the present day. White's thought has been influenced by his own idiosyncratic reading of continental philosophy and Zen, and while living in France he has been receptive in a somewhat singular manner to the French interpretation of German thought. Specifically, his understanding of continental thought has informed his geopoetics.

White left Scotland in the 1960s, a decade that Edwin Morgan considers 'a Scottish spring', adding that '[i]t was genuinely a time of beginnings, a time of openings, and I always felt that those who left Scotland then – e.g. Kenneth White, Douglas Dunn – were too impatient and should have stayed' (Marsack 2009: 164). While Dunn returned to Scotland, White settled in France permanently, no doubt striving to escape what, in *The Idea of North*, Peter Davidson calls 'Scottish modes of writing about Scotland (often anger and lamentation) [which} have gone far to support the myth of dearth, the idea of an impoverished north' (2005: 234). For White, 'Alba is Scotland un-couthied, un-cruddied, re-discovered. Scotland itself after all is a colonial term, and Scotland has been over-colonised. Imagining postcolonial Scotland means getting back down to Alba, to original landscape-mindscape, and, connecting them, wordscape' (1998: 3). That is why he needed 'to get away from constricting ideology and very curtailed outlook of this type, away from such historically dictated, historically dated situations that I felt the need to leave the Scottish context at one point' (White 1996: 54–5). Leaving Scotland was for him 'a question of scope and breathing space' (White 1996: 54–5).

Thus, this chapter is about White's highly idiosyncratic manner of looking at and responding to the world, as much as it is White's own sense of being an outsider from his homeland. As such, it is not as specifically about the Scottish landscape or seeing the world; and yet Kenneth White is an important source for a poetic thinking of landscape originating in the memory of Scotland and its land and seascapes, its elements and organic, non-human forces, which determine not only how White reads the world, but also provide a semiotic template for thinking the self and world. White's poems evoke the immersion of the self in the environment, emphasising the inseparability of humans and the more-than-human world, which is about 'the simple and immediate grasp of being in our own "being-in" the open-ness of place' (2006: 2), to use Jeff Malpas's words. Thus my discussion will be informed by phenomenology, particularly by Maurice Merleau-Ponty's work on the emplaced body and Martin Heidegger's on the mind reflecting on dwelling. It will be expanded by references to recent writings in the field of the environmental humanities, especially material ecocriticism. Furthermore, and specifically, two concepts have had an impact on this chapter: that of the vitality of things, proposed by Jane Bennett in *Vibrant Matter* (2010), and Gilles Deleuze and Félix Guattari's material vitalism, or 'matter-movement, this matter-energy, this matter-flow' (1987: 407) in 'Treatise on Nomadology'. Moreover, because so much of White's writing focuses on the ground, rocks and stones, it exhibits what Jeffrey Jerome Cohen calls 'geophilia', or 'an ecological allure . . . a propulsive and conjoining force that draws earth and water into a union generative of stone, that draws stone and other worldly things together to create, compose, produce' (2015: 25–6). I shall return to Cohen's work further on.

In his poetry as well as his essays, White constantly returns to the necessity to live 'on the earth, with a cosmic sense, but *living on the earth*, moving towards a finer earth-living' (1989a: 167). Reaching for the ground means, for White, attempting to abandon the world of late modernity and travelling in a three-fold manner: to the past in order to access ancient cultures, away from Scotland with its sentimental self-representations, and towards territories untainted by Western civilisation. According to White, our modern age has become the time of 'the Mastery of Man over Nature', 'with disastrous consequences' (2003: xxi). As Michel Serres notes, we observe the calamitous effect of human activity on the world due to 'Mastery and possession: these are the master words launched by Descartes at the dawn of the scientific and technological age, when our Western reason went off to conquer the universe' (1995: 32). We have moved, as far as Serres and White appear to agree, away from the earth, forgetting that Being-in-the-world is associated with being grounded.

White's work divides critics. Some consider his poetry '[e]rudite, elemental, big and bold, a manifestation of the kind of poetry MacDiarmid hoped for' (Dunne 1990: 111) and 'a significant contribution to technique and possibility, repeatedly laying out a Scottish autobiography in other locations and perspectives, often exotic and always effectively rendered' (Brown and Nicholson 2009: 136). Some critics express their reservations concerning White's poetic project: 'Questions remain about the poetic success of any exploration of emptiness, yet the work has achieved a considerable following in a present-day Scotland perhaps hungry for new articulations of spiritual experience' (Gifford et al. 2002: 784). Mostly critics point out White's constant self-referential, self-congratulatory manner, finding it irritating and indigestible, and stressing White's 'dreary narcissistic digressions' (Kennedy 2007: 174), 'the sheer narcissistic tendency in his work . . . hindering the quality of many a poem and many a page of prose (Jamet 2009: 108), and '[t]he "me"s and "I"s and even "I myself"s [that] accumulate in certain essays so that his approach might be construed as being overly egocentric, narcissistic even' (Graham 2011: 222). Further, Graham writes that White

> attempts to defuse the effect of self-centeredness by referring to himself in the third person as 'the traveller poet and wandering scholar' . . . [just as elsewhere he refers to himself as our 'gallivanting Glaswegian', 'our Scottish-born intellectual nomad', 'our adamant author', and 'our erratic author' (*On Scottish Ground* pp. 120–1)]. The ruse is not entirely successful. (Graham 2011: 222)[1]

Innes Kennedy, cited by Graham, writes that 'Absolutely no other British writer is as prepared to risk being so embarrassingly pretentious as White. As he himself says, such pretension contravenes Anglo-British strictures on taste' (Graham 2011: 222). Graham observes that, 'increasingly obviously', White focuses his work on himself 'without being apologetic for it' and instead 'he is moved to explain his overt and recurrent presence in his texts' (Graham 2011: 222–3). One of the difficulties with reading White is precisely that he engages actively in the myth of self-creation, largely turning his poetics into a process of self-aggrandising polemics. Moreover, he wears a series of interrelated personae that give the reader nothing on to which to grasp.

On the other hand, a proponent of White's work, Cairns Craig, has remarked, 'White remains somewhere in the margins of modern Scottish literature and yet if there is one Scottish writer with a truly European reputation, it is him' (Craig 2013: n.p.). White has 'continued to extend European connections that had been built since the early 1960s', while his 'psychogeography-influenced work described the experience of travelling, writing and environment, often deliberately pitching between genres' (Gardiner 2009: 190). Published frequently in France rather than in the English-speaking world, White's work garners the attention initially, if not principally, of French readers and scholars (even if, as Pierre Jamet argues, a lot of this is a myth of self-creation; see Jamet 2009). At the beginning of his career in France in the 1960s, 'several personalities, some of importance in the French literary landscape of the twentieth century, . . . eulogised White's writing . . . namely Pierre Leyris, Philippe Jaccottet, André Breton and Swiss travel writer Nicolas Bouvier' (Jamet 2009: 105). In his brief Foreword to *The Handbook of the Diamond Country*, Gary Snyder sees in White's poetry 'clarity, emptiness, purity of spirit' and calls it 'poetry of the one world' (White 1990b: n.p.). Yet, as already remarked, it remains the case that White has been widely criticised (see Kennedy 2007; Kelman 2002; Jamet 2009), especially for his grandiose, self-centred style and for bathos (Kennedy 2007: 174), as well as the excessive number of references that he employs in his essays, which 'his detractors call mere name-dropping' (Jamet 2005: 98), and which Innes Kennedy sees as 'the constraining of a tremendous heterogeneity to a surprisingly limited reservoir of concepts' (2007: 175).

In his vast project, White proposes an engagement with geological earth based on a phenomenology of being, whereby an incarnate subject is attuned to the 'rhythms of the world' (2004: 63), or radical openness and response to the world. He moves from what Fazzini describes, somewhat vaguely, as 'the local to the international through a spaciousness of voyaging and extended horizons' (Fazzini 2009: 111), whereby 'the local' refers to the locality of place, groundedness in the local landscape, its flora and fauna. Though Fazzini does not clarify White's poetics but relies on the reiteration of a somewhat occluded and visionary polemic, what takes place is a focus on the locality of place and a groundedness in the local. White's movement from the local to the general is a typical strand in certain thinking, from thinkers as disparate as Marx and de Man. Following James Hutton's words, 'Let us open the book of Nature and read in her records' (Hutton qtd in White 2006: 18), White foregrounds the importance of open, physical space in search of 'a new event in poetics: a space of being, allied to a transpersonal language' (1998: 199). Attempting to collapse divides, White's writing acts against binaries, leading towards a deepened exchange between Eastern Zen aesthetics and philosophy and Western metaphysics, for a unity of opposites. His writing is marked by a rejection of a historical or sociological approach in favour of a more universal one focused on deep time, the groundedness of consciousness in the body and, through the body, in the world. It may also be said that White's approach is vague and deliberately provocative because it relies on surfaces of becoming rather than having depth.

White works in various genres: essays, poetry and travel writing, which he calls 'way-books'. He believes that he offers a coherent vision of his writing, transcending traditional genres and giving each type a different function and a place in his work. As he expounds in the Preface to *Travels in the Drifting Dawn*, he thinks of his 'triple literary activity' as an arrow:

> the essays, maintaining direction, are the feathers, the prose, ongoing autobiography, or what I like to call 'way-books' (alias transcendental travelogues) is the arrow's shaft; and the poem is the arrow-head. And of course the whole arrow is in movement, going somewhere. (1989b: 8)

In all these genres, there is an emphasis on an 'outward movement' (1989b: 8), a decentred drift. In place of a grand narrative or essential 'truth', White proposes a poetry constantly in flux (Gairn 2008: 136). Poems are not separated from the rest of his work, but combined with prose books, some of which are 'concentrated moments of illumination en route' (Graham 2011: 217). He employs various poetic forms, such as long itinerary-poems, as in the open sequences of an 'Atlantic Atlas', haiku, 'diamond poems'. He writes in the belief that 'maybe you can push things farther by not settling on any one tradition' (1990b: 191), reading widely in philosophy. Both his essays and his poems abound in references and allusions to numerous texts and authors, presenting the reader with a complex network of literary and philosophical references, which results in a complicating of his work through many philosophical and literary traditions' wide net of references.

White focuses on the elemental world – stone, sea, birds, trees recur in his poems – stressing the need for groundedness in a phenomenological experience of the landscape, which explains his geopoetics and then blossoms into the greater field of the metaphysical. His work proposes a poetics that comes 'from contact with the earth, from a plunge into biospheric space, from an attempt to read the lines of the world' (White 1989c: n.p.). A response to the Scottish landscape, this thus predates, or anticipates, much ecocritical work. A 'pathbreaker for a new ecological awareness' (Craig 2009: 154), he proposes a poetry of that focuses on the perception of the world in moments of being in a clear voice and with a lucidity of vision. While White's essays show a number of limitations, pointed out by such critics as Jamet, Kennedy and Graham cited above, his poetry realises something because poetry is an expression of the self perceiving the world. He offers another way of reading the world, an ontology of becoming, which foregrounds change, flux, movement and becoming, bringing his work close to process metaphysics, represented by such philosophers as Heraclitus, Friedrich Nietzsche and Martin Heidegger, all of whom occupy an important place in his writing. Among White's many inspirations, as he likes to underline, are Ezra Pound, Walt Whitman, T. S. Eliot, W. B. Yeats, Hugh MacDiarmid, Neil Gunn, William Carlos Williams and Gary Snyder. Specifically, Scottish influences pervade his work through landscape (the Atlantic and hyperborean), through poets (Hugh MacDiarmid and Neil Gunn), and finally, through philosophers and thinkers (John Scotus Erigena, Duns Scotus, James Hutton and David Hume). Among his most important poetic influences, White lists two major figures in twentieth-century Scottish literature: Hugh MacDiarmid and Neil Gunn (1998: 15).

The word 'eccentric' recurs in descriptions of White (cf. Gairn 2008, Craig 2009 and Fazzini 2009) and in his own writing. He celebrates exile and exodus, 'the wandering life' (2003: xxii), considering himself 'Scotus vagans' (1990b: 188), like John Scotus Erigena. The tradition of *Scotus vagrans*, the Scottish intellectual who settled in France and dissipated Scottish knowledge, 'represent[s] one of the major traditions of Scotland's intellectual history', which justifies White's choice to make his life and work there 'as the territory for the development of his Scottish agenda' (Craig 2009: 155). Against nationalism and national identity, White perceives regionalism as something that threatens to 'replace a field of creative energy' with 'identity ideology' (White 2006: 59). Instead, he prefers the word 'territory', foregrounding the concept of openness, which will be discussed further in this chapter: 'Every territory, while maintaining its presence and compactness, is open, if one knows how to read it' (White 2006: 76). His work, informed by geology, zoology, linguistics and hydrography, 'ignore[s] national or regional fixity by straying over borders, thereby contributing to his idea of an

... open world poetics' (2006: 76). It makes White 'a Scottish speaker for adventures in cross-border relationships that refuse confinement by nationalist narrative' (Brown and Nicholson 2009: 136).

There is something else that connects White with MacDiarmid and Gunn: namely, his predilection for the East. White notices that MacDiarmid writes about the connection between Celtic culture and Eastern thought in *Aesthetics in Scotland* (1984) (White 1990b: 190). 'The more I walk / this northern coast / the closer I am to the East,' writes White in 'The Gannet Philosophy' (2003: 93). Similar to Neil Gunn, White 'gathers inspiration from Celtic sources that are seen as closely linked as Eastern religions' (Craig 2009: 158). As White suggests in his essay 'The Birds of Kentigern', 'It is far from being a rule, but I find that it's often minds with a Celtic background that get closest to the Far East' (1998: 73). This turn to the East results in a better, more real grounding. White also finds affinity with another Scot, Patrick Geddes, and his geotechnics, which is 'the means for human beings to learn how to really and fully inhabit the earth' (White 1998: 142). His poetry resounds with the 'stone voices', as Neal Ascherson calls 'the way in which human experience in this difficult northern place has been so intimately into the geology and the post-glacial ecology of Scotland that a people and its stones form a single cultural landscape' (Ascherson 2002: viii). An affinity with the geological world is visible in White's writing, which displays elements of 'the post-glacial ecology', as Ascherson puts it. By reaching far into the Indo-European roots of language, White finds a correspondence between the Latin word *homo*, denoting man, and earth, *humus* (2006: 7), thus foregrounding the connection between humans and the terrestrial sphere, celebrating 'inhuman nature', to use Jeffrey Jerome Cohen's term. As Cohen writes in *Stone: An Ecology of the Inhuman*, the lithic is a 'substantial force that exists outside of particular humans and often bluntly disregards their intentions, shaping and working and using and making with a startling autonomy, language responds to stone as matter to matter' (2015: 8). White's poetic language recognises and responds to this autonomous power, which makes his poetry chthonic, reaching beneath the surface of the earth, concerned with the spirit within and the unconscious impulses of the self entwined with the world it inhabits.

Land and *Logos*

Before turning to White's poems, I wish to describe briefly some of his concepts, which are linked to his other forms of creation. It is necessary to establish the parameters of his project first, and to offer these in the broader sense of continental thought.

In White's view, '[m]aybe thought can be like a landscape – with fields and running waters (fluid concepts). A landscape-mindscape. That's maybe what we could make our way towards' (2004: 63). The above words come from the collection *The Wanderer and His Charts: Exploring the Fields of Vagrant Thought and Vagabond Beauty*. Essays on Cultural Renewal (2004), in which White explores various themes in sections devoted to geopoetics, the intellectual nomad, place and space. All these concepts converge in a major theme, occupying a central position in White's writing: the interconnectedness of mind and land, 'a thinking-in-the-territory (implicated in it, not imposed upon it)' (White 2004: 63), as he argues. Even though White believes that thinking is not imposed on the land, paradoxically, in his work the ego obscures the land. Throughout his work, White attempts to construct a total vision, setting out into a new ground, a new spatial poetics, 'looking for a new space-art, a new spatial movement, which means new mindscape' (1989b: 8). This new mindscape, based on space on the move, White argues, necessitates a new language, a 'topology of being' (1992: 169). This is a clear reference to Heidegger's concept of topology, which, according to White is '[b]eyond subject and object, the "being" is thrown into an ex-static presence (a *Dasein*)' (1992: 169). It is important to discuss in more detail here this crucial concept in Heidegger's late writing.[2]

A fundamental concept in White's writing, geopoetics,[3] the aim of which is to reconsider, redefine and reformulate relations between humans and the planet, has proved a culture-making concept, stimulating a number of responses.[4] Even though White argues that he began addressing the issue of geopoetics 'around the end of 1978' (1992: 172),[5] his approach is just one of the existing, often quite disparate approaches. In 1989, White funded the International Institute of Geopoetics (with centres in many countries) and *Cahiers de géopoétique*. An attempt to re-consider human relations to space, White's concept of geopoetics combines geography with cosmology and philosophy, 'concerned, fundamentally, with a relationship to the earth and with the opening of a world' (White 2004: 243). White argues that geopoetics begins 'with the lie of the land, remaining close to the elements, it opens up space, and forms a new mindscape. Its basis is a new sense of land in an enlarged mind' (2006: 52). According to White, it is necessary to 'get back an earth-sense, a ground sense, and a freshness of the world' (1998: 48). White insists on the geographical aspect of his writing, situating it in space, a comment about the world, the self and poetics. This approach foregrounds the significance of a close human relation with the earth that is sensuous and sensible, based on presence and embodiment. In Aldo Leopold's words, 'Land, then, is not merely soil; it is a fountain of energy flowing through a circuit of soils, plants, and animals' (1949: 216). When human contact with the world is sensitive, subtle, intelligent, there emerges 'a "world" (a culture) in the strong, confirming and enlightening sense of the word' (White, qtd in McManus 2005: 17).

The prefix 'geo' can be understood to signify various things: earth, geography, geologically, planetary. For White, the word *poetics* transcends poetry, prose, thought and politics, having a universal significance, a synthesis. It involves another concept developed by White, that of intellectual nomadism, which will be discussed in further sections of this chapter. White's claim is that, being partly theoretical and biographical, geopoetics is not egotistical or linguistic, for such a view would narrow it down to those categories, while the concept needs to remain fluid, dynamic, mobile. Yet, given his work, this claim cannot really be made. This is a major limitation of White's project as, being (auto)biographical, it is also highly egotistical. The thought in relation to geopoetics attempts to put world before self, but that is impossible. There is no world before self. The self sees the world, the self names the world. Perception is always before world; there is no world without perception. What I call the world is my perception of it, however much that is confirmed by objective fact. There is no objective fact that is not perceived. It remains 'there' and not 'here' that the 'I' thinks; thus the claim that the world comes first cannot be made.

There are traces of the Romantic tradition in White's geopoetic project, with its premise that the world can be transformed in and through art. Suspicious of history and narrative as human-centred creations, geopoetics, according to White, aims at focusing on the 'real world' in order to perceive things-in-themselves. For him, a 'real grounding', as he calls it, is possible only after 'the end of history', which will expose the occluded 'nature of things' (2004: 207). The employment of the word 'real' is highly problematic and ignores the impossibility of defining what this concept would be. White seems oblivious to the problem, repeating the adjective when he argues that '[i]t's from the nature of things that real writing emerges, not from any I–Thou dialectic' (2004: 207). This statement carries another problem that looms in White's writing, in part characterised by declarative, wishful thinking. When White announces the emergence of 'real' writing without specifying what it would be, he seems to ignore the fact that, based on language, writing cannot bypass human consciousness. What is more, his own writing does not eschew focusing on the ego.

This is one of the reasons why his geopoetic approach has met with some criticism. Bertrand Westphal, a proponent of a geocritical approach to literary texts that involves 'a geocentred approach' (Westphal 2011: 111) and abandons 'an egocentred approach' – whereby 'discourse on space is made to serve the discourse on the writer, who becomes the ultimate object of critical attention' (Westphal 2011: 111), is critical (or, indeed, dismissive) of White's geopoetics. As he argues, '[u]nlike most literary approaches to space – such as imagology, ecocriticism, or geopoetics (à la Kenneth White) – geocriticism tends to favour a geocentered approach, which places *place* at the center of debate' (2011: 112). Focused on place, Westphal's approach rejects elements of autobiography present in White's concept. It should be said that, for all his vaunted 'self free world' poetics, White does not avoid placing the ego at the centre. In this, his argument becomes *a negative performative*. In claiming that we have to put the world, the natural world, first and so give it a real grounding, he is, in fact, performing just such a reading that is centred not on the world but on himself.[6]

Another concept used by White is 'cosmopoetics' or 'biocosmopoetics'. Every epoch is shaped by different 'cosmological' ideas, he argues. As has been mentioned above, he deplores the turn taken by Western civilisation that has resulted in moving away from the non-human world with all the disastrous consequences. A possible solution may lie in reaching beyond Western metaphysics and becoming 'pre-socratic', as he writes in 'Interpretations of a Twisted Pine' (2003: 213). The necessity to search for what he calls a 'real writing' (2006: 7) began during continental Romanticism, as White suggests, with authors such as Novalis and Hölderlin and his *Weltgeist*, or world spirit (2003: xxi). According to White, the paradigm shift that occurred in the Romantic era was expressed in

> a journey from self to Self, from confusion and ignorance to a cosmo-poetic reading of the universe', giving 'a sense all along the way of what is open and flowing and cannot be defined in any cut-and-dried fashion. . . . All is essay, fragment, approach. (2004: 96)

The word 'cosmos', concerned with the origin and structure of the universe, from the Greek *kosmos*, emphasises the order and spheres of the world. White's term 'cosmo-poetics' comes from the fusion of two words: *poïesis*, the act of creation, of making, and *kosmos*, signifying order, orderly arrangement, a harmonious universe. The importance of the latter concept is stressed in an epigraph to an essay, 'Elements of Geopoetics', which is extracted from Alexander von Humboldt's major work, *Cosmos*: 'As intelligence and language, thought and the signs of thought, are united by secret and indissoluble links, so in like manner, and almost without our being conscious of it, the external world and our ideas and feelings' (Humboldt, qtd in White 1992: 163). From these two words – *kosmos* and *poïesis* – White coins a concept of cosmopoetic, which he further expands, adding a prefix *bio*, signifying life. Thus 'biocosmopoetic' suggests a relation to living things co-existing in a harmonious, orderly arrangement; it suggests the making – *poïesis* – of an onto-theology grounded in the ideology of a harmonious organic structure. According to White, cosmopoetics proposes 'a heightened sensitivity towards the environment in which we try to live' (White 1992: 165).

This heightened sensitivity may be expressed only through poetry and White emphasises the significance of poems for a grounded, rooted being. Poetry in White's world view is not a projection of the poet's imagination but a work of the world on the poet's mind, as he prefers the word 'intelligence' to 'imagination' (2003: xxiv). This claim implies a connection between intelligence and how the world works on the poet's mind. Poetry resonates with life, seeking the depth of being together with philosophical thought: 'For art and philosophy *together* are precisely not arbitrary fabrications in the universal of the "spiritual" (of "culture"), but contact with Being precisely as creations. Being is *what requires creation* of us for us to experience it,' as Merleau-Ponty puts it (1968: 1970). And furthermore, in a note from 4 June 1959, he reflects, in a manner that anticipates much in the thought of White, on how

> philosophy, like a work of art, is an object that can arouse more thoughts than those that are 'contained' in it (can one enumerate them? Can one count up a language?), retain[ing] a meaning outside of its historical context, even *has* meaning only outside of that context. (Merleau-Ponty 1968: 199)

A concept borrowed from Oswald Spengler's *The Decline of the West: The Downfall of the Occident* (1918) is that of the intellectual nomad, one of the personae assumed by White. It was a theme of his doctoral thesis, developed in *L'Esprit nomade* (1987), in which White moves from culture to culture, tracing the history of nomadism in various locations such as America, India, Tibet, Polynesia, China and Japan. Intellectual nomadism, in White's view, is embodied by the 'Scot abroad', including 'wandering scholars and travelling monks' (1998: 100) of the early Middle Ages, a lot of whom were 'Scotic', by which White means both Scottish and Irish (1998: 100), characterised by 'the exportation of energy and intelligence' (1998: 107). He provides examples of such intellectual nomads throughout history, including Duns Scotus, John Scotus Erigena, Robert Louis Stevenson and Hugh MacDiarmid. (In other texts,

White also writes about other men who represent intellectual nomadism for him, such as Arthur Rimbaud and Friedrich Nietzsche.) In his essay, 'The Nomadic Intellect', White continues to focus on Scottish references, every so often including autobiographical comments. In one such remark, White recalls an image created at the age of thirteen by reading Emerson, who 'describes intellectual nomadism as the faculty of seeing far in all directions' and for whom 'the house of the intellectual nomad is a chariot in which, like a Kalmuk, he will traverse all latitudes, never forgetting his own "inner law"' (2004: 8). This image made White collect texts from Mongolia and 'adjacent territories' (2004: 8) later in life. Such remarks may create considerable reservations about White's concept. In 'Treatise on Nomadology', Deleuze and Guattari notice 'the dangers' (1987: 379) in White's vision of nomadism and his emphasis on 'this dissymmetrical complementarity between a race-tribe (the Celts, those who feel they are Celts) and a milieu-space (the Orient, the Gobi desert . . .)', noticing 'the profound ambiguities accompanying [him] in this enterprise' (1987: 379). White seems to demonstrate an egotistical privileging, a bourgeois blindness where the ego asserts itself by colonising tropes that are non-Western.

It is difficult not to notice that too often White makes grandiose claims and appropriates ideas without much profound insight. For Deleuze and Guattari, nomad thought

> does not ground itself in an all-encompassing totality but is on the contrary deployed in a horizonless milieu that is a smooth space, steppe, desert, or sea. An entirely different type of adequation is established here, between the race defined as 'tribe' and smooth space defined as 'milieu'. A tribe in the desert instead of a universal subject within the horizon of all-encompassing Being. (Deleuze and Guattari 1987: 379)

Pierre Jamet extends the thought of Deleuze and Guattari further, arguing that even if 'White's nomadism and geopoetics echo Deleuze's nomadism and geo-philosophy', the concepts are 'radically different', as according to Deleuze [and Guattari, it should be added], being a nomad 'starts with a capacity to disregard any concept that puts a stop to the ever-interpreting and creative nature of thought', whereas White's nomadism 'means primarily to travel and to open one's senses to the world outside, then to read many different authors from many different disciplines and try to hammer this all into a unity thanks to the earth paradigm' (Jamet 2009: 113). For Deleuze and Guattari, nomad thought shies away from fixedness and dogmatism, it is free, singular and mobile, given to movement, a co-habitation with other beings. All thought is 'becoming, a double becoming, rather than the attribute of a

Subject and the representation of a Whole' (Deleuze and Guattari 1987: 380). Deleuze and Guattari write that nomads 'have no history; they only have geography' (1987: 393). This is echoed by White, who puns that the nomad 'follows his paths from well to well. He's concerned with well-being. So doing, he works in close to geography, and with the parameters of sensitive space' (White, qtd in Dósa 2009c: 267). In this, again, he reverberates with what Deleuze and Guattari write about paths (even if it seems to be a very faint echo of Deleuze and Guattari's complex nomadology): 'The nomad has a territory; he follows customary paths; he goes from one point to another; he is not ignorant of points (water points, dwelling points, assembly points, etc.)' (1987: 380).

In White's nomadic geopoetics, the figure of the path, understood both literally and metaphorically, understandably occupies a significant place. Paths emerge as a result of dwelling; they

> occur almost naturally. People dwelling in a place, however briefly, tend to leave footprints . . . Path . . . is a trace formed incidentally by people walking more than a few times, not made expressly for travel . . . [Trace] connotes a way which vanishes, leaving behind nothing when foot traffic ceases. (Stilgoe 2015: 173)

Paths are also *Holzwege*, Heidegger's metaphorical concept of paths, or tracks that follow no order, randomly leading us to *Lichtungstehend*, a clearing, bringing moments of epiphany. Thus following tracks and traces, the nomad moves from one clearing to another, as '[t]he life of the nomad is the intermezzo. Even the elements of his dwelling are conceived in terms of the trajectory that is forever mobilizing them' (Deleuze and Guattari 1987: 380). Not following any route, the nomad chooses a landscape with paths off the beaten track. It does not mean that he is deprived of roots, as the aim of nomadism is 'extending them, enlarging them, recovering scope and energies, able to apply them within any specific socio-cultural context' (White 1998: 42). The recovery of scope and energies occurs through *stravaiging* across the expanses of the earth. The spirit of *stravaiging*, a Scottish term meaning to wander about aimlessly, fills White's writing in all its forms. 'True' literature and everything else recommences on the blue road (2013: 13), *voie-de-vie* (2013: 11), the road of life, according to White.

The spirit of wayfaring stretches on to the essays, founded on intellectual *stravaiging* across cultures and periods. It is also present in the collections of poetry, the structure of which often quite randomly follows a map. There are also a lot of poems characterised by what J. Hillis Miller calls, 'atopical topography', a 'description without place' (1995: 258). Tracing topographies, other poems contain place names, which map brief impressions and encounters, which lead to a deepened metaphysical observation. For instance, the title of the collection of longer poems published in English in 1989, *The Bird Path*, explores the theme of wandering, each section embedded in a place. Some titles are general but still suggest a geographic orientation, as, for example, 'Walking the Coast', 'North Roads, South Roads', 'The House at the Head of the Tide'. Others, such as 'Out of Asia', 'Pyrenean Meditations' and 'The Atlantic Movement', point to more specific, if vast, locations. Within each section, a similar rule governs the poems: for instance, 'Remembering Gourgounel', 'Hölderlin in Bordeaux', 'Letter from Harris', 'Early Morning Light on Loch Sunart', 'Labrador', 'The Armorican Manuscript', to mention a few. In 'Europe in the Fall', the poetic subject is 'stravaiging round the Black Sea' (1990b: 104). White employs similar technique in *Latitudes and Longitudes* (2013), arranging the poems in five sections: 'Alba', 'Up and Down in Europe', 'American Territories', 'The Oriental Act' and 'Armorica', within which many poems refer to specific place names in their titles. These are poems given to exploring edges and peripheral regions of the North with their hyperborean haecceities. For instance, 'Walking the Coast', a long poem comprising fifty-three numbered stanzas, or, as White puts it in a brief note, 'fifty-three waves', offers 'a map of new co-ordinates', focusing on 'the glow that can be found within the apparent dullness of nature' (Newell 2003: 10). The sense of North returns time and again in 'the Atlantic poetics' (2003: 125) and various tidal analogies. In *On the Atlantic Edge*, White writes about the importance of the Atlantic understood as a vast region, suggesting one body of water.

Walking 'is a state in which the mind, the body, and the world are aligned, as though there were three characters finally in conversation together, three notes suddenly making a chord. Walking allows us to be in our bodies and in the world' (Solnit 2002: 5). Following the footsteps of ancient peripatetic philosophers, such as Xenophantes, the Japanese poet Hakuin, who practised a walking meditation instead of *zazen*, Henry David Thoreau and many other thinkers and poets, White practises walking, wandering, *stravaiging* in various forms. From a very early age, walking around on the Ayrshire coast gave White 'the feeling of being in touch with a larger, more-than-human context' (Dósa 2009c: 261), living through a sensible field of the body.

Openness

The concept of openness is a fundamental element of White's work, defined by him as a capability to apprehend the world directly. The idea of 'world-opening' resembles Merleau-Pontyan dehiscence, whereby the self opens to the world. Opening may be read therefore as being 'of the essence of the thing and of the world to present themselves as "open", to send us beyond their determinate manifestations, to promise us always "something else to see"' (Merleau-Ponty 1962: 388). Dehiscence is related to the notion of chiasm, which denotes 'the motion of perpetual dehiscence, in which perception is understood as a being in momentum' (Vasseleu 1998: 30). White privileges random, decentred movement, theorised by Guy Debord as *dérive*, or drifting, a situationist practice, which involves passing through various places, subjecting oneself to psychogeographical currents. He continues to foreground 'direct contact with the outside, the acquiring of a non-panic sense of dispersion, disaggregation, dissolution' (1992: 165). After all, as he asks, '[t]o "have space", isn't it a prerequisite for any kind of decent living?' (1992: 166). This seems to echo Merleau-Ponty's conclusion: 'The true solution: *Offenheit* of the *Umwelt, Horizonhaftigkeit*' (1968: 196).

The *stravaiger* chooses open spaces, unmarked by human presence, moving between 'geometric' and 'anthropological', and between 'striated' and 'smooth' spaces. The former distinction was made by Merleau-Ponty, who considers 'geometric' space to be homogenous and empty, and 'anthropological' space to be experienced, or 'existential', space, which is subject to individual perception (1962: 324–334). Deleuze and Guattari distinguish between 'striated' and 'smooth' space, whereby in the former 'lines or trajectories tend to be subordinated to points: one goes from one point to another' (Deleuze and Guattari 1987: 478), whereas the latter occurs when 'the dwelling is subordinated to the journey; inside space conforms to outside space: tent, igloo, boat'. And further, 'There are stops and trajectories in both the smooth and the striated. But in smooth space, the stop follows from the trajectory; once again, the interval takes all, the interval is substance (forming the basis for rhythmic values)' (Deleuze and Guattari 1987: 478).

Following the lines of the world along an unknown trajectory, the nomad engages with place, which in White's work becomes a poetic space of inhabitation. As Jeff Malpas points out,

> in Kenneth White's work, the nomadic refers precisely to a mode of engagement with place, and certainly not to any mode of disengagement from place

or indifference towards it. It is through journeying out into the world that place is encountered, and though such journeying always stands in relation to sojourning, as movement and rest implicate each other. For White, it is not the nomad who is apart from place but the obsessive stay-at-homer, the one who refuses to see the necessary implication of the home-place with the foreign, who fails to see, even in the home-place, the horizon that opens up the world beyond. (2018: 174)

In the modern world, the 'House of Being' has come to be reduced to 'a villa . . . an asylum, or a sanatorium at the side of the technological Highway' (White 1989a: 60). The proper dwelling may be achieved in the state of openness that combines encountering the world in releasement through journey with home-making. 'Might it be possible to conceive of a "great residence" that would reconcile movements and things, removing and remaining, stravaiging and staying?' (White 1989a: 177). It might be attainable to couple a wandering life and Heidegger's dwelling following his concept of *Gelassenheit*, or a state characterised by dwelling in openness, exposure and ability; the nomad must dwell in 'releasement toward things' and nomad thought which 'is tied not to a territory but rather to an itinerary' (Deleuze and Guattari 1987: 557).

Openness is also the attitude of non-domination and non-possession, the relation modern humans have with the land, as '[r]efusing to take possession of the land they cross, the nomads construct an environment out of wool and goat hair, one that leaves no mark at the temporary site it occupies . . . .They leave space to space' (Deleuze and Guattari 1987: 557). The assumption that humans are at the centre of the world – that they inherited the earth – should be cast off. The two verbs – dominate and possess – that came to describe the 'fundamental relationship we have with the things of the world' (Serres 1995: 32) should be re-evaluated. As Norman MacCaig asks in 'A Man in Assynt':

Who possesses this landscape? –
The man who bought it or
I who am possessed by it? (1969: 49, ll. 36–8)

White's wayfarer traverses territories, staying close to the ground when

the land ceases to be land, tending to become simply ground (*sol*) or support. . . . The nomads are there, on the land, wherever there forms a smooth space that gnaws and tends to grow, for it has been established that the nomads make the desert no less than they are made by it. (Deleuze and Guattari 1987: 381–2)

The attitude of openness means to be outside, out there, grounded, in a state of releasement, radically dehiscent.

This interconnectedness of self with the environment is emphasised in moments of perception that arise from a phenomenological being in the world when in the 'desire of a whole world', 'the mind cries out for unity, for a unitive experience' (White 1998: 60–1). In 'Region of Identity' (2003: 202–4), landscape and mindscape are intertwined, the poetic subject wishes

> to go beyond signs
> into the light
>   that is not the sun
> into the waters
>   that are not the sea. (ll. 25–9)

The repeatedly used preposition 'into' suggests a movement within, penetrating the surface of things in order to reach their essence. It is possible if we are attuned to 'that kind of living system of meanings which makes the concrete essence of the object immediately recognizable, and allows its "sensible properties" to appear only through that essence' (Merleau-Ponty 1962: 151). To attain this requires a renunciation of the faculties of the mind, redundant in the encounter with wild Being. In 'Region of Identity', 'the intelligence trembles/at the approach of naked being' (2003: 202, ll. 13–14). The expression 'naked being' suggests an image of existence stripped off until pure essence appears. After 'the opaque burned out / the heaviness dissolved' (2003: 204, ll. 43–4), there emerges an intertwining of transparencies and opacities through an interfolding of the material and immaterial: 'the physical absolute' (2003: 204, l. 42). Similarly, '*Fuzeshin, fuzebutsu, fuzemotsu*', from *The Gateless Gate*, translated as '[n]either mind, neither Buddha, nor a thing' (2003: 609) in the epigraph to 'Last Page of a Notebook' (2003: 123), signifies for White an 'absolute reality' (2003: 609). The triple negation emphasises the impossibility to choose one of these elements. As such, the negation stands as synecdoche for all of White's work in its inextricability and as a figure for a total work toward which he strives.

In the epigraph to 'Cape Breton Uplight', we read 'Always the search for the place and the formula, the essential locality and the few necessary words' (2003: 217). This poem is composed of a series of brief glimpses and emergent reflections, governed by the rule: 'express only the essential' (l. 9). The word 'essence' comes from the Latin *esse*, or 'to be'. White's attempt to reach the root of being follows the premises of phenomenology, or

> the study of essences; and according to it, all problems amount to finding definitions of essences: the essence of perception, or the essence of consciousness, for example. But phenomenology is also a philosophy which puts essences

back into existence, and does not expect to arrive at an understanding of man and the world from any starting point other than that of their 'facticity'. (Merleau-Ponty 1962: vii)

Related to a corporeality or materiality, Husserl's *'vague and material* essences (in other words, essences that are vagabond, inexact and yet rigorous)' were different from 'fixed, metric and formal, essences' (Deleuze and Guattari 1987: 407). Essences are at the root of all the relationships of experience; 'Husserl's essences are destined to bring back all the living relationships of experience, as the fisherman's net draws up from the depths of the ocean quivering fish and seaweed' (Merleau-Ponty 1962: xvii). Thus to search for essences is to seek the essence of existence, the very being. The essence of the thing is its 'thisness', or 'haecceity', a concept coined by Duns Scotus, meaning that 'a season, a winter, a summer, an hour, a date have a perfect individuality lacking nothing, even though this individuality is different from that of a thing or a subject' (Deleuze and Guattari 1987: 261). In constant relations, haecceities affect and are affected as between two bodies or things there occurs 'a natural play of haecceities, degrees, intensities, events, and accidents that compose individuations totally different from those of the well-formed subjects that receive them' (Deleuze and Guattari 1987: 253). Haecceities is a word that defines all of White's work, what it does and how it proceeds, how it all relates.

'To return to things themselves is to return to that world which precedes knowledge,' writes Merleau-Ponty (1962: ix–x). In a number of poems, such a return to the world through direct contact is attempted where 'space is blue and birds fly through it' (White 1992: 165).[7] This is the world that does not necessitate a scientific apparatus to be experienced fully. For instance, in 'Tractatus Cosmo-Poeticus' (2003: 195–6), the poetic subject ponders the possibility of entering in direct contact with things as they are without attempting to impose a meaning. Following Hume, the speaker aims at 'forgetting the human / at least the all-too-human' (ll. 2–3), moving to places ranging from Scotland to Iceland, North America, Japan and back to Europe, to Wittgenstein's house in Vienna, to ponder on the nature of reason:

> the mind loves elements
> related to one another
> in a determinate way
> and from there reaches out
> to the sum-total of reality. (ll. 17–21)

The speaker observes the relatedness of things and strives to see it in its entirety, avoiding particularisation of 'forms and void / bulk and blanks' (ll. 22–3). Yet any attempt at a direct contact is thwarted by the mind, which cannot stop the mind doing its work, 'drawing distinctions and conclusions' (l. 25). The return to 'things themselves' is prevented by the intellect, which accesses knowledge and language. Thus 'the less you say / the more is said' (ll. 30–1). In the final stanza of the poem, in the haiku-like image the speaker struggles once again to 'forget the human', hopelessly thwarted by the Cartesian 'I think' (l. 32).

The idea of essences is a theme that recurs in White's poetry. For instance, in a haiku titled 'Example' (1990b: 56), glimpses of quartz in sandstone demonstrate layers of deep time lying behind the surface of the rock, 'and in its purity is beyond perfection' (l. 3). The rock persists longer than the biological beings forming the ecosystem around it, which makes the poetic subject ponder the intractability and profundity of time. As Craig observes, in his pursuit to touch the essence of the world, White resembles Hugh MacDiarmid, who 'had come face to face with the "primordial" and discovered "a metaphysical vision of the Light as conceived by Plotinus: contact with the light that makes it possible to see"' (Craig 2013: n.p.). Both pose 'the ultimate question': 'How to enter into this world of stones, this elementary world, rather than just describe it' (Craig 2013: n.p.). Yet how to achieve that without the use of language? White's poetry often demonstrates the tension between an attempt to go beyond anthropocentricity and the difficulty of doing that. Time and again, he returns to the lithic, '[p]rimal, enduring, and intractable', which 'stands in for nature itself: the given, the really real, a trope for the inhuman' (Cohen 2014: iii).

Thus the primordial, elementary world, made of stone and light, constitutes a major preoccupation in White's poetry. Reflected from the seeing eye, the visible spectrum of light is composed of wavelengths, which results in various colours, yet in White's writing only two colours return regularly: the blue of the sea and the sky, and landscape in the distance, the colour 'of solitude and of desire' (Solnit 2005: 29), and the white of the rock and the vast expanses of snow and ice.[8] The blue is 'the blue of land that seems to be dissolving into the sky . . . the blue at the farthest reaches of the places where you see for miles, the blue of distance' (Solnit 2005: 29). 'The world is blue at its edges and in its depths,' it is 'the light that got lost' (Solnit 2005: 29). The white returns time and again. Scotland and 'the whole Scottish mindscape' (White 2003: 125) are represented in the colour white, as the idea of Scotland (conceived of as 'Alba', or 'white world')

> added the whole hyperborean, circumpolar complex, which brings together Celtic culture, Indian-Inuit culture, and Siberian shamanism. And then again,

the white background of Zen Buddhism, where supreme identity is described as 'a white heron in the mist' – all of which again, both territorially and ideationally, belongs to the 'white world' of the Hyperborean North. (Dósa 2009c: 265)

White pervades all being, constituting 'the pure pathology of my body and mind', as we may read in 'Into the Whiteness' (2003: 109, l. 4). Thus 'white' is a concept that occurs in White's writing with a particular frequency, endowed by him with a special meaning, connected with what he calls 'white phenomena', which constitute 'an experience, centering on the real body – a psycho-physical experience that can be of the utmost intensity' (White 1998: 63). As he explains, '"White world" 'brought together the phenomena I was moving among (breaking waves, quartz pebbles, wings of gulls, birch-bark), the country I was living in (its ancient name: Alba), and, as a bonus, my person, but in an almost anonymous way' (Bowd et al. 2005: 199).[9]

The idea of 'white phenomena' is employed in poems such as 'White Valley' (2003: 52). In the overarching silence and emptiness, the mind '*breathes*' (l. 12), moving with ease, gliding over things 'without doing too much naming' (l. 16). The self merely is. By employing the word 'here' at the end of the poem in a repeated sequence – 'Here I am, here' (l. 20) – White opens the place to everything that is changeable and relative, linking it with the self: 'here' is inextricably bound with the speaking I. It is a significant gesture, as it may be read corporeally, through the speaker's body: 'here' is where I am, I am in a place that is linked with me through my physical presence. This word, which grounds the self, appears recurrently in White's poems, functioning as an anchor of presence. To capture phenomena before they are constituted by consciousness as 'things', the pure essence of meaning/consciousness, 'that union of essence and existence' can be found in, or through, perception (Merleau-Ponty 1962: 170).

White light unites the visible with the invisible; '[t]he Total experience of the earth is also a *luminous* experience' (White 1998: 38). If we treat light as texture, as Vasseleu proposes, it is no longer transparent, as '[i]n its texture, light is a fabrication, a surface of a depth that also spills over and passes through the interstices of the fabric' (1998: 12). Thus we may talk about the tactility of perception, a palpating eye. Such an understanding of light challenges the division between senses that upholds other divisions and dichotomies: between body and mind, between feeling and thought, between the visible and invisible. This approach privileges objective knowledge based on perceptive distance, only possible after the mind is separated from the body with its sensations. Following that, 'as a texture, the naturalness of light cannot be divorced from its ... embodied circumstances' (Vasseleu 1998: 12). It is 'neither visible nor invisible, neither metaphoric nor metaphysical' (Vasseleu 1998: 12).

> In its sensible indeterminacy as both feeling subject and object being affected, tactile perception is defined as a loss of objectivity in relation to the infinitude of vision's scope. The distance and space for reflection and insight that comes with vision through the mediation of light is lost as the sense of sight passes to the sense of touch. At the point of light's contact with the eye, the objectivity of the visual standpoint becomes a perception of the presence of difference, where light is experienced as a non-rational subjection to feelings such as being penetrated, dazzlement, ecstasy or pain. (Vasseleu 1998: 12)

The intertwining of vision and touch, the mind with the land, the self with the world, being in 'the ultimate union / of matter and space' (2003: 100–1), a chiasmic intertwining of substance and spirit.

Poetic Language

Openness is also a faculty that gives the poet a chance for direct apprehension. Poetry should be written, suggests White in a highly enigmatic manner, 'in the name of the Outside', this Outside that, according to White, somewhat paradoxically, 'has no image, no meaning, no subjectivity' (1989a: 176).[10] White's choice of poetic forms such as haiku, with its minimalistic form, reflects his interest in Zen aesthetics, the simplicity and purity of which suggest the desire to avoid unnecessary decoration in the form of metaphorisation and other language flourishes. For the poet, poetics lies, as he puts it, 'in those rock piles' (1992: 173); thus poetry is an attempt to effect a union with the landscape, and an 'attempt to get back into the living forest, the archaic ground' (White 1998: 31). With this primordial contact is a correspondence with a primordial way of speaking that the West no longer knows. In White's view, the landscape, speaking as *logos*, pre-exists the world (Merleau-Ponty 1962: xxiii). Thus, in pursuit of a new language, White returns to the figure of the shaman, who lives at one with the world and thus is able to communicate with it:

> If the shaman imitates the movements and voices of animals and birds ... it's in order to learn the language of the whole of nature, this desire for complete language leading eventually to the practice of incantation (providing enchantment) and/or the development of a jargon (the language of the jars, that is, the wild duck). (1998: 38)[11]

Shamanism enables a direct contact with the earth by 'seeing again', which, White argues, 'means both perspective and clarity of vision, is, at least for a start, to open up the whole northern circumpolar complex' (White 1998: 32–3). A renewed vision is possible only if one leaves history and society, transcending their limitations and constraints in pursuit of something larger. Strictly speaking, of course, this is impossible. Whether Kenneth White actually achieves what he states as his goals is a problematic issue, so again, I would remind the reader that I am, here, merely seeking to delineate the contours of White's thought. The ultimate or total transcendence may be achieved by a shaman or 'the dawn-man, according to the Ojibwa, who has 'a capacity for experiencing (and also expressing) total life' (White 1998: 38). Isolation and loneliness offer a path to totality; outside of the community, the shaman brings it 'breathing space' (White 1998: 38). Thus ec-centric, the shaman seeks ecstasy – 'getting outside one's self as well as outside history' (1998: 38) – and what White calls 'de-conditioning', which entails a jettisoning of social identity. The aim is a transcendence, 'a capacity for experiencing total life' (White 1998: 38). And so, as in 'Winter Wood' (1990b: 23), the intellectual puts away the books, ready to touch and be touched by the world.

The primordial language may be accessed only after removing the urge to represent the self and the world through poetry. Following Heidegger's concept of language, White argues that real poetry should not be the emanation of the poet's ego ('a person thinking in his inner self and who thereafter "expresses" that self for the speech of a world' (2004: 157)); nor should it strive for representation:

> We leave the idea of a representation of the world for a presence in the world, which is the *Dasein* (literally, 'being there'). 'The Dasein', writes Heidegger in *Being and Time*, 'doesn't emerge from some inner sphere, its primordial way of being means being always outside.' (White 2004: 158)

In this anti-Romantic gesture, White proposes the poetry of presence, which stands against the expression of emotions through the description of the world. Naturally, language cannot contain the world but the poet attempts to 'unearth a prehistoric language spoken in things, or if beneath our stammering there is a golden age of language in which words once adhered to the objects themselves' (Merleau-Ponty 1973: 6). Speech, though, for White (and to reiterate an earlier point, necessarily), is somehow out there, found in the natural world, which resounds with 'the music of the landscape' (White 2003: 594). Words 'come from mental territories still unknown', appearing suddenly in response to the world, answering 'the need to voice it' (2003: 275). In 'Crow Meditation Text (2003: 279–82), the subject seeks for a possibility to

> say the world anew
> dawn-talk
> grammar of rain,
> tree, stone blood and bone. (ll. 53–6)

The final line evokes a vegetal, animal and mineral intertwining, foregrounding what Stacey Alaimo calls, in *Bodily Natures*, 'the interconnections, interchanges, and transits between human bodies and nonhuman natures' (2010: 2). In White's lines, language seeps from the natural world, from the engagement with a place, with the plant, mineral and weather-world, all entangled with the flesh. The act of joining these elements in a chain in the last two lines foregrounds a relation that occurs beyond language, a pre-cognitive moment of wild Being, 'an irreducible nexus of language and materiality' (Vasseleu 1998: 25). Glimpses of this imagined 'prediscursive inter-world' (Vasseleu 1998: 72)[12] are also visible in many other poems such as 'Winter Wood' and 'Late August on the Coast', ending with the words 'wild spirits / knowing what they know' (White 2003: 597), focused around a pre-cognitive knowing. The words 'wild spirits / knowing what they know' evoke a Merleau-Pontyan image, in which *logos* 'pronounces itself silently in each sensible thing . . . which we can have an idea of only through our carnal participation in its sense, only by espousing by our body its matter of "signifying"' (Merleau-Ponty 1968: 208).

Knitted together – 'As flesh, the interwovenness of language and materiality in perception is embraced as an irreducible complexity that is necessary for a sense of self' (Vasseleu 1998: 23) – various consciousnesses are chiasmically intertwined: when other beings enter one's field of perception, they become part of one's subjectivity. To understand White's practice of language in phenomenological terms, 'transcendental subjectivity is a revealed subjectivity, revealed to itself and to others, and is for that reason an intersubjectivity' (Merleau-Ponty 1962: 421). The embodied consciousness, transcending oneself in the movement towards the intercorporeal world, relies on an exchange. The web of other beings 'establish[es] relations in the heterogeneous' world (White 1989a: 176) in order to enter into contact with them. Other consciousnesses enter one's field of perception, becoming part of one's subjectivity in 'the network of experiences' (Merleau-Ponty 1962: xx). White's language reveals how gaining knowledge of one's own consciousness occurs through the possibility, as Husserl imagines it, of transcending oneself, and also in an exchange of perceptions as 'worlds of experience . . . may be united together through actual empirical connexions into a single intersubjective world' (Husserl 2012: 93). Creative perception helps unveil the 'Lebenswelt logos', as

Merleau-Ponty calls it, or 'language of the living, perceivable world' (Vasseleu 1998: 24).

Moments of transcendental intersubjectivity occur rarely, emerging from fragments, flashes, junctures. Many of White's poems are brief glimpses of the world, a few lines of each contained in one blink. Even his longer poems are, in effect, constructed as a series of self-contained images, so many fragments forming a whole. Although seemingly a paradox, White insists on a whole formed of fragments, which, in cohering, lose none of their fragmentary nature. For instance, 'Walking the Coast' (1989a: 42–74), mentioned above, is a sequence composed of fifty-three short, numbered poems, creating a chain of interlinked beads, a recurrent technique for White. Each separate poem is a haiku-like glimpse, loosely combined with the other poems through a unifying vision. For example, poem III, 'a hymn to chaoticism' (2003: 129), is an expression of secular reverence, foregrounding the randomness of the world. In turn, poem XI emphasises 'a power of synthesis / at one with life'. Chaos and unity recur in White's poetry, both working together in 'founding and grounding / a world' (2003: 146).

Secular reverence reveals itself in enchantment and wonder at the beauty of the world evoked in some poems. In the embodied self, a degree of transcendence is possible; 'the mind cries out for unity, for a unitive experience', moving beyond to a pre-verbal moment of wild Being, whereby it encounters the 'sheer experience of the nakedness and loveliness of everything, an ecstatic existence, expanding to the sense of cosmic unity' (White 1998: 60, 64).[13] For instance, in 'Wakan' (1990b: 158), the word 'beautiful' is repeated four times in a five-line poem. The speaker is able only to repeat the phrase, as if short of other words to describe the feeling created by the landscape. As the poet explains in the note, the title is a reference to the concept of sacredness among the Indians of North America, adding that 'it's not absolutely forbidden to read also into the title of this poem the word "waken"' (1990b: 199). 'Wakan', then, would suggest an awakening to the beauty of the world and the sublime that exceeds the power of language to grasp. The use of the common expression 'there is nothing more', which returns as a refrain, emphasises the impossibility of verbalising the impression and yet, paradoxically, the effort, in the iteration, to overcome the aporetic experience of the impossible verbalisation. The citation preceding the poem points to a waking of the mind; it is unspecified and yet there is 'something' stirring in the mind. The economy of words appears to arise from an awareness that, as Merleau-Ponty would argue, 'I point to a world around me which already speaks' (Merleau-Ponty 1973: 6).

For White, language emerges from what he calls 'radical silence' (2003: xxiii), during which we 'must link ourselves, by a long silent process, to the reality' ('Valley of Birches', White 1989a: 160). Quieting one's mind and immersing oneself in the experience of silence constitutes a prerequisite condition for all utterance. This is a recurrent motif in White's poems, appearing in various contexts: for instance, 'the wind of silence' (1990b: 44), 'a ring of silence' (1990b: 45), 'in the silence under Orion' (1990b: 180), 'I talk grotesquely to myself / and the silence answers' (1990b: 46), 'but there is no landscape, and no / language, only a ragged silence' (1990b: 47), 'the roaring of nothingness in my ears' (1990b: 24). Silence in the self is achieved through space ('silence – spaces'), after quietening the mind in order to hear the world and keep 'the language open' (1998: 78). We hear the world, which hears us, and through the world we hear ourselves: a reversibility that allows us to experience the world made of the same flesh as we are. As Louise Westling explains, 'Human language intensifies this coiling back of self-reflection by allowing us to articulate the meanings we find sedimented in our experience' (2013: 118–19).

While 'listening only to the wind' (1990b: 20), what emerges is a simple, pared-down, direct language, stripped as far as possible of decorations and metaphors in order to avoid the imposition of subjectivity to prevent tinting the image and contaminating it with imaginative phantasms. The directness of language ensures that the poem remains undiluted, the sparsity of language reflecting minimal expectations, marking with this a withdrawal of the self, as if it 'would be / almost too much' (White 1990b: 67). It is language, 'not as a sum of statements or of "solutions", but as a veil lifted, a verbal chain woven' (Merleau-Ponty 1968: 199). Perception does the work of unveiling in a Husserlian *epoché*, or a suspension of judgement, a technique for the examination of essences. All things in the world should be approached with the suspension of commonly held views, focusing on the appearance of things with their full awareness. Such an observation of natural processes dissolves the objects that appear or are given. Similarly, the use of a technique of juxtaposing images is intended to serve to avoid providing links that might falsify the impression through their linguistic nature. In a number of poems – for instance, in 'Letter to an Old Calligrapher' (1990b: 65) or 'West Labrador' (1990b: 139) – there are no verbs in finite form but predominantly nouns, threaded together. The proliferation of nouns and the withdrawal of verbs foreground the rejection of a utilitarian vision of things; things are, and that, in itself, is a wonder to be noticed. In this poetry, things *are*. In 'Theory' (1990b: 108), a simple statement, 'It is there' (l. 3), suggests an uncontaminated vision given by the world, which none the less hides an unveiled mystery. Similarly, as the final line of a brief poem titled 'A Snowy Morning in Montreal' (2003: 400) suggests, 'it's all out there' (l. 3). More words would be redundant, as inventing titles or naming things would be. The title contains the whole poem and expresses the vision, encompassing everything, all the significance given to the poetic subject. On the one hand, the real constitutes the ground for poetry; on the other, it gives to poetry the ground that grounds it.[14]

Elemental Poetics

White seeks to ground much of his poetry in elemental phenomena, focusing particularly, repeatedly and insistently on the sea, rocks, wind, rain, snow, mist and light. The elemental powers of the tide, along with earth, air, water and fire, signify those forces characteristic of the physical universe, elements that are primal. The brevity of White's preferred poetic form, the haiku, and its variations affords a fragmentary urgency and directness in keeping with the elements' direct force that come to inform the tripartite structure of *Handbook for the Diamond Country: Collected Shorter Poems 1960–1990*. This volume demonstrates a movement through regions, cultures and traditions, foregrounding their interconnectedness: the middle section, 'Open World Poems', is bracketed by 'Scotland Poems' and 'Brittany Poems'. The dedication – 'For the land, the light, the mind' – foregrounds the poetic subject's relation to the elements and world in a triad of interlinked themes prevalent in White's poetic work. Once again, haiku proves an appropriate poetic form to combine the three elements in a pared-down language, stressing the elemental aspect of these poems. A major pursuit in his poetry – a renewal of language – resembles the Mallarméan aim, to purify the language of the tribe ('purifier la langue de la tribu'): 'to speak a language freed of principal structure, a language simpler, more direct, closer to the "physics" of the universe' (1989a: 170). As the title suggests, the collection is meant as a book to provide reference or instructions. This may explain the careful paratextual devices that include the preface, the dedication and two epigraphs, as well as the notes, which, as White offers, '[b]y no means exhaustive, . . . are there just to give a few discreet pointers' (1990b: 13). The notes point outwards, directing the reader.

Beginning with 'sea, wind, earth / clouds and rivers' (1990b: 81, ll. 9–10), let us consider the elemental in White's poetry. The elementals arrive and recur in these poems as something inevitably, corporeally experienced when being outside, on the move. In 'Morning Walk'

(1990b: 17), consisting of eight lines, four conjunctions, 'and', connect the features of the landscape with all the elements: the weather-world with 'a cold slow-moving mist' (l. 1), the sun, the earth, the beeches, the bird and the boy. It is a world subject to time, and through it, to destruction and decay, as witnessed by broken shells and 'mouldering leaves' (l. 8). Through the body, the subject experiences various attributes of place, including its atmospherics. The weather-world dominates perception; the self is attuned to corporeal, sensual experience, experiencing moments of attunement, that which Heidegger identifies as *Stimmung*.[15] '[W]rapped in weather' (1990b: 181), the self is enveloped in the folds in the world. This is further expressed in the interrelation between the rhythmic alignments of body and world. Corporeal attunement to the rhythms of the world involves the self being open and responsive to the regular movements of the earth, such as the tides. Tidal movement serves as a formal device, a number of poems being dominated by waves, the rhythms of the natural world co-existent with the rhythms of the mind. This fusion of form and theme, an attunement to bodily and world rhythms, offers a movement towards something that Merleau-Ponty considers a disclosure of 'an ontology through depth and rhythm', which 'would have to be not grasped but performed' (Wiskus 2015: 123). The world is experienced not only subjectively, but intersubjectively, in a constant dialogue with the landscape, with other animate beings and inanimate objects.

Interweaving Landscapes

In contrast to (and complementing) the impermanent, ephemeral aspects of the weather-world, there are poems concerned with geological, deep time. They underline an interconnectedness of beings and things, their embeddedness in the ecosystem, pointed out by Aldo Leopold in an often-cited passage from 'Thinking Like a Mountain': 'behind these obvious and immediate hopes and fears there lies a deeper meaning, known only to the mountain itself. Only the mountain has lived long enough to listen objectively to the howl of the wolf' (1949: 129). As Lawrence Buell points out, Leopold provokes people 'to make a concerted effort to think against anthropocentrism . . . [which] amounts to nothing less than a new Copernican revolution at the planetary level – this insistence that the world must no longer be thought of as revolving around "us"' (2005: 105–6). Dominated by ice and stone, 'Scotia Deserta' evokes a withdrawal of the self in a deglaciated and deserted landscape. Another poem, 'Sun Yoga' (1990b: 57), comprises three elements: the sun, the 'rock-like' self and breath, or light, stone and air. The self merges with world in its most basic form. Similarly, 'Fossil' (1990b: 95) combines the rock formed millions of years ago and the print left by a bird mixes with drops of rain. There is thus given to the reader a sense of synergy between self and world, a 'human-lithic enmeshment' (Cohen 2015: 26), an interweaving that is organic and ineluctable for White:

> Why would not the synergy exist among different organisms, if it is possible within each? Their landscapes interweave, their actions and their passions fit together exactly: this is possible as soon as we no longer make belongingness to one same 'consciousness' the primordial definition of sensibility, and as soon as we rather understand it as the return of the visible upon itself, a carnal adherence of the sentient to the sensed and of the sensed to the sentient. For as overlapping and fission, identity and difference, it brings to birth a ray of natural light that illuminates all flesh and not only my own. (Merleau-Ponty 1968: 142)

Synergistic relations recur in White's poems, which often evoke a 'sheer experience of the nakedness and loveliness of everything, an ecstatic experience, expanding to the sense of cosmic unity' (White 1998: 64). Such a unity may be possible in moments of being-in-the-world. In 'Interpretations of a Twisted Pine' (2003: 213–14), the words of Matsuo Bashō cited in the epigraph – 'Learn of the pine from the pine' (2003: 213) – remind the poet of the need to pay attention to the world and so notice things as they are. In the poem, the pine becomes one with the mind:

> The branches of my brain
> are alive to sun and rain
>
> my forest mind
> is in tune with the wind
> there is reason in my resin. (ll. 24–8)

The subject's self-identification with a pine tree emphasises an interfolding of a mind with the natural world, thus forming an inseparable bond. It is thanks to 'our own mineral composition' (2010: 46) that we can experience affinity with the trees and the rocks, as David Abram argues. The repetition of a possessive pronoun, in phrases such as 'my forest mind' and 'my resin', in combination with words associated with the plant world, stresses a reciprocal enfolding and intertwining. Reason combines with resin in a phonological adherence, combining *logos* with sap, two essential constituents, foregrounding an elemental, as well as a semantic and sonic sense of interweaving. This in turn may be read as illuminating how Being-in-the-world is a phenomenological experience, involving one's being attuned to the rhythms of the weather responding to sun, wind and rain.[16]

The intertwining of the mind with the vegetal world in 'Interpretations of a Twisted Pine' gives way to a 'Sun Yoga' flesh. In 'Autobiography 1' (1990b: 25), the speaker dwells in 'the breathing emptiness' (l. 6), leading a lowly, animal existence. The most elemental, essential function of existence, the breath connects him to other living beings, despite the loneliness prevailing in this image. In the dark and uncertain, he is

> groping my way through the undergrowth
> with only
> the feeling of existence
> as it trembles in an animal belly. (ll. 10–13)

Deprived of vision, the speaker is left with a sense of touch, as foregrounded in the tactility in the gerund form of the verb 'groping', the form suggestive of a repetitive aspect of this action. With its consonantal sounds – the repeated fricative 'th' which falls at the beginning, in the middle and at the end, tightly clasping the three words together – the expression 'through the undergrowth' stresses the difficulty with which the speaker moves. What remains is the basic, primordial feeling shared with other animals. Thus in an acute moment of a creaturely life, the speaker experiences what Merleau-Ponty describes as 'the culmination of subjectivity and the culmination of materiality', when 'my body is made of the same flesh as the world (it is a perceived), and moreover that this flesh of my body is shared by the world, the world *reflects* it, encroaches upon it and it encroaches upon the world' (1968: 248). The speaker is enmeshed with the world through breath in a supreme moment of subjectivity and materiality.

Glimpses of the interfolding appear in 'Crab Nebula' (1990b: 39), which opens with the words 'In this lighted chaos I' (l. 1). The visual bracketing achieved with the repetition of the letter 'I' emphasises the chiasm between beings. The personal pronoun suspended at the end of the line stretches the existence of the subject and carries to it the next line, composed of three verbs – 'live', 'move', 'have' – strung in a chain linked by two conjunctions, 'and', and capped by the expression 'my being'. Strong, one-syllable words are connected through the dental consonant 'v' and a variant of a vowel. In a circular motion, the third line returns to the first line in its situation work but reverts concepts: 'chaos' becomes 'mass', whereas 'lighted' becomes 'incandescence': 'in this mass of incandescence'. The opening line recurs in the same form in the first line of the second stanza, when the remnant of a supernova folds into itself a cosmic chiasm. Once again, light returns in this poetry, becoming endowed with a materiality, and assuming a carnal, synergistic form.

An awareness of the interweaving landscapes is visible in the attempt to refrain from imposing an order that would falsify the organic arrangement foregrounded in a number of poems on a formal level. For instance, 'The Chaoticist Manifesto' (2003: 550) refrains from imposing an artificial order that comes with language by attempting to arrange the world into a logical sequence, endowing it with a teleology. Typographically irregular, the poem's visual structure suggests a scattering of signs, a refusal to impose fixed points of departure. It abandons a syntactic order and coherence for breath, moments of vision, the present, the real. Our participation in the world is fragmentary: we may have a glimpse of the wild Being, we may briefly, sensually experience the interconnectedness, but it is momentary and does not extend beyond that instant. White's poems attempt to probe what is behind such acts of responsive surges of fragmentary mapping. The world exists as a seriality of topographies in a recurrent entwining between the open self and the world that is there, that gives, the world as other, as constellated alterity. The elements are aspects of phenomena of the conscious perception of the world's state as one of constant and unending repetitive fragmentation. White's poetry is a process of consciousness mapping of the signals of the world, which it picks up, the elements and other atmospherics being the pulses of the world's semiotic that the conscious self minimally orders as so many iterable coordinates to give a sense to the world, to what it is, which is – as with a map – all surface, no depth. His directionless peregrinations foreground the significance of the interaction with the environment, a renewed relation with the world, through a geopoetics that is '[p]oetry, geography – and a higher unity' (1992: 174). Through grounded subjectivity and corporeal mediatedness of perception, in sparse, minimal language this poetry strives to reject fallacious representations in order to focus on objects that arise in becoming, and flow through. Thus in movement, the new poetic mindscape wanders in an open space, or 'sky, or sea, the Ocean, the Unlimited' (Deleuze and Guattari 1987: 495).

Notes

1. Other names may be added, such as the 'intellectual nomad', a concept that will be discussed briefly in this chapter, or the 'navigator–wanderer', which White employs in his collection of essays *The Wanderer and His Charts* (2004: vi).
2. Jeff Malpas, who discusses the concept in depth in his study *Heidegger's Topology: Being, Place, World*, stresses the significance of 'placing', arguing that Heidegger's examination of being always entails 'presencing or disclosedness as this occurs in terms of the happening of a "*Da*", a there, a *topos*'

(Malpas 2006: 14). Heidegger draws from the origin of two Greek words, *topos* and *logos*, which gives 'the sense of a "saying of place" (*Ort-reden*)' (Malpas 2006: 33). Thus topology is 'an attempt to "say" the place of being' (Malpas 2006: 305), to find language to evoke place. In 'The Thinker as Poet', Heidegger writes, 'poetry that thinks is in truth the topology of Being' (2013c: 12). It is where different elements gathered in one unity, a place where we find ourselves, where truth is disclosed to us.
3. Mohammed Hashas devoted a whole book to the concept. See *Intercultural Geopoetics in Kenneth White's Open World* (2017).
4. For instance, in Elżbieta Rybicka's and Anna Kronenberg's studies from Poland, both titled *Geopoetyka* and published in 2014 White's term occupies an important place. Other critics and writers who refer to White's geopoetics include Kazimierz Brakoniecki (2010) and Mariusz Wilk (2012). White's concept also resonates in the Middle East, as Omar Bsaithi demonstrates in his book (2008).
5. Pierre Jamet points out that it was Michel Deguy 'who actually invented the concept of geopoetics twelve years before White', giving it a different meaning (Jamet 2009: 111).
6. I would like to thank Julian Wolfreys for suggesting this.
7. White mistakenly ascribes these words to Niels Bohr (White 1992: 165). In fact, they were uttered by Werner Heisenberg. Bloch remembers how, during a walk with Heisenberg, they started talking about space. After having read Hermann Weyl's *Space, Time and Matter*, Bloch 'was proud to declare that space was simply the field of linear operations. "Nonsense," said Heisenberg, "space is blue and birds fly through it"' (Bloch 1976: 27).
8. If one wished to be pedantic, one would specify that white, reflecting all the visible wavelengths of light, has no hue and thus is achromatic.
9. This last remark stands in opposition to White's claims of selflessness and the erasure of ego, a contradiction that seems to compromise his project.
10. The capital letter is another example of the pathos that is so characteristic of White's style. The concept of 'the Outside', which 'has no image, no meaning, no subjectivity', is highly problematic. It may be argued that the 'outside' is an image, a result of both perception and language. As Jacques Derrida puts it, '[t]here is nothing outside of the text [there is no outside-text; *il n'y a pas de horstexte*] (1997: 158).
11. Yet, White himself risks being accused of white Western idealism of the other, as such fetishisation could be considered insulting to non-Western cultures.
12. This echoes the concept of the sublime introduced by Kant in his *Critique of Judgment*, in which he explains the pre-cognitive in the face of the landscapes that creates an aporetic experience. In the face of a sublime object, characterised by 'unboundedness' (1987: 98), imagination fails to apprehend it. For Kant, the sublime resides in 'crude nature' (1987: 109), in the 'wildest and most ruleless disarray and devastation provided it displays magnitude and might' (1987: 100). The idea of infinity evoked by the experience of the sublime reminds us of the inadequacy of imagination, a feeling comparable to 'an abyss in which the imagination is afraid to lose itself' (1987: 115), as our cognitive powers, including the power of language to express, prove limited. As Kant explains, 'our imagination strives

to progress toward infinity, while our reason demands absolute totality as a real idea, and so . . . our power of estimating the magnitude of things in the world of sense, is inadequate to that idea' (1987: 106).

13. 'Language is so often considered only in terms of inter-human communication. But you're not only in the human context; you're in the universe. You have to have some awareness of non-human and cosmic language too. I keep *logos* in touch with *eros* and *cosmos*, and it all started back then' (Dósa 2009c: 261). Alluding to Matsuo Bashō, White admits that it is 'Ah!' that appears 'in front of some astounding scene. Exclamation comes before communication' (Dósa 2009c: 262).

14. Apropos such thinking, Levinas calls *il y a*, 'element', whereas for Merleau-Ponty, *il y a* is Heidegger's homeland (Tymieniecka and Matsuba 1998: 11). Indeed, Merleau-Ponty's *il y a* is a translation of the Heideggerian expression *es gibt*, developed in *Being and Time*. For Heidegger, different uses of the verb 'to be' are connected to existence, to being present and to being there, or *Dasein*. The fact that the word *gibt* 'is the present tense third-person singular of the verb *geben*, which means "to give"' is 'crucial' for Heidegger (Philipse 1998: 237). As Herman Philipse notices, by 'giving this very gift, Being conceals itself and remains mysterious' (1998: 238). In 'The Specter of a Pure Language' from *The Prose of the World*, Merleau-Ponty suggests that 'expression involves nothing more than replacing a perception or an idea with a conventional sign that announces, evokes, or abridges it' (1973: 3).

15. A polyvalent word, *Stimmung* appears in Martin Heidegger's *Being and Time*, where he writes about it in reference to the attunement (*Befindlichkeit*) of Dasein, its openness to the world, a thrownness (*Geworfenheit*), or the facticity (2010: 134–7). The term has manifold meanings, which change according to context as Heidegger expands it by a number of derivatives such as *Bestimmung*, *Übereinstimmung* and *Stimme*. Krzysztof Ziarek underlines the significance of the concept of *Stimmung* in Heidegger's work, offering an illuminating analysis of various meanings of the word, which includes 'a tuning or a disposition and a voicing' (2013: 64). Hubert L. Dreyfus notes that, for Heidegger, *Stimmung* might be mood as well as affect, affectedness (1991: 169), as it is the manner in which *Dasein* is affected. According to Rodolphe Gasché, in *Stimmung*, which 'must be understood beyond all psychology of moods' (1999: 117), *Dasein* 'is shown to be capable of being "affected" by the world and directing itself toward things in a world that in every case has already been disclosed to it' (1999: 116). 'Dasein's being attuned in a state-of-mind is the existential a priori of all possible linkage, connecting, or relationship,' Gasché argues (1999: 116). White writes that *Stimmung* is a 'tuning', 'which isn't just an internal psychic event, but is a delivered way of being in the world' (1992: 169).

16. Heidegger's concept of the four-fold earth, sky, divinities and mortals, gathered by a bridge in a 'simple oneness of the four' (2013a: 147), brings together human beings with the divinities on the surface of the earth and beneath the sky. As Andrew Mitchell writes in his study, *The Fourfold: Reading the Late Heidegger*, things 'unfold themselves ecstatically, opening relations with the world beyond them' (2015: 3). For Heidegger, the interconnectedness is crucial, as being 'consists in dwelling . . . on the earth. But

"on the earth" already means "under the sky". Both of these also mean "remaining before the divinities" and include a "belonging to men's being with one another". By a *primal* oneness, the four – earth and sky, divinities and mortals – belong together in one' (2013a: 147). Humans stay on earth, under the sky, with other mortals and things, interconnected with 'gods', which represent customs and traditions, as 'the world-as-fourfold appears to be an integrated combination of nature (earth and sky) and culture (divinities and mortals)' (Wheeler 2011: n.p.).

Chapter 2

'Buried in the flesh': Home, Embodiment and Interanimality in John Burnside's Work

Radiant Meditations

This chapter aims to provide a discussion of the role and significance of concepts such as home, dwelling, language and, in general, the question of embodied Being in relation to John Burnside's writing. It can be viewed as expanding and supplementing elements of the original analysis in the essays on Burnside that I have written over the past few years.[1] This is especially so as regards my discussions surrounding the idea of dwelling and the place of human animals within the living world (as part of an attempt to decentre the human), which I consider as constituting predominant themes in Burnside's work, and which I will develop through the thinking of Martin Heidegger and Maurice Merleau-Ponty specifically, and phenomenological thinking more generally, but with reference to other modes of critical apprehension. This belongs to a larger project of exploring, through several exemplary Scottish poets who complicate the notion of 'nature poetry', the relation between human selfhood and the non-human world proposed in the Introduction. Burnside's writing offers a broad constellation of themes, tropes and topics; there is a richness and multifarious investment on his part. However, the ideas I have developed in the essays focus mainly on the impermanence of home, *Mitsein*, or Being-with other animals, and the question of naming things. In this respect, this chapter can be viewed as providing not only a particular way of reading Burnside's poetry, but also a more detailed investigation of the way in which the concept of dwelling relates to certain aspects of place, understood as a dynamic nexus of relationships, the concept of 'silent knowing', as well as concepts of the creaturely and unity. I see these themes, together with the problem of language, as dominating Burnside's poetic work. Apart from being a prolific poet, Burnside writes novels, essays and short stories, and regularly contributes to the *New Statesman*. I shall preface my reading of Burnside's poems with a consideration of his essays in a separate section.

Critics have noticed the 'rare, intense, unsettling beauty of John Burnside's poetry and prose', which 'gives us a momentary glimpse of a magical realm that runs parallel to the everyday world' (Brewster 2006: 179). Other scholars write about Burnside's ability to combine various elements, focused on 'mixing the civilised with the savage, the spiritual with the material, and Christian with gnostic or pagan imagery in unsettling ways' (McGonigal 2006: 235). Don Paterson has called Burnside's poems 'radiant meditations [upon the] transparent natural world numen' (Paterson and Simic 2004: 26, qtd in Bristow 2009: 50). Radiance is often combined with menace, which has been pointed out by such critics as Scott Brewster, who writes that 'the wonder of the natural world, the unassuageable longing for transcendence, and the ever-present potential for startling cruelty – are woven together by the ever-present fascination with retreat and (self)obliteration' (2006: 179). Some critics, such as Steven Matthews in his review of *The Hunt in the Forest*, point to the limitations of Burnside's 'enterprise', '[t]he unremitting earnestness' of which can sometimes become a 'burden', as often 'the sequences lapse into the near-pretentiousness of a rhetoric about the subject, rather than revealing the marvellous potential in the subject itself' (2010: 91). This 'near-pretentiousness' might be seen as a possible link to both Kenneth White's foreground of self, in a poetry that struggles to reconcile the oneness of self and non-human world on the one hand, while also speaking to the mutability, the ineluctable protean nature of a self barely there (yet all the more felt in its withdrawal and the trace it leaves) in an ever-changing world in the poetic world of Kathleen Jamie and Robin Robertson. David Borthwick and James McGonigal find elements of Scottish literary tradition, folk culture and communal identity in Burnside's work. As Borthwick claims, '[i]n his verse Burnside taps into vestigial and almost forgotten Scottish traditions' (2011: 134) and sees similarities with Neil Gunn and George Mackay Brown. McGonigal argues that Burnside's poems emerge 'from passivity, which 'contrasts with the technologically driven and positivist vision of MacDiarmid and Morgan' (2006: 236). Furthermore, he points to 'a blending of the Scottish/continental tendency towards analysis of arcane experience or supernatural glimpses with the more English tendency ... towards pastoral escape and contemplation of detail' (McGonigal 2006: 238). All the poets discussed in this book are 'Scottish continentalists', and so embody the greatest traditions of Scottish literature in its historical opening of itself toward European thought in its many forms, as well as to non-Western thought, concept and belief (North American and Asian) that passes over the country to the south. Louisa Gairn helpfully situates Burnside among 'writers consciously setting out to explore constructions of "self" and "other" in the context of ecological theory', such as Iain Crichton Smith, Ian Hamilton Finlay, Kenneth White, George Mackay Brown and Kathleen Jamie (2008: 5). She recognises 'older traditions in Scottish writing, such as Lewis Grassic Gibbon's *A Scots Quair*, or the poetry of Edwin Muir', which echo in some of Burnside's poems (2008: 185). Finally, Tom Bristow's excellent and necessary work on Burnside's poetry situates it in the philosophical tradition, particularly in the context of Henri Bergson's, Martin Heidegger's and Gregory Bateson's thought.

'One glimmering lattice of interdependence'

Burnside's voice on matters of ecology and sustainability resounds powerfully, urging us to relinquish our pretences of domination over the world. In his essays and articles Burnside consistently points to the necessity of opposing the damaging effects of encroachment on the land. The pernicious effect of the Anthropocene, a concept that has had a brilliant career in the past few years – defined by some as 'hubristic, elevating the human species by assuming it has godlike powers to shape the planet' (Morton 2016: 19)[2] – is a frequent concern in Burnside's essays and articles. He is not interested in the issues of Scottish identity and politics, appealing to the feeling of belonging that is not nationalistic, but instead is both local and universal, and strongly related to place: dwelling is made on earth, among other beings, and not in a particular country separated by borders. Yet, as he puts it in the essay *Otro mundo es posible*,

> Every good poem proposes this world and, to that extent, every *published* poem is a political act. I don't mean political in the party sense, of course, and I want to widen – or rather, to redefine – 'political', not merely to include, but to revolve around a question of right dwelling. (2003: 9)

This is a poetry that aims to undermine dominant discourses, where the poem becomes a political act, a statement of being, whereby its phenomenological opening is the 'right dwelling' and thus the redefinition of the political. Disagreement with the established order, as well as criticism of political leaders, corporations and banks, is necessary and may be practised through literature in a form of poetic dissidence explained as a refusal, 'a quiet yet dogged *Non serviam* on every level'

(2003: 4–5). Burnside's opposition is to contemporary global culture in its broadest sense: dissent from imposed views, the worst aspects of globalisation and commercialisation, a refusal to accept greed, consumerism and monetarisation of every aspect of life. Thus, the *non serviam* is a possibility of showing one's freedom and independence from the ever-growing demands of politicians and businesses. The poet's privileged position allows him or her to oppose the pressure of these forces and counter violence with another vision of the world. Consequently, the poem performs a certain kind of spiritual labour, as Burnside writes, while at the same time being irreducible to 'some kind of political or social recipe' (2003: 10); as he suggests,

> every poem contains, or implies, the proposal that *another world* is possible. ... A world where the nature of things is recognised as the rightful basis of our laws and customs and – not to put too fine a point on it – something holy. A world of dwelling. (2003: 10)

Unlike the critic, in placing the self in the world in a poetic way, the poet admits that the two – the self and the world – are not separate, a project Burnside shares, albeit a project effected in different ways, with White, Jamie and Robertson. To criticise merely the Anthropocene as such is to remain within the dialectics of criticism, which is subject to the empirical thinking that places the world at a remove. Writing a poem is both an act of a different politics and a politics – and poetics – of difference, of seeing and responding to difference. Making a political statement in effect means making an ethical difference that performs the difference through the close, the intimate intertwining of self with world. In its labour to imagined worlds, poetry performs a crucial role, opening new spaces: it has the power to experience the world whole, foregrounding the indivisible nature of phenomenal reality. This exceeds the work of critics such as Timothy Morton in their objectification of the problem through a recuperative discourse of the Anthropocene. In the world, which is often 'divided by sectarianism and tribal resentments' (2013: 147), the poetic act emphasises interweavement and interconnectedness. Poetry performs an essential role in tracing unity, as it is recognised through such poetry that we have lost the connection with the non-human world, frequently writing about our disconnection from a wild nature (to recall Merleau-Ponty's phrase) arising from increasing isolation caused by technological advances, which in turn distance us from the natural world further and further, while allowing, in that distancing, a fetishisation of the 'natural world' as simple dialectical opposite, itself a misrepresentation and misunderstanding. However, as Burnside demonstrates in his poetry, we are never entirely cut off from the non-human world: the poems point to the necessity of reuniting a broken relationship with the animal and vegetal worlds, and he admits that his books are 'about the continuity and the discontinuity between human beings and the natural world' (Dósa 2009a: 118). Foregrounding the feelings of separateness and calling for mending the gap, Burnside urges for the non-destructive sharing of the habitat. In the essays and interviews, he stresses that the purpose of 'ecological art', which is to reconnect us. Poetry acts against the impossibility of wholeness in its effort to combine and associate.

Burnside's writing frequently transcends borders of various kinds – whether of a national, geographical or generic nature. His cosmopolitan influences and intertextual references suggest a transnational ambition, an aspiration to go beyond borders, and find connections and correspondences. An incorporation of poetic traditions converging in his work demonstrates an openness that is also an opening to, for or of the other. There are numerous references to the Bible and religious writings, such as those of St Augustine of Hippo and Hildegard of Bingen, which give his texts a spiritual dimension. Literary and other aesthetic references form a bridge through accessing a language of aesthetic figuring and cultural or philosophical representation, which arrives in the poetry to stand in for those places where the poet's language would otherwise fail, or fall silent. In allowing the various voices of writers, philosophers, theologians et al. to speak, Burnside's poetry constitutes a constantly constellated performative act, wherein the stitching of voices across time and discourse produces a bricolage that is the world, the subject engaged in the world and responding to the world across time and cultures. Thus Burnside mobilises those voices in the service of a poetics of the 'other world'. In doing so, Burnside discounts and challenges the assumption that we are separate from the world, but suggests that there is a continuum, of which we have lost sight: a continuum made manifest in the mapping and tracing of his constellated references. The song of the earth appears alongside resurrection symphonies and blues tunes in Burnside's canon, being in harmony with one another. Similarly, Christian as well as animistic thinking of non-Christian cultures informs the thinking in the core of this poetry, together with Heidegger and other philosophers. Burnside's writing shows a connectivity that we have never lost but merely forgotten, because the composition of the poetry comes from all the places where humans think, and so affords a re-thinking of the Anthropocene through a weaving together of various discoursing strands. He uses alternative belief systems to point us towards a different politics of being, as they are important discourses that afford Western thinkers an alternative mode of apprehension and articulation, when placed alongside phenomenological thought.

Burnside frequently voices his disagreement with modern approaches to the idea of nature developed since Romanticism and marked by oppositions: the source of beauty for poets and the laws of physics for scientists. However, a shift can be noticed in recent years, in which 'the viewpoints have been moving towards a common appreciation of nature, where function and form, beauty and objective fact, the laws of nature and a sense of mystery can coexist' (2003: 14), foregrounding the need for re-enchantment, as is captured in the essay *Otro mundo es possible*. This opens with a description of a Sami myth, which describes how the god of creation set the heart of a young reindeer at the centre of the earth. Against such re-enchantment, or as a way of stressing its importance, Burnside also foregrounds the vision of loss and destruction, and exhorting us to mend what can still be mended, Burnside urges us to share the habitat in a non-destructive way. He underlines the necessity to mend the broken relationship, stressing in the essays and interviews that the purpose of 'ecological art' is to reconnect us: 'Such a reconnection seems to me the basis of a new way of thinking, a way of thinking that, in turn, may change the way we dwell in and with the rest of the living world' (Crawford 2006: 105). We have forgotten the connection with the non-human world, he argues, but poetry has the potential to perform an important role in finding unity: 'poetry itself can be seen as a means – a discipline, a spiritual path, a political–ecological commitment – to wholeness and reconnection with the earth itself'. He continues, '[f]or an ecologically-*mindful* poet, the task is one of reconnecting, of rediscovering, as it were, one's own nature through connection with a wider reality, with the more-than-human' (Crawford 2006: 99–100). The reconnection can take place in the poetry of 'we', defined as 'preserving the environment and studying how we, human beings, should dwell on the Earth without destroying' (Dósa 2009a: 117). Burnside often uses 'we' about children and memories of the past, which makes these appear not only a 'present' but a 'temporal' concern. Childhood appears in his writing as a time when connection with other beings is the most powerful. Even though our relationship with the living world is fraught, there is still a possibility to mend the broken connection, and this can be achieved by proper dwelling.

If poetry may offer a chance to alleviate the effects of the disconnection of humans from the world, as Burnside stresses when he talks about a fundamental concern with healing, in its broadest sense, it is 'not the healing of the world, or of the other, so much as a healing of oneself, sufficient to allow for a continuation of meaningful and non-destructive play between self and other' (Fazzini 2009: 121–2). There are hopes for healing through poetic form by abolishing harmful divisions, stressing familiarity and sharing. Re-establishing the connection, and thus hoping for unity, is possible, thanks to a mode of reflective and immersive mindfulness (which is itself discontinuous – it cannot be endless) and the faculty of listening. Poetry invites us to listen attentively to the song of the earth, as writing and reading poetry constitutes 'a heightened self-awareness, in which we are capable of knowing the self, and laying it to rest, for a time, in order to be open to, to attend to, to *listen* to that world' (Burnside 2003: 9), which results in an intimate feeling of seamless fabric forming what we think of as reality.

Re-establishing the connection, realising the interlacing between the self and the world and thus striving for unity, Burnside argues, is possible, thanks to full awareness and the faculty of listening, as human alienation from nature can be mended by listening. He urges us to listen attentively to the song of the earth: 'everything – everything – is continuous, *everything* belongs, the world of being is seamless and entire, one fabric, one glimmering lattice of interdependence. One extended heartbeat' (2003: 10).[3] The repetition of the word 'everything' and the emphasis placed on the word are particularly significant here, as 'everything' includes everything human, non-human and technological. It is also important to note the use of nouns – 'fabric', 'lattice', 'interdependence' – that foreground the sense of interconnectedness, the interweaving of elements. Furthermore, adjectives such as 'continuous', 'seamless', 'entire' and 'glimmering' strengthen this vision, foregrounding oneness. It is luminous but perhaps also unstable, dynamic, in a constant process of becoming. Finally, the metaphor 'one extended heartbeat' points to the vital quality of this interdependence, which resembles a living organism. Burnside assures us that the song of the earth 'is not a metaphor, but an actual sound, one that can be listened to' (2006: 102). Music is there in poetry, a reflection of the fabric of the world, its intricate weft, all the threads and strings requiring playing from the poet and inviting the reader to attend to the dehiscence of the ear. Music is also poetry, poetry being the recording of the music. Thus poems are a form of dehiscent existence, attuned to the world and the other, attentive to the quotidian and mundane, and at the same time an evocation of the enchantment and wonder, close to the earth, and its 'mystery of the simply living being' (2003: 70), to use to Giorgio Agamben's words. Music and mystery will return in this chapter as they recur in Burnside's poetry.

Home, 'a random matter'

Burnside insists repeatedly that we should learn to dwell properly with respect for all beings and things. It means a quiet, yet relentless dissent, an opposition to an imposed world view, a resistance to rational, critical objectivity, which can be realised poetically. For Burnside, artists in general – and poets in particular – should demonstrate dissent from established opinions, as he sees the role of the poet in a refusal 'to serve the apparatus of commercial and cultural imperialism' (2003: 4). His poetry exemplifies this approach, straying from the hegemonic, human-centred *Weltanschauung* and instead seeking to highlight connections and correspondences between humans and the world, the lyric being the fullest expression of the intertwining of the self with the world. Burnside underlines that habitat matters more than tribe, place more than nation and state (Crawford 2006: 93) in a world where there is '[t]he beauty of the real, as opposed to the virtual' (Crawford 2006: 93). Informed by Martin Heidegger's thought,[4] Burnside argues the importance of a 'philosophy of dwelling that includes all things, living and non-living, and informed by the principle of *ahimsa*, of doing, if not no harm, then the absolute minimum of harm' (Crawford 2006: 93). Ensuring 'a continuation of meaningful and non-destructive play between self and other' (Burnside, qtd in Fazzini 2009: 122) would create a possibility of what would constitute a proper, mindful dwelling on earth. Burnside emphasises the necessity to share one's home with other creatures, but also highlights the impossibility, the impermanence and the fleeting and frail nature of home. One of the epigraphs to *The Asylum Dance* comes from Heidegger's writing on dwelling, explicitly suggesting that this is the poet's preoccupation:

> The proper dwelling plight lies in this, that mortals ever search anew for the essence of dwelling, that they must *ever learn to dwell*. What if man's homelessness consisted in this, that man still does not even think of the *proper* plight of dwelling as *the* plight? Yet as soon as man *gives thought* to his homelessness, it is a misery no longer. Rightly considered and kept well in mind, it is the sole summons that *calls* mortals into their dwelling. (1993: 363)

'The plight of dwelling' is about finding or negotiating one's place in the world, temporary and provisional as it is, a transitory home that humans share with other beings, which has to be learned anew because it is *the* plight, the most fundamental predicament of human existence. The word 'proper', used in this translation, a word to which Burnside returns in reference to the question of dwelling, emphasises two aspects: its rightness and individuality. The dwelling plight is experienced individually and thus must be undertaken by everyone continuously, as the 'essence of dwelling' is that one must never settle but continue to learn how to achieve it. This crucial passage and the fact that the paradox is the location of consciousness and reflection for Heidegger, mean that one must remain with the problem rather than seek a solution. Paradoxically, it seems that it is this very homelessness that allows for the condition of constantly dwelling and for allowing a return to the past as collective memory. This sense of togetherness is created by a frequent use of the first person plural. Thus there occurs a tension between solipsism and sharing the experience with other beings.

The sense of the frailty and temporariness of home is often combined with a memory of a familiar place, where memory forms the abode, becoming the domain of dwelling. Such memory is that which connects Burnside in his homeless dwelling to both White's walking the earth and Robertson's enfolding of the self in the atmospherics of place as this returns in poetic language, to stand in for the memory of the self's past in the places of the north-eastern Scottish coast, which abide in the poet as the tropes that open the self to the world in the present act of writing. Foregrounding the provisionality of dwelling, Burnside argues that 'the perpetual need for settlement, like the quest for the moment's grace, is necessary because home, like grace, is a temporary, sometimes fleeting thing, and cannot be occupied as such' (2011b: 23). There exists an inherent paradox in the human need to have a safe, stable abode and the constant impermanence of things, and Burnside embraces the contradiction that forms the central theme of the Heidegger epigraph. The necessity to negotiate one's place in the world is thus a major concern of Burnside's poetry, and the need for home recurs with the words 'home', 'haven' and 'harbour', reverberating in many poems. There also appears to be a connection between home and a port, where a harbour is home but also a departure point, a place that is merely passed through; the figures of the sea and the traveller often recur. For instance, in 'Ports', the opening poem of the collection *The Asylum Dance* (2000), the title of the last part, 'Moorings', echoes both the title of the poem and the epigraph, foregrounding plurality. The title of the first section – 'Haven' – in turn suggests protection against danger, a place of safety, as well as something pertaining to seafarers, which further strengthens the temporariness of place. McGonigal believes that it 'is unclear whether such travel is freely chosen or whether the poetic persona is driven by a deeper restlessness to undertake his agnostic pilgrimage into alien territory' (2006: 243). It may be argued, however, that the necessity of being on the move – commensurate with Merleau-Ponty's ontology, which 'rests on the significance of movement' (Buchanan 2008: 116) – that is foregrounded in the collection stems from the nature of home, which is never given and must be learned anew. In the troping of his language about the non-human world, Jamie and Robertson also foreground the significance of motion, as does White in the act of walking the world, the steps of the poet becoming the movement of the poetry through the world. The dwelling place is not defined by anything solid or concrete, but rather by a changing light, which is elusive and fleeting. The second part continues this motif, its title 'Urlicht', or 'Primal Light', alluding to Mahler's Symphony No. 2, also referred to as the Resurrection Symphony, thus foregrounding renewal and revival, a returning of light. Experienced corporeally, perceived and felt, light foregrounds the relation between embodiment and consciousness. According to Merleau-Ponty, light initiates the visibility of things, inaugurating 'the openness of my perception upon the world' (1968: 42) as the body opens itself to the natural light, becoming dehiscent, 'in order for the visible there to become my own landscape' (1968: 118). Light 'illuminates all flesh' of the world (1968: 142) in the elemental alliance of things.

At times it is merely a slant of light that creates a dwelling place for us, an understanding that highlights its fleeting nature to remind the poetic subject that while everything passes, only light, wind and rain will remain. 'Nothing's impermanent here, where nothing is ever untouched by the wind, or the salted rain,' as we read in the fourth part of 'Epithalamium' (1997: 50). In this line, four negations – 'nothing', repeated twice and the negative prefixes 'im-' and 'un' – powerfully emphasise the only certainty that remains: everything is of a 'fleeting nature'. An inherent feature of the landscape, the motif of impermanence returns in a number of poems. In 'Remote Viewer with Three Moons' from *A Catechism of the Laws of Storms* (Burnside and Maclean 2014), the self surrenders to things falling apart – to becoming-transient, to the experience of panic that remains. In the line ' – so nothing to do but submit to this gap in the wind', the dash preceding the verbal expression is indicative of the silence that arises in the experience of the moment. This gap resonates in the self that stands watching the dereliction reinforced by such words as 'splinter', 'topples' and 'dredges away', bracketed by the expressions 'in the cold salt air' (l. 3) opening the sentence and 'in the cold salt tide' (l. 6) closing it, the three single-syllable words echoing one another in the movement of vowels. Acceptance of the world's transitory nature echoes through the poem, as the word 'submit' returns in the expression 'we only submit' (l. 20), followed by 'and what else to do but give thanks, though things fall apart' (l. 23), which expresses a calm realisation of the nature of things.

Home is never owned for long; one may even say it is never owned. Burnside perceives it as ephemeral, momentary, unstable, achieved merely in a glimpse before the feeling of impermanence returns. As we read,

> and home a random matter: transitory,
> provisional;
> somewhere you find by chance. (ll. 41–3)

The lines come from 'Poem on a Line of George Seferis' (2017: 78–91), published in the collection *Still Life with Feeding Snake*. 'A random matter' in the lines above gestures to an understanding of home as something that happens, something unknown, occurring without definite aim or pattern, given to chance. It is substantial, solid, but sometimes it can also be redolent of air, scent or musk (as in 'Field Mice' from *The Light Trap* (2002)), thus brief, impressionistic, ungraspable. Burnside often balances between materiality and immateriality, fusing the two, as, for instance, in the lines from 'Harunobu: "Catching Fireflies"' (2002: 14): 'as gravity // makes light / material' (ll. 54–5). His speakers vacillate between materiality and immateriality, organic and inorganic matter, flesh and wood or stone. Home in his poetry is something tangible as familiar birds and plants, and that which cannot be grasped, like an emotion, a memory, something unnameable. 'Inherent in the spine' (2000: 5), the urge to find a dwelling place is primal, wild. This yearning resounds in us, reverberating endlessly like bats in 'Echo Room' (2009: 23), which 'flicker' (l. 2) and 'skim' (l. 5), 'all skitter and echo, / gathering, then forgetting' (ll. 14–15), the short vowel and the guttural consonant repeated – echoed – in the first three verbs, the final gerunds prolonging the effect, emphasising their continuous, cyclical nature.

In many poems, connections are constructed on both the thematic and the technical levels. On the structural level, there are frequent enjambments, including intrastanzaic ones, which signal possible divisions, but simultaneously highlight cohesiveness as the separate lines come together to form a poem. The form of many Burnside's poems is marked by a high degree of irregularity: there are no regular stanzas, and the lines are broken, scattered, which emphasises the sense of rootlessness. What is achieved in these poems is an organic form. Regular prosody is merely alluded to, skirted, and a large number of lines are broken, with many enjambments. Irregularity of form thus foregrounds the recurring themes and reinforces the expressive force of the poems. Charles Bennett writes about 'the odd prosody' (2002: 150) typical of

Burnside: 'his strange placement of lines and the lilting divisions – have a tendency to cohere toward the end of the poem. Burnside seems to be suggesting that things fall together, not apart' (2002: 150) and 'He is absorbed by the sense of attachment and simultaneous detachment. . . . He is continuously present and utterly absent: connected and fractured at the same time' (2002: 150). Burnside understands and presents the experience of the world in terms of synchronicity. Fiona Sampson suggests that Burnside's 'stepped lines' be named 'scoring', as they direct the eye (2012: 248). According to her, the manner in which the lines are arranged on the page is suggestive of 'air, space or a resonating chamber' (2012: 248). As she puts it, Burnside's 'concertinaing techniques' emphasise what she calls 'longitudinal unity', whereby parts of the poem are combined 'by *aural* logic' (2012: 249). Indeed, Burnside achieves unity in a seemingly disjointed manner (as if unity were a chance that befalls the poet). Connections are also constructed by means of poetic devices, such as metaphors, which act against the impossibility of oneness. Moreover, Burnside's predilection for one-syllable nouns that are frequently combined to form internal rhymes emphasises the dynamic relationships that occur between beings. The most frequent system of versification involves broken lines, which form and reveal iambic pentameter when combined, heightening the urge to mend – or at least form a kind of a hinge within the fabric that is self and world – the relationship with the non-human world and foreground the longing for unity pervading Burnside's writing. The fragment in such forms of versification is suggestive of something greater, while remaining complete in itself. The fragment is whole and therefore never the fragment it seems at first to be; its own unity resists suggesting an ontology greater than itself, even though in the laying out of fragments a greater image emerges or is suggested implicitly. In Burnside's method, the fragment is complete, but in the suggestion of greater connections, immanence is always there, as the formal revelation admits.

In this poetry, the quotidian is imbued with the extraordinary, the self is immersed in the now but also a form of memory work. The wild seeping in through porous borders reminds us of our creaturely lives, in a phenomenological entanglement with the flesh of the world. Such encounters constitute epiphanic moments, forms of the realisation of *Weltlichkeit* of *Geist*, or Worldliness, the enworlding of spirit, a realisation the transcendental relationship, or the chiasmic intertwining between the self and the world. Those moments when we experience 'the fragments of the luminous field' (Merleau-Ponty 1968: 152), when my flesh adheres to the flesh of the world, remind us of 'the cohesion of my body with the world' (Merleau-Ponty 1968: 152). Time and again, memories of collective childhood return in the poems: while the novels often focus on a solitary child, in poetry, childhood is often a collective experience or one that connects (to others, to the mother, to the world) rather than alienates. Bristow writes that 'Burnside's poetry is littered with dispersed structures of consciousness: epiphanies; dreams; memories; meditations' (2011: 162). Yet the verb 'litter' does not seem to be a fortunate word in relation to Burnside's method, as it suggests that there is formed an accumulation of objects, scattered about in disorder. Epiphanies, dreams, memories and meditations are not thrown into these poems yet they constitute their essence, their very body. Furthermore, representing a phenomenological experience of the world, they give the poetic self a chance of 'apprehending essence' (Husserl 2012: 134). These negotiations are related to his poetic search for reconnection with the non-human world, demonstrating a longing for oneness, *Sehnsucht*. Nostalgia recovers the home and presents it as lost, and it is the lost status, spoken from the position of a present homelessness, the condition of the modern man, that the poet constructs in order to imagine a connection to the world that abides, that dwells and on which we can dwell, and which therefore begins the thinking of a politics and an ethics of difference.

Sehnsucht is embedded in the flesh, as '[t]he body as the sum of all nostalgias' (l. 1), to borrow a line from 'Abiding Memories of Christian Zeal' (Burnside 2017: 7), which evokes a longing for a prelapsarian world. An idea we carry in us, *Sehnsucht* is the ghost of a home, or a haunted house we carry around with us. Neither material nor immaterial, *Sehnsucht* is something felt but not tangible, and therefore always in the experience; with a yearning it experiences and memories it carries within, nostalgia makes itself materially present through the form of flesh and bone, evoking the enfoldedness of phenomenology. This powerful, pervasive longing, a dream of belonging and a dream for something lost, recurs throughout Burnside's poetry. For instance, in 'Bird Nest Bound' from the collection *Black Cat Bone* (2011a: 42–3), the thought of home – a powerful yearning for a dwelling place – is signalled in the opening lines, 'In the slow time, after the end, all you want / is home' (ll. 1–2). The title of the poem, 'Bird Nest Bound', refers to a blues album from 1930 by Charley Patton, and the line in italics is a travesty of a line from the song, 'Take me home, sweet home, baby, to that shining star.' The longing is further emphasised at the end of the poem, with 'the true self' (l. 32), finding

> an old belonging, something he couldn't believe
> till now.
>   *Safe sweet home, sweet home, through that shinin' star.* (ll. 34–6)

'The true self' can be reached only in a dream, where 'an old belonging' is also experienced. The dream ends in a rude awakening when the speaker wakes 'in the cage of my bones, / on the same cold ground' (ll. 37–8), homeless and alone. The liminal state between dreaming and waking is suggestive of unreality, situating genuine being beyond the realm of our terrestrial existence. Inhabiting the world in a constant yearning for finding one's 'true self', the speaker longs to be home, truly and permanently, yet realises the impossibility.

'Buried in the flesh'

Many poems evoke the difficulty of describing the experience of the world, of verbalising something that is lived, something that can only be sensed apperceptively. That is why the undecidable, the ill-defined dominates Burnside's lyric. While in Burnside there is in this a modernist sensibility, the effort to define through negation, Robertson solves this through the affirmation of the protean. One grasps after the event the nature of the phenomenon, after it has metamorphosed into another figure, another form, another trope. The flesh folded with the flesh of the world, the poetic subject experiences things sensually, intuitively. In 'Viriditas' (2002: 78–82), the title refers to greenness, vitality, fecundity, and is a reference to Hildegard of Bingen's text in which she praises the divine force of nature. Things are not fixed or stable: there is a prevailing sense of instability and shimmering movement. Aiming to avoid 'any kind of reification of the subject, either as a mind *or* as a body', Burnside's poetry, just like Merleau-Ponty's philosophy, 'seeks to understand subjectivity as a dynamic and open-ended process of emergence' (2012: 2), in Scott Marratto's words.

> Subjectivity emerges with the emergence of meaning in the world on the basis of the self-articulating character of living movement. What Merleau-Ponty calls 'perceptual meaning' thus arises on the basis of a dynamic that is, as it were, older than subjective *consciousness*. (Marratto 2012: 2)

Meaning emerges dynamically and so words and expressions suggesting an approximation abound in 'Viriditas', as in many other Burnside poems: for instance, 'something like guesswork / happens amongst the leaves' (III, ll. 11–12), 'somewhere in the gap between // the last faint gust of birchseed and the point / where rain is blue again' (III, ll. 9–10). Crossing the interstanzaic boundary, the image introduces the combined effects of air and vision: seeing and cultivating the greenness in our bodies and souls. Subject to the laws of the natural world, nothing is a static being but is a Deleuzian becoming, which is emphasised at the end of the third section: 'becoming mildew, slut's hair, / random birds' (III, ll. 19–20). The poem closes with the phrase 'lost in wonderment' (IV, l. 18), which foregrounds the rapture felt at the living world in the epiphanic moments and reminds us of our interconnectedness with things. Between the two leaves of the world, we carry traces of the living world in our bodies, planted there, interwoven with our tissue:

> It's buried in the flesh
> with avocet and lizard and the last
> glimmer of rock-salt
> ravelled in the spine. (I, ll. 20–3)

The vitality of nature, its *viriditas*, resides in the flesh and stone. *Viriditas* is *there* in our flesh – in the flesh of the world; it forms part of it just as animals do, and sediments of minerals occurring in the landscape. It is all 'ravelled', or entangled, where 'ravel' also means to undo the texture, to become unwoven or unwound, suggesting both presence and absence: a ghost, a trace. It is *there* but remains unnamed, unknown, unknowable, its spectral presence felt but invisible, just like 'xylem' (l. 26), one of the transport tissues in vascular plants that conducts water from the roots upward. The word is echoed in the neighbouring 'flexed' (l. 26), the meaning transported as the guttural sound turns into the dental one, starting in the throat and travelling on the tongue to reach the teeth. The verb 'blet', in the expression 'bletting in the bone' (l. 28), suggests a further vegetal–human entanglement, a process of decay, over-ripening of a fruit constituting part of human body matter. This is not a rational process, as is suggested by the verb 'think' repeated twice, and replaced by 'never think it' toward the end of the first section of the poem: 'but never think it; / let it go unnamed' (ll. 24–5). Thought does not yield; it is the pre-conscious knowing, a kind of sensual knowledge hidden in the flesh, 'a preconceptual cohesiveness between body and world' (Buchanan 2008: 132). With it come the abundance, the energy, the sustaining power of nature. The self strives to situate itself in the world until it becomes intertwined with it: this is something still to come. On the cusp of change, Burnside speaks frequently of experiencing epiphanic moments, which may offer glimpses of *kairos*, the right moment in which something significant happens. 'Kairos' is a title of one of the sections of 'An Essay Concerning Time' (2009: 36–41), standing in opposition to 'chronos', or chronological time, in another part of the poem. *Kairos* is a spot of time, it is indeterminate, while *chronos* is a measurable string. *Kairos* suggests a rare, elusive glimpse of the ineffable, the 'ungraspable', as 'the present is from close-up, in the forceps of attention, it is an encompassing' (Merleau-Ponty 1968: 195), in which the sensible world is woven, passing threads, an instant when an opening appears. Phenomenologically experienced, 'nature' is understood as 'intra-structures, intersections, not things or exterior substances, but glimpses of the world for someone who is of it and inhabits it in the cohesion of his life' (Merleau-Ponty 2003: 228). Being *of* the world, the self in Burnside poems touches and is touched by it in moments of epiphany, glimmers 'we salvage / from the instantaneous' (2002: 14, ll. 54–6).

Many poems are dominated by the awareness that even if we are of the world, our understanding of it is most often limited. The impossibility of assigning words, of naming the experience that overwhelms in moments of epiphany is a brush with the undecidable. There is often a sense of the unknowable, the real lying within all phenomena but impossible to apperceive through processes by which the mind comprehends phenomenal objects. This reflects a Kantian approach, in which '[p]henomena and noumena, or the natural and the supersensible realms, are not wholly unconnected ... but our knowledge of how they are linked is extremely limited' (Bennett 2001: 41). The truth that underlies the real but remains impossible to know, remains beyond human understanding. This is often when our creaturely nature brings an embodied 'knowing'. Such Merleau-Pontyan 'silent knowing,' or 'pre-knowing' (1968: 178), brings us closer to wild Being. In 'Epistemology' (Burnside 1994: 43), the speaker begins to 'suspect' (l. 1) the existence of creatures 'to match us, under the earth' (l. 2): fish 'dreaming us alive' (l. 4) and 'moles' decoding a muffled existence they would guess // was music, or a story being told / in cipher' (ll. 6–8). These animals dream, decode, 'guess' (l. 6), just as we do when we try to comprehend them because humans may explain non-human animal worlds only in anthropomorphic terms. Knowing based on intuition, or as Burnside often puts it, on 'guesswork' (a word that recurs in his poems: for instance, 'and what they leave behind / as guesswork' (2007: 33) and 'experiment / in guesswork' (2002: 23)), offers a chance to make sense of the world. Instrumental in knowing the world, the body must remain dehiscent in order to recognise the natural order of things, where facts are not known (if they can be known at all).

In 'Yird' (meaning 'earth' in Scots), the second part of 'By Pittenweem' (2007: 56–66; the first part is titled 'Home'), the speaker is

> alone in the dark and looking to see what there is
> between the near field and the kitchen door:
>
> the old familiars shifting in the grass
> beyond the garden. (II, ll. 5–8)

Immersed in darkness, the self senses the world of betweenness, endeavouring to decipher 'what there is', unnamed, though familiar. The self's positioning is indicated by the inclusive preposition 'in', which suggests that the self is contained *in* the dark, which also contains the house, the garden, the field and, further, the sea, the circle extending further and further with every place. 'Familiars' gesture towards a companion, someone who is often seen and also a spirit that may be embodied in an animal, guarding a person. Thus we exist in a chiasmic intertwining, even if we are often unaware of it.

Night and darkness recurring in a number of poems suggests that the subject remains in the dark, literally and metaphorically, frequently suspended between states. As the self immerses itself in the night, the visible is folded, or as Merleau-Ponty puts it, 'this coiling over of the visible upon the visible' (1968: 140) happens. In the dark, but also in the rain, fog or haar obscuring the vision – on the cusp of the visible – the sense of hearing dominates, enhancing the openness of the ear. The music of poetry, its musicality, thus becomes an expression of the song of the world, of which Burnside is aware, introducing complex phonemic patterning in his poems, which is also the material of blues albums and popular song. Merleau-Ponty writes about the 'carnal texture' (1968: 150) of light and sound. Music, as light, opens a dimension with the first contact, 'it is the invisible *of* this world, that which inhabits this world, sustains it, and renders it visible, its own and interior possibility, the Being of this being' (1968: 150). Music is what remains:

> where the nothing that happens in time
> is the one thing we have
>
> for keeps:
>   the seep of music through the bone:
> a wavelength of owls, where everything is static. (ll. 84–8)

The recurrent pronouns 'something' and 'nothing' suggest an oscillating movement between the indeterminate and the non-existent, emphasising what is indefinite, imprecise, vague: the poet's favourite images. The above lines come from part one of 'Responses to Augustine of Hippo', titled 'De Corporis Resurectione' (2007: 3–6). The body is reborn cyclically with the appearance of snowdrops and the arrival of song, 'the black / transformed to green' (ll. 41–2). The poem is imbued with the atmosphere of expectation, the speaker remembering the wait for the coming of god every spring, 'more atmosphere than flesh' (l. 52). Memories of childhood mingle with the impressions of transitional states, with glimpses, snapshots and oneiric scenes, juxtaposed to form unusual combinations: for instance, 'apples, mole-runs, tiny birds' (l. 38), 'dew trails and traces of frost / in a downstairs cupboard' (l. 46), 'aconite; meltwater; cinnabar; Prussian blue' (l. 12). These lines exemplify Burnside's focus on things that are 'minor, commonplace, even trivial', as he says, emphasising the significance of this gesture in poetry (Crawford 2006: 93). Yet, things perceived and mentioned are often 'approximate' (l. 11); the only manner in which the speaker achieves the effect that they create, how they appear, is 'something like' (l. 69), an expression recurring in Burnside's writing. This is another difference between Burnside and Robertson. While things are 'approximate' for Burnside, they are precise for Robertson; having appeared for the latter, they transform almost immediately through the unstoppable motion of the grammar. As in many of Burnside's poems, cohesion is achieved through rhythm and sound patterning. The sense of ungraspability continues in the next parts of the poem. This is the case with the poem 'Responses to Augustine of Hippo' (2007: 12–15), which refers to St Augustine's work of the freedom of will. In the lines cited below we may recognise the motifs mentioned above: the dark, indeterminacy, betweenness, guesswork:

> – something that comes
> from the dark
>   (not
> self or not-self)
>
> but something between the two
>   like the shimmering line
> where one form defines another
>   yet fails to end. (III, ll. 1–8)

In the above lines from the third section of 'Responses to Augustine of Hippo', titled 'De Libero Arbitrio' (2007: 12), the sense of uncertainty, of ungraspability, dominates, where the pronoun 'something' repeated twice foregrounds the hesitation of the speaker in naming things. This 'something' is barely perceived, ill defined, in between two forms or emotions, its definition infinitely deferred. There remains only an approximation, a comparison to something similar but not quite the same, the ungraspable never possible to pin down. The sense of ungraspability is further emphasised by the form of the poem. The lines are of variable length, and the poem lacks regular rhymes but contains numerous enjambments, suspending the meaning across the lines; this is a formal indication of betweenness, making borders hazy and porous. As in many poems, it is a stream of memories and instances of dreamlike epiphanies, accessible as mere glimpses when we experience 'kinship of flesh with flesh' (2002: 5).

This kinship extends beyond the life we know, or perhaps there remains a hope of such connection in '[t]he absence of another here-and-now, of *another* transcendental present, of *another* origin of the world appearing as such, presenting itself as irreducible absence within the presence of the trace' (Derrida 1997: 47). At times there is a suggestion that the human animal connects with other animals through the transmigration of the soul, which comes to inhabit the bodies of other beings. The idea of transmigration resembles the work of poetry itself, a kind of translation, a metaphorical mobility, a flow that allows for such imagination to take place. In the third part of the poem 'Blackbird' (2002: 63–9), titled *'metempsychosis'*, which opens with the question 'Who would be born again in the plated flesh / of the armadillo?' (ll. 1–2), the speaker further wonders

> and shall I follow, taking up the life
> that waits to happen: creature memories
> and blood-heat; colours; stitchwork in the bones;
> the singsong heart that beats amongst the leaves? (ll. 18–21)

The poem is filled with questions, the tone hesitant and uncertain, the speaker musing on the possibility of creaturely lives, experienced in other corporeal forms, 'a body of fish-scale and fur' (l. 6). Imagining rebirth, the speaker performs a thought experiment of another embodiment, adhering to the flesh of the world where the elements are mingled: human craft with blood and bones, the intertwining of the animal and the vegetal. A figure of betweenness, the blackbird is believed to go between worlds, functioning in the whole collection as a messenger, a guide making possible the connection.

Encounters with the Wild

In Burnside's poetry, the concept of home is not necessarily tied to a place but is embodied by kith and kin of the animal kingdom. Reappearing in a number of poems, the word 'kith' points to such concepts as 'homeland' and 'home', and is also related to 'knowledge' and 'familiarity'. It comes from *cuð* 'known', the past participle of *cunnan*, 'to know'. The original meanings of 'kith' were 'knowledge' and 'one's native land'; thus what we know leads us to a dwelling place, 'choosing our landmarks, finding the best way home' (Burnside 1997: 52). The speakers are often homesick, suggesting a yearning for a place but also for other living beings, as in the line 'homesick for the other animals', ending 'History' (2002: 20) and opening 'The Light Trap' (2002: 23–5).

In 'The Soul as Thought Experiment' (2011a: 64), the speaker catches a glimpse of belonging, a moment in time, a place 'where you cannot help but think // of kinship' (ll. 16–17). In the lines 'sweet as love // and feral, like the soul you disallow / to call this home' (ll. 7–9), the liquid consonant in the nouns 'love' and 'soul', the adjective 'feral' and the two verbs 'disallow' and 'call' weave the sound and prolong it until 'home'. The soul becomes a thought experiment, a device of the imagination used to investigate the nature of things, bringing us closer to wild Being. As a result, a sense of kinship occurs, a transcendental relationship, 'some black road you thought was yours alone, / made bright and universal' (ll. 18–19), leading to the enworlding of spirit, a gesture in which self and world are mutually enfolded in the moment of vision or awareness.

The human/non-human intertwining is experienced particularly powerfully in moments of encounter, when animals cross our paths – or when we cross theirs. Such brief moments, often mere glimpses, bring a brief realisation of the transcendental relationship of the self and the world. Sightings of the wild are a reminder 'of something / lost, a creaturely / awareness I could only glimpse // in passing' (2014: 52, ll. 44–5). Entangled with the flesh of the world, the poetic subject becomes momentarily one with other beings. Oneiric images recur frequently in Burnside's poems. On the boundary between dream and waking, the poetic subject is immersed in an unrepresentable experience. In 'Five Animals' (2007: 36–41), it resembles ' – a rumour of flight, / a gift from the legible world' (III, ll. 26–7), or becoming bird, 'my fingers a flurry of light' (III, l. 3). There are mere glimpses of another being, as if they were glimmers of the interwoven threads of *viriditas* showing through the fabric, as in part V, titled 'Coyotes (Sonora)'. The speaker 'hurries on', repeatedly, through images of the desert and a house, going between the inside and outside. The faint traces of something ungraspable, 'a gust of wind; a thread of green' (V, l. 16), evoke a powerful yearning that presses on the speaker and makes him run 'towards some / epicentre' (ll. 9–10), towards the open. Drawn outside by the sounds of the living world, which remain unintelligible, the speaker experiences a moment of wholeness, possibly evoking an image created by Kant, who believed that 'nature speaks ... it utters enough to assure us that, or at least give us enough hope that, the world is a coherent order' (Bennett 2001: 44–5). The self is summoned by voices coming from the desert, speaking of a long-forgotten connection in another time, reminiscent of a wholeness, until he is called back by 'the voices calling from the present tense / restoring him' (ll. 19–20) to 'the nothing of the self' (l. 21), an emptiness of the current existence.

In another poem filled with non-human animals, titled 'Varieties of Religious Experience' (2007: 23–35), part six, 'Totem', evokes the realm of a dream, 'the animals further away / and indistinct' (VI, ll. 3–4), as spirit beings, emblems that remind us of our ancestry, their existence a hint of our creaturely nature. In part nine, titled 'The Adept Owns Nothing but Has the Use of Everything', the mice remind the speaker

> how a man might
>   prosper
>   if he dared
> making himself at home
>   without a sound,
>   adept
>   unledgered
>   loyal to his burden. (IX, ll. 36–43)

The word 'prosper' is echoed in the word 'dared', which follows it. It comes from Latin *pro* and *spere*, 'according to one's hope', burying hope in these lines despite the modal verb 'might', which enhances the sense of unlikelihood of man rendering himself happy. The word 'unledgered' – unrecorded, uncounted – suggests a yearning for a life in which the economic, transactional dimension and the keeping of ledgers, all obscuring access to wild Being, are not needed. Not counting money paid and received, people might finally become 'adept' at making a dwelling, attaining 'an animal / propriety' (IX, ll. 31–2), a true nature. As the title suggests, such a dwelling of the adept would entail no ownership. Animals are *there* as a quiet presence, often sensed merely through traces such as footprints, scent, musk, spoor; they are a remainder of wilderness from our anthropocentric perspective, but also a reminder of our creatureliness. For Burnside, they are a model of making oneself at home, something that humans cannot do properly.

At times the subject's engagement with the world is total, as in the poem entitled 'Transfiguration' (2011a: 31), in which the speaker finds a dying bobcat and relates the experience, how he 'stole the tattered remnant / of its soul' (ll. 2–3). In 'the man–animality *intertwining*' (Merleau-Ponty 1968: 274), the breath of the dying animal inhaled by the speaker tastes of 'blood and catpiss and a thread / of spirit . . . like gasoline' (ll. 6–7). Combining disparate elements such as an immaterial being, bodily fluids and a chemical mixture, the simile admits how we inhabit the animal world as much as the technological one, forming the bridge, as poetry bridges the space between human and world. Therefore, Burnside does not oppose the modern world as such; he merely laments its negative forces. He sees a human capability of connecting everything with everything, thereby reminding us of what we have forgotten but not lost. This is why the memory of childhood is important in his poems, for children do not 'know' their being. Returning to the poem, the human–animal intertwining in the moment of death brings a powerful metamorphosis, a mystical experience: the eponymous transfiguration, alluding to the Transfiguration of Christ described in the New Testament, as a result of which Jesus became radiant in glory. The effect of the union is the poetic subject's transformation into the Alpha and Omega, the beginning and end of all, 'the First and the Last' (Apocalypse 2: 8), a symbol suggesting divinity. The human and divine elements combine, the connection evoking the temporal and eternal dimensions coming together. The final line – 'my blood exchanged for fire, my thoughts for stone' (l. 14) – emphasises the promethean power of the intertwining, the daring creative force.

The total, elemental immersion takes the form of fire and is redolent of the creative force of spirit. In 'Rain', from the collection *The Hunt in the Forest* (2009: 26), the epigraph 'And thou shalt renew the face of the earth' comes from the Office of the Holy Spirit. A prayer for guidance, 'Come, Holy Spirit' contains lines about rekindling the fire of divine love (Psalm 104: 30), which suggests active spirituality, beyond the power of language to convey. The poetic subject watches the bats and moths flickering, the world shifting 'from lit to dark, from unseen to seen', which usher in the chiasmic reversal. The creatures imitate, echo and reiterate the motion of light and dark, here in the form of darkness and light stitched together by the animals that cross the borders between them:

> though the spirit is creeping, inchwise, through
>   mortar and blood,
> unpicking the fabric, renewing the face of the earth. (ll. 17–18)

As in the line from 'Transfiguration' discussed above, the spirit of connectivity prevails, once again with three elements – spirit, blood and mortar – uniting the immaterial and material world, as well as the human and non-human world. Holy Spirit, or *Pneuma*, air in motion, breath and wind are recurrent images in Burnside's poetry. Air mediates between us and the world, ensuring a passage from our bodies to the flesh of the world; breath coming in and out of the body becomes a link between the outside and inside. At the same time, the forgetting of air is the main destination of Being, as Luce Irigaray argues (1983: 5). Furthermore, the weather-world is where perception begins, with the wind and the rain, as

> [p]erception is not first a perception of *things*, but a perception of *elements* (water, air . . .) of *rays of the world*, of things which are dimensions, which

are worlds, I slip on these 'elements' and here I am in the *world*, I slip from the 'subjective' to Being. (Merleau-Ponty 1968: 218)

The self experiences Being first and foremost through immersion in its elements. In the words of Luce Irigaray, we all participate 'in a universal communion through air' (Irigaray and Marder 2016: 41). The motif of air is frequently employed in Burnside's poems to foreground impermanence and fleetingness, emphasising that temporality and finitude are the main features of dwelling where states in between dominate. References to air, fog, phosphorescence and ether suggest the immaterial, the ungraspable realm of being that is sensed and perceived by Burnside's poetic subjects, representing the ineffable, which remains hidden behind the materiality of things.

As has been mentioned above, betweenness is a recurrent trope in Burnside's poetry, visible on many levels: between language and thought, between self and the world, between inside and outside, between animal and human, between being and animality, between presence and absence, between the visible and the invisible, between dreaming and being awake, between this life and the next, between the poet and the reader, thresholds between the house and the wild. It is not so much an abolition of the gap but the making possible of a communication – a communion – a crossing over. Proposing a non-dualistic, non-binary vision, Burnside is concerned with what happens in the seam of things. His is a poetry that lies 'at the borderline between "self" and "other"' (Fazzini 2009: 121–2), striving to connect, healing the gap, abolishing the separateness. In his discussion of the borders, boundaries and bounds in Burnside's poetry, Ben Smith suggests that 'the other selves and twins', appearing frequently in Burnside's poetry at the borders of a familiar world bring with them 'connotations of haunting and gothic figures such as the doppelgänger', as they 'unsettle and destabilise the perceived notions of identity', not fixed in space or time, suggesting that 'the self not only transcends the Cartesian "shell" of the body to become defined along with its environment, but that it continues to exist, simultaneously at different times, in different potential situations' (2013: 70).

In part VII of 'A Process of Separation', titled 'Mandrake' (1997: 13), the images evoke disparate worlds crossing one another:

> I know this ghost. It's only a drift of smoke
> in the summer darkness,
> fox-piss lining the hedges, road-kills and dew.
> Something from nowhere. (VII, ll. 11–14)

The speaker claims to know – a curious choice of verb, knowing, 'if there is such a thing' (2008: 7), as Derrida says – something vague, a composition of many elements, becoming known, coming to be present. Other words are worth looking at closely here. For example, in the line 'It's only a drift of smoke', the word 'drift' suggests a mass but can also be a drift as in drifting: a course, a current, movement. It may be a certain scent lingering in the air, or perhaps an after-image left by animals. At the end of the stanza, the word 'thing' appears, embedded, 'some thing': what is that thing? The ghost is 'a thing which is unnameable or almost: something, between something and someone, whoever or whatever, something, this thing "this thing", but this thing and not another, this thing looking at us, defying semantics as much as ontology, psychoanalysis as much as philosophy' (Derrida 2006: 26). Ghosts and hauntings recur in Burnside's poems, reminding us that there are things that defy semantics, things – 'some things' – that leave a trace yet cannot be grasped or articulated.

Foxes and the unnamed, unnameable road-kill, mutilated beyond recognition, leave a trace – a scent, a smear of blood, shreds of flesh, a print. The trace suggests an absence but not a lack, according to Derrida:

> The trace is not a presence but is rather the simulacrum of a presence that dislocates, displaces, and refers beyond itself. The trace has, properly speaking, no place, for effacement belongs to the very structure of the trace. . . . In this way the metaphysical text is understood; it is still readable, and remains read. (1973: 156)

Thus, it is not presence but its simulation. In the absence of things, we strive to read traces. In Burnside's case, these are often texts of the living world. The metaphysical text of the natural world, its grimoire, or grammar, remains uncoded. The trace, the scent, is something alien, marking the outside, contaminating it with misapprehension. 'We live inside a grimoire we cannot read . . . and we write, in that same book, random and possibly unintelligible graffiti across the pages' (Burnside 2013: 264–5). The grimoire glimmers, remaining partially visible and invisible simultaneously. Burnside constantly looks into this textbook of magic, playing a sorcerer, in an attempt to decipher and decode its grammar and to learn its rules. The word 'grimoire' comes from the Old French word *grammaire*, meaning all books. But grimoire also came to mean a book of spells that perhaps only writers are capable of reading, capable of becoming animal, of becoming other. As Deleuze and Guattari argue, 'writers are sorcerers because they experience the animal as the only population before which they are responsible in principle' (1987: 280). 'If the writer is a sorcerer, it is because writing is a becoming, writing is traversed by strange becomings that are not becomings-writer, but becomings-rat, becomings-insect, becomings-wolf, etc.' (1987: 280).

Being, belonging, becoming niggle incessantly at Burnside, nibble at him. A recurrent motif in his writing is indeed belonging, a constant crossing of borders in search of a dwelling place, which is part of our creaturely nature:

> when I go back inside, my mind falls quiet again and, as I settle by the stove, that sense of belonging returns, which is to say a belonging that is not to this or any specific place, or to any community or faction or tribe, but to the dust from which I came and to which my body will return, and to the entire corpus of the creaturely. Spring tide and chert and blizzard. Flamingo and bobolink and pine. The lives of unknown others who are awake in the dark, watching fires, or writing in tattered notebooks like this one. (Burnside 2013: 265)

The lives of other beings remain unknown, unknowable, despite the attempts to read from the grimoire of the living world, the grammar of belonging, which is about being:

> in a world we do not know
> and name the things
> one object at a time:
> fishing boat, lighthouse, herring gull, clear blue sky. (ll. 11–14)

The above lines end the poem 'Pentecost', from *The Good Neighbour* (2005a: 25–7). The title of the poem refers to the descent of the Holy Spirit, as a result of which the Apostles started speaking in many languages. Naming is a recurrent trope in Burnside's poetry, the speaker recognising home by the ability to name things round about, as in the poem cited above, or encountering animals that escape naming, as in the poem titled 'Animals', which contains the line 'They cross our path, unnameable and bright' (2002: 18, l. 7). The intensity of illumination seems to be a substitution, or a replacement for the unnameable, giving to it a more profound eidetic function. Thus, Burnside vacillates between the knowledge of a slice of a familiar reality and the inability to name the world, where naming is 'the sole and unbreakable limit between man and animal' (Derrida 2008: 47); yet Derrida aims to '[accede] to a thinking [. . .] that thinks the absence of the name and of the word otherwise, and as something other than a privation' (2008: 48). The labour of language that we should undertake is to find names for *animaux*, or *animots*, the plural forms in French of the word animal and *mot*, signifying 'a word', 'a noun': 'The suffix mot in l'animot should bring us back to the word, namely, to the word named a noun [nommé nom]' ('Le suffixe mot, dans l'animot, devrait nous rappeler au mot, voire au mot nommé nom') (2008: 48). However, names do not come naturally, and Burnside often remarks that so many of the animals we cross cannot be given a name. There is nothing 'natural' about the 'proper' name; the name signals what is proper to the self, the manner in which one marks as property that which is most proper, and which accords with its imprimatur the propriety of that which is, and is not something else. This experience is 'Chanced upon a mystery of eyes / They cross our path, unnameable and bright' (2002: 18, ll. 6–7). The exchange of looks brings to mind Derrida's realisation that 'an animal looks at me' (2008: 58). Animals look at me, they concern me, and I try to meet – reciprocate? – 'the bottomless gaze' (2008: 12). The gaze hides an undecipherable mystery. We could try to reverse the order to decentre the human and say that *we* cross their paths, unnamed, unrecognised. The poet further explores unknowability and unnameability in 'A Process of Separation', which opens with a question: 'What animals are these, / come from the fields, / shifting from form to form / in our clouded garden?' (Burnside 1997: 15; VIII Leaving, ll. 1–3). The lines foreground the plurality of animals, as well as their shape-shifting qualities as they cross the borders between the fields and the garden, the wild and the tame. The next stanza focuses on the movement of the animals, emphasised by the speaker's immobility as he watches them 'become invisible / then reappear an arm's length further on' (VIII, ll. 4–5). When they return, the animals are found immobile, no longer 'flitting' (l. 16) but lying in the porch, 'decaying slowly, lingering for days, // or lost between the floorboards and the wall: / a knot of hair; / an aftermath of feathers' (VIII, ll. 18–21). Watching a bird in flight, we may perceive a 'feathery commotion still here which is already over there, in a sort of ubiquity'; we may observe 'the unity of its movement' (Merleau-Ponty 1962: 288). When the animal movement is interrupted, when it no longer flies, swims, runs, crawls, it no longer has 'this adhesion of the multiple', which gives 'meaning to its surroundings' (Merleau-Ponty 2003: 156). The poem creates a contrast between the animals appearing, shifting and flitting in the first part and their fixed, lingering presence in the form of rotting flesh and, later, traces of hair and feathers. The instability, the shape-shifting nature of the animals spotted in the fields is foregrounded in the first stanza, establishing the speaker's relation to beings that are 'shy; evasive; grounded in the shadows' (l. 6). The sound effects in the line 'shifting from form to form' start with a sibilant 'sh' and follow with the accumulation of the fricative consonant 'f', interspersed with the liquid 'r'. The cluster 'th of f' in the expression 'an aftermath of feathers' enhances the presence of their trace. The animals remain unnamed, their *Umwelt* unreadable for the speaker. And yet they are there, close but impossibly far, as other, and we are open to their mystery, their alterity.

Animals return, and traces are found, then lost. Burnside's speaker often expresses a yearning for wilderness, gravitating towards the edges of existence. As he admits, the aim of his poetry is to bridge the gap between humans and the world:

> My poetry works at the borderline between 'self' and 'other' – partly with a view to undermining the feelings of separateness that make us capable of damaging the world in which we live, the meta-habitat that we must share with all other things. (Fazzini 2009: 121–2)

The threshold, a frequent trope in Burnside's writing, crossed between the inside and outside, is foregrounded by the full stop. Limitrophy is therefore his subject, to paraphrase Derrida: 'what feeds the limit, generates it, raises it and complicates it' (2008: 29). It is very much about 'questioning . . . the limit between Man with a capital M and Animal with a capital A' (2008: 29). There is a limit – some call it the abyss (a 'double chiasmatic invagination of edges' (Derrida 2013: 20), suggesting that once you open yourself on to the abyss, all meaning disappears and the very limit by which the human defines and separates itself from the animal finds itself as always already deconstructed[5]) – between humans and non-human or more-than-human beings. But this is our human limit. Animals know no limit, no limits. They are everywhere, invisible to us; they inhabit every nook and cranny of our houses. In 'Ahimsa Bee Sutra' (2009: 44), Burnside focuses on animals and their *Umwelt*, listing insects inhabiting the house, which include 'woodlice and gnats' (l. 3), 'craneflies and death-watch beetle' (l. 4), 'lice and moths' (l. 5). The list, which comes at the beginning of the poem, foregrounds the proliferation of animals tucked away and is topped with ticks in the penultimate line, a word that performs a double function: it can be a verb and a noun – a tick, belonging to the arachnid family. The cupboard 'ticks like a heart, or a cloud, / in the kindly dark' (ll. 7–8). We too share the 'place in the far end of the house . . . where the body seems truest, where it seems most creaturely, but I have no idea what the local fauna makes of' us (Burnside 2013: 264). The presence of barely or rarely visible creatures, tucked away in the nooks and crannies of a house 'in the kindly dark', shares a suggestion of the self and the other merging together. The acknowledgement of the presence of other creatures is visible in the careful choice of words, suggesting something imperceptible and inexpressible, founded on intuition rather than cognition. The third stanza unveils the conceit, as it is 'the house of the self' (l. 9) that is inhabited by such beings, and where bees are akin to a lion, 'rooms of honey in the bones, / the mane a haze of crimson and forgetting' (ll. 17–18). The long vowel sound in the middle word of the title joins the other two words, providing a thread, foregrounding the etymology of the word 'sutra'. Originating in Vedic literature, sutras are spiritual teachings, weaving various strands of knowledge. Combined with 'ahimsa', or doing no harm, the title thus proposes an alternative version of the fifth commandment, 'Thou shalt not kill,' teaching about the sanctity of life, all life.

As for ticks, the limit, the boundary, the difference seems to rely on their ability to wait. In *A Foray into the Worlds of Animals and Humans: With a Theory of Meaning*, Jakob von Uexküll writes

> At the Zoological Institute in Rostock, they kept ticks alive that had gone hungry for eighteen years. The tick can wait eighteen years; we humans cannot. Our human time consist of a series of moments, i.e., the shortest segments of time in which the world exhibits no changes. For a moment's duration, the world stands still. A human moment lasts one-eighteenth of a second. We shall see later that the duration of moment is different in different animals. . . . But time stands still in the tick's waiting period not just for hours but for years, and it starts again only when the signal 'butyric acid' awakens the tick to renewed activity. (2010: 52)

Uexküll's work, especially his concept of *Umwelt*, was important for both Heidegger and Merleau-Ponty in their writing on animals, as well as Deleuze and Guattari, and more recently, in environmental humanities, especially in the field of biosemiotics.[6] Giorgio Agamben picks up on this passage in *The Open*, noticing that the tick 'effectively suspended its immediate relationship with its environment, without, however, ceasing to be animal or becoming human' (2003: 47). He then enquires:

> But what becomes of the tick and its world in this state of suspension that lasts eighteen years? How is it possible for a living being that consists entirely in its relationship with the environment to survive in absolute deprivation of that environment? And what sense does it make to speak of 'waiting' without time and without world? (2003: 47)

adding 'Perhaps the tick in the Rostock laboratory guards a mystery of the simply living being' (2003: 70). These words, already cited, deserve another mention here in the context of the poem discussed above. The animals that inhabit the house, as well as those the speaker encounters on his path, present an unsolved and insoluble mystery of being.

We can say that, very simply, a living being experiences vulnerability as we share our finitude with non-human animals. They may not talk, but they too suffer and die. Jeremy Bentham's question 'changes everything' for Derrida (Wolfe 2010: 46), who writes about the finitude that binds us with the animal: physical vulnerability and death (Wolfe 2010: 126). The suffering and death of animals is a recurring theme of Burnside's poems. The poet takes the answer to Bentham's question further: not only do they suffer, but we suffer with them, seeing their pain, witnessing their death. For instance, the epigraph to the poem entitled 'Alcools' (2014: 70) – a line from Apollinaire's 'Cors de chasse', *'Passons passons puisque tout passe'* – reinforces a pervading sense of transience. So do poems then become testimonies, acts of bearing witness to the animal other, through the making visible the trace that remains, which survives beyond the death of the animal? In tracing the trace, they translate the untranslatable, voicing for us that which we otherwise cannot hear. In Burnside's poem, the speaker finds an injured goldfinch in the grass and takes it inside 'for a moment's shelter' (l. 4), demonstrating a momentarily child-like faith in defying death. From what does he want to provide shelter: from the inevitable? Yet the inevitable arrives as it always does and the speaker announces in the next couplet: 'It didn't live / and that was no surprise' (ll. 5–6). Perhaps, knowing this to be inevitable, what is important is that there is a witness to death, to record its event, acknowledge its coming to pass, the poet as the survivor who enables the trace to be repeated.

In 'Penitence' (1997: 60–1), ending the collection *A Normal Skin*, in which the speaker talks about hitting a deer with his car, the death of an animal is closely experienced. The poem takes a form of a confession, already announced by the title, in which the speaker, despite a willingness 'to go, to help, to make it well' (l. 24), admits to fear: 'not fear of the dark, or that presence / behind the trees' (ll. 30–1) but touching the agony of another being. The withdrawal from sharing pain with the other being becomes a sin, which the speaker regrets sorrowfully. The end of the poem suggests an intertwining, a chiasm through death (that chiasm is where the act of witness is 'felt', registered as trace): 'my own flesh in the body of the deer / still resonant, remembered through the fender' (ll. 44–5). Chiasm is 'adherent to *location* and to the *now*' (Merleau-Ponty 1968: 140); experiencing it, the self becomes powerfully intertwined with the world, emplaced in the present, as in the line 'a hard attention / boring through my flesh / to stroke the bone' (ll. 13–15). The expression 'through the fender' foregrounds the difficulty of remembering and talking about the event in the pronunciation of the initial sounds. The speaker seeks forgiveness from the animal for accidently hitting it with his car and possibly ending its life, acutely experiencing 'the dread / of touching, of colliding with that pain' (ll. 32–3), the harm 'still resonant' long after. The longing for connection with all sentient beings is expressed in the phrase 'own flesh in the body of the deer', a yearning to merge with another being ensconced in the wish to transgress bodily borders, for intercorporeity, or 'interanimality', which for Merleau-Ponty constitutes '*Selbstheit* of the *world*' (1968: 172). The expression 'tuning in' occurs twice: 'and something beyond the trees was tuning in' (l. 12) and 'the woods tune in' (l. 37), the latter immediately followed in the same line by the expression 'I listen to the night' (l. 42). He remains listening in darkness, *to* darkness, in a chiasm of the senses.

They cross our path and we are to follow as we are always after the animal, in both senses. Our 'evolutionary' moment is later than the animal's, but we follow the animal, we come (after the animal) to understanding belatedly that which the animal knows intuitively. There is closeness, the overlap of being and following; to be is to respond to someone's, some thing's call, to correspond. Burnside's animals are not separated from us by the abyss, a point which Heidegger makes in 'Letter on Humanism'. Rather, they tell us about our limits and limitations. Both singular and iterable, they remind us of 'the abyssal limit of the human: the inhuman or the ahuman, the ends of man' (Derrida 2008: 12) demonstrates that there are no limits to thinking of animals, to thinking poetically. When lost in the maze of unnameable beings, we turn to poetry, as 'thinking concerning the animal, if there is such a thing, derives from poetry' (Derrida 2008: 7), and poetry is like a hedgehog: 'rolled up in a ball, turned toward the other and toward itself [. . .] close to the earth' (Derrida 1995a: 36).

Re-attunement to the Continuum

The encounters with other animals that recur so often in Burnside's poems gesture towards a yearning for the recovery of the forgotten connection, which would lead to an 'illumination, a re-attunement to the continuum of objects and weather and other lives that we inhabit'; a poem is 'another source of that clarity of being that alchemists call *pleroma*' (Burnside 2005b: 60). A Gnostic concept, pleroma signifies 'fullness' or 'totality'. In the poem 'Pleroma', from an early collection, *Feast Days* (1992), the concept is represented by 'pure space'; the pre-existing if elusive light is a reminder of continuity and resonates in 'life'. In the endeavour to abolish divides and in the search for reconnection, the poems are marked by the yearning for fullness. From his first volume of poetry, one of Burnside's main preoccupations is unity. The eponymous poem entitled 'The Hoop' is preceded by a citation from Black Elk: 'The nation's hoop is broken and scattered. There is no centre any longer and the sacred tree is dead' (1988: 37). For Burnside's poetic subjects, the world frequently seems fragmented, disjointed, decentred, only coming together in brief moments of epiphany indicative of worldliness, the brightness of the unnameable. Perhaps this is not a negative aspect of Being, not a condition of our existence but simply the nature of who we are. As discussed above, connectedness comes from the realisation that humans share their provisional home with other creatures, which needs to be learned. Many of the poems foreground an interlaced quality of being, connection, correspondence, continuity, lyrical explorations of belonging. The epigraph to the first section of the collection *The Light Trap* (2002), 'Habitat', contains words by Paul Shepard, who writes about 'something more mutually and functionally interdependent between mind and terrain, an organic relationship between the environment and the unconscious, the visible space and the conscious, the ideas and the creatures' (1998: 35). The above words well express the motifs to which Burnside's poems return: the interdependence, the chiasmic intertwining of beings, which embodies the hopes for fullness, wholeness, pleroma.

As discussed above, Burnside often expresses this yearning for fullness in connecting the human with the non-human. Phenomenologically oriented, Burnside's poems mark a continuity with the more-than-human world, to use David Abram's expression. As Burnside repeats, his books are 'about the continuity and the discontinuity between human beings and the natural world' (Dósa 2009a: 118). 'A Theory of Everything' (2002: 83), which echoes the collection's epigraph, draws attention to the fact that the world may be accessed through immediate, corporeal knowing, appearing whole and complete even if this unity is elusive. Combining the senses of hearing ('the sound of water rushing through the pines'), smell ('a scent / unfolding from the earth, to draw us in') and sight (light, sea, 'sunlit track') makes the world seem instantaneously 'entire'. This is when the direct experience of phenomenological reality is not fragmentary or partial. Yet the glimpses of fullness are transitory, the feature foregrounded by the structure of the poem: the last two words separated by a line break yet linked with the conjunction, the run-on line allowing for one breath. Burnside's ambition to fuse various life forms suggests an attempt to abolish formal borders.

The interstices of the self and the world, human–animal and non-human animal, form an interrelated, fluid, endless continuity in Burnside's poetry, which is a thought experiment into the nature of things. Through the openness of *Umwelt*, the embodied animal subject may briefly experience cohesion with the milieu. The sense of briefness, of instantaneity, pervading Burnside's poetry reminds us that our dwelling place is a fleeting, temporary thing. Home is made *in* language, *through* language, as we name the things we know and recognise: things that make the world familiar to us. As many poems demonstrate, Burnside's speakers feel at home in a place if they are equipped with the capacity to recognise and name what they see. This gesture grounds them, makes them feel at home. We dwell in a world that remains unknown and unknowable, Burnside tells us, yet we endeavour to familiarise ourselves with it, finding a language to name the things we see, even though it may appear insufficient. As Derrida points us, we constantly experience 'the irremediable absence of the proper name' (1997: 106–7). As long as there is no name, there is no limit, no end, no totality, no ontology. Naming is frequently problematised in Burnside's poetry, as it is both positive and negative as an act. It might be said to give us back a connection to what we had lost touch with. It may also fix and order things, give them labels and a structure, and close them in categories, thus taming the unknown and harnessing the chaos in an anthropocentric gesture of colonisation. Burnside eschews this through his language of approximations, which emphasises the avoidance of succumbing to the illusion of knowing the world, being capable of deciphering its grammar. The language of the living world remains unknowable, and speech, which forms part of it, 'is mostly human twitter and bark, and sometimes merely the rustle of leaves' (Paterson 2018: 173). Aware of this, Burnside makes a home in poetry, making a poetic home everywhere, which may be realised only through coming to terms with our human–animal homelessness.

Notes

1. '"The Wider Rootedness": John Burnside's Embodied Sense of Place'. In: Monika Szuba and Julian Wolfreys, eds, *The Poetics of Space and Place In Scottish Literature*, 2019. '"A temporary, sometimes fleeting thing': Home and Dwelling in John Burnside's Poetry'. In: Ben Davies, ed., *John Burnside: Contemporary Critical Perspectives*, 2019. '"Beyond our Illusory Homelands": Representability, Deception, and Epistemological Angst in John Burnside's *A Summer of Drowning*'. In: Stephen Butler and Agnieszka Sienkiewicz-Charlish, eds, *Crime Fiction. A Critical Casebook*, 2018. 'Burnside's Bestiary: The Significance of Birds and Other Animals in John Burnside's Poetry'. In: Aniela Korzeniowska and Izabela Szymańska, eds, *Polish Scholars on Scottish Writers: An Interpretative Collage*, 2018. '"The *terra incognita* of the whole": John Burnside's Writing and the Entangled Bank of Culture'. *Litteraria Pragensia*. '"Peering into the dark machinery": Modernity, Perception, and the Self in John Burnside's Poetry'. In: Julian Wolfreys, ed., *New Critical Thinking*, 2017. '"That Essentially Scottish Virtue of Openness": Literary and Philosophical References in John Burnside's Poetry'. In: Aniela Korzeniowska and Izabela Szymańska, eds, *Scottish Culture: Dialogue and Self-Expression*, 2016. '"I think of them as guests": John Burnside's Encounters with Nature.' In: Philippe Laplace, ed., *Environmental and Ecological Readings: Nature, Human and Posthuman Dimensions in Scottish Literature & Arts (XVIII–XXI Century)*, 2015.

2. The concept is highly problematic, as has been pointed out by such critics as J. Hillis Miller and Tom Cohen. As Miller argues, the problem lies in the prefix 'Anthropo-', which 'begs important questions by buying into the Greek definition of "man" as male, reasonable, and Greek, that is, the prefix is intrinsically exclusionary, as the Greeks excluded women and all non-Greek others, the "barbarians" from the category of "man"' (Cohen et al. 2016: 146). This creates another problem with the concept: namely, that a number of thinkers consider the dominance of the human in the present geological age to be somehow separate from 'nature', overlooking the fact that nature is a concept of the Anthropocene.
3. As I write elsewhere, the importance of listening to the heartbeat of the earth, its song, is a major theme in Burnside's poetry, but also in the work of other poets discussed in this book. Martin Heidegger, Alain Badiou and Jacques Derrida point to the advantage that poetry holds over philosophy in this respect. In an interview, Derrida asks, 'I wonder if philosophy [i.e. rational thinking] . . . has not meant the repression of music or song. Philosophy [and criticism] cannot, as such, let the song *resonate* in some way . . . I do not write *about* these voices . . . I try to let them speak . . . The music of voices, if there is any, I do not sign it . . . first of all I listen to it' (Derrida 1995b: 394–5).
4. See Gairn (2008) and Bristow (2012).
5. There is implicit in this, as a gesture beyond Merleau-Ponty, Derrida's notion of the chiasmatic invagination. In two essays, 'The Law of Genre' and 'Living On: *Border Lines*', Derrida reads Blanchot's *La Folie du jour* through the notion of 'chiasmatic invagination'. By invagination, Derrida refers to the 'inverted reapplication of the outer edge to the inside in a form where the outside then opens a pocket' (1979: 97). In other words, invagination (which is necessarily double and chiasmatic) occurs at the moment when a text marks its border – but, by marking its closure, it introduces an opening; Derrida adds in 'Living On' that 'the chiasma of this *double invagination* is always possible because of . . . the iterability of the mark' (1979: 100). This leads, says Rodolphe Gasché, to the possibility of challenging all formal identities. There is, for Gasché, a fundamental difference between the notion of the chiasm in Merleau-Ponty and in Derrida. In both thinkers, chiasm prevents totalities from ever coinciding with themselves, but for different reasons: for Merleau-Ponty chiasm is marked by finitude, whereas in Derrida the chiasm is a '*structural* possibility affecting in principle all totalities precisely because their borders refer to an outer, to an other, and hence because iterability characterizes them as traces' (1987: xxii).
6. In his early work, *The Structure of Behaviour*, Merleau-Ponty cites Uexküll, 'Every organism . . . is a melody which sings itself' (1967: 159).

Chapter 3

'Gifts of the Wild': Dwelling, Temporality and Landscape in Kathleen Jamie's Writing

Coexisting with the Landscape

Born in the west of Scotland, Kathleen Jamie is a poet and essayist. Considered to be one of the foremost poets of her generation, Jamie is undoubtedly an important voice. Kirsty Scott notes that Jamie's 'trademark is a simplicity in seeing, a willingness to look, the resulting poetry and prose as close as writing gets to a conversation with the natural world' (Scott 2005: n.p.). The 'trademark simplicity' and the 'conversation with the natural world' are a result of, on the one hand, her grounding in philosophical reflection and, on the other, her travels. Jamie studied philosophy at Edinburgh University and made her poetic debut early, receiving the Eric Gregory award at the age of nineteen. At twenty she published her first poetry collection, *Black Spiders* (1982). She spent some time travelling in Pakistan and Tibet. Travels in the 1980s, exploring the world, resulted in the collection *The Golden Peak: Travels in North Pakistan* (1992; a new edition was published under the title *Among Muslims* in 2002) and *The Autonomous Region: Poems and Photographs from Tibet* (1993). Her travel writing has been collected in *Among Muslims*. In 2005, Jamie published a collection of essays, *Findings*, followed by *Sightlines* seven years later, both focusing on local places where plants and birds mark home. The Scottish landscape is an important theme in her latest poetry volume, *The Bonniest Companie* (2015).

Even though it would be limiting to call her merely 'a Scottish author' or 'a nature writer', terms that Jamie herself dislikes,[1] Scotland has an important place in her writing, as many of her essays and poems explore the relation of the individual and terrain. Intertwining landscape, language and history, Jamie's poetry is concerned with interrelations between land, perception and poetic form. The major concerns in

Jamie's early poetry collections – national and sexual identity – have yielded to the examination of the natural world in her latest volumes *The Tree House* (2004), *The Overhaul* (2012) and *The Bonniest Companie* (2015). Sparse verse marked by innovation and technical variety constitutes an important feature of Jamie's poems. As William Logan puts it, she has a 'modest, insinuating voice, one often with a surprising sting to it' (2007: 66), adding that her poems are 'taut, closely rendered' (2007: 66). Hers is a minimalistic poetry, pared down, devoid of unnecessary decorations. It suggests a formal relation to dwelling and perception, as poetic 'minimalism' is a way of perceiving more phenomenologically, because it is the work of the *epochē*, a concept coined by Edmund Husserl, meaning the radical reduction of perception so that all that exists is the subject and world, spatially and temporally. Close observation of nature is accompanied by a unique clarity of language that is linked with its musicality; precise style, elliptical sentences and economical use of poetic devices are its main characteristics.

There has been considerable interest in Jamie's writing, though there has been little sustained work on it, with the exception of Rachel Falconer's excellent collection with contributions from Alan Riach, Robert Crawford, David Wheatley, Timothy C. Baker and Lucy Collins, among others. Authors such as David Borthwick and Louisa Gairn have written on Jamie in the ecocritical context. Gairn notes that Jamie, together with John Burnside and Alan Warner, whom she discusses together, is 'not only reviewing human relationships with nature, but also the role writing has to play in exploring and strengthening that relationship, helping to determine the ecological 'value' of poetry' (2008: 10), thereby 'ensuring that a 'biodiverse' Scottish literature of the twenty-first century continues to discover new ways of exploring our crucial relationship with the natural world' (2008: 148). Employing Jamie's phrase 'lines of defence' (Fraser 2001: 20), Gairn argues that the poet's engagement with the natural world expresses her political commitment. Laura Severin sees Jamie's attempts to re-envision our relation to the natural world as necessary, but notes that 'the quest to create a more radical nature poetry is always marked by a process of struggle with the limitations of past environmental narratives' (2011: 99). Similarly, Deborah Lilley notes

> Consideration of what is encompassed by the term 'nature' recurs throughout her writing from different perspectives, and in the process, the category of 'nature writing' is reconfigured to accommodate those perspectives. Her versions of the form are composed from ecological, social and historical viewpoints, challenging both the idealisation of nature and the perceived externality of nature that enables such idealisation. (2013: 16)

Peter Mackay rejects the idea that Jamie's poetry expresses the song of the earth or dwelling plight, arguing that hers is a poetry 'as a stymieing and troubling of communication' (2015: 91). He suggests also that Emmanuel Levinas's ethics of the respect for the Other may be applied to Jamie's poetic project with better results than Heidegger's concept of dwelling (2015: 87–8).² Following Levinasian philosophy, which expresses the unknowability of other beings, for Mackay, argues that *The Tree House* offers 'a consummate communication of this non-communion' (2015: 91). Together with David Wheatley, Mackay disagrees with aligning Jamie with ecopoetry, thus refuting Matt McGuire's presentation of Jamie as a neo-Romantic poet (McGuire 2009: 146–7). For Wheatley, McGuire's analysis means 'steering clear from political stridency' (Wheatley 2015: 56) and he disagrees with what he sees as 'a strangely depoliticised response' (Wheatley 2015: 56) to Jamie's writing. It should be remembered here that, as Jamie herself states, writing about nature is a political gesture. McGuire, Mackay and Wheatley seem to draw from the understanding of Heidegger developed by Jonathan Bate.³ Jamie cannot be considered a neo-Romantic poet, as she moves beyond Romantic visions of the self and the natural world, refuting the ego- and anthropocentric tilt. What her writing proposes is a re-envisioning of the facile representations and appropriations of nature.⁴

Recognising the intrinsic value in landscape and renegotiating our place in the world, Jamie examines various approaches to the non-human world. The choice of prepositions is crucial, as the poet insists that she does not write 'about' the world, but rather 'from' or 'toward', or occasionally 'through' it (2004a: 5–7), thus stressing the intertwining. 'Writing towards nature' constitutes 'the pivotal figure', as Falconer puts it, which introduces new directions in Jamie's writing (2015a: 4). David Borthwick suggests that Jamie's writing is a response 'to contemporary alienation from place and disconnection from nature' (2011: 135), particularly in 'the latest phase' that began with the publication of *The Tree House* in 2004, which Jamie herself 'calls her shamanic mediation between various worlds . . . moving between the human and nonhuman world, seeking resonant connections' (Borthwick 2011: 139). This turn occurs at a point when the concept of the Anthropocene assumes greater importance. As Tom Bristow points out, 'the metaphor of the Anthropocene asks us to think of the human as one part of the More-than-human world, which is to think of us not within the world but of the World' (2015: 3).⁵ Jamie often insists on the need to diminish the role of the ego so that being does not dominate over the world, and one does not impose oneself. Diverse worlds conjoin in her work: the world of plants and animals, which intermingles with the human world and the intimate world of the body, demonstrating how to live deeply in the enveloping world, or what Merleau-Ponty calls a chiasmic intertwining with the world's flesh (1968: 130–55). Her writing foregrounds the fact that 'Human beings and their cultures are deeply enmeshed in the coevolutionary history of life forms, as well as being dynamically involved with the nonliving forms, materials, and energies of the world' (Westling 2013: 13). Poetic language serves to emphasise the enmeshment. Through poetry we come to experience 'the fragments of the luminous field' (Merleau-Ponty 1968: 152) but these moments of being are mere glimpses, transient and passing. Language is a site of slippage and absence, reinforcing human limitations. As Amanda G. Michaelis suggests, Jamie's poetry 'foregrounds the *instability* of the word, the body, and the self' (2010: 671). An important theme in Jamie's writing, which will be explored in this chapter, is transience, or a sense of temporality, which pervades her poems and essays; the phrase 'Everything else is provisional' reverberates throughout, foregrounding fleeting sensations and underlining brevity.[6] Jamie demonstrates that perception of the land – our co-existence with it – is affected by an awareness of the passage of time and how it is inscribed in the landscape. The analysis focuses on texts recording the experience of landscape stretched over time: how a sense of permanence is intermingled with a pervasive sense of transitoriness. It centres around Jamie's emphasis on human intrusions into landscape (the residue of human presence described by Jamie includes littered beaches, light pollution, and settlements that 'stain' the land), juxtaposed with the brittleness of flora and fauna, their transience underlining the temporality of dwelling. Offering a reflection on the passage of time embedded in the land, Jamie points to the necessity to negotiate our own dwelling place within a temporal framework. Temporality, represented in past, present and future considerations of change, is a major preoccupation; thus part of this chapter is devoted to an exploration of the interweaving of permanence and impermanence.

According to Jamie, poetry is a 'connective tissue where [the writer] meets the world, and it rises out of that, that liminal place'. As she says,

> I am interested in the world which is more-than-human, which is beyond the human. . . . The role of the poet is not to be political but shamanic (it's the only word I can think of), mediating between various worlds and bringing messages back and forth between them. (Dósa 2009b: 142)

Connectivity is an important aspect of Jamie's work, indicating numerous interrelations between land and poetic form, and emphasising the enworlding of spirit – *Weltlichkeit* of *Geist*, or worldliness. Following the poet's statement, 'I rub up against the world', sections of this chapter concern Jamie's phenomenological approach to the chiasmic intertwining between the self and the world. Hers is a writing concerned with what happens outside and beyond the domestic realm, but also inside it, at home, these two domains frequently intertwine, as in the essay 'Peregrines, Ospreys, Cranes' (2005: 29–47), in which ospreys observed from the attic window add to her everyday concerns, or in 'Fever' (2005: 102–13), where she notices cobwebs under the gutter of the house 'acutely' (2005: 102) when her husband falls ill but never 'with such intensity since' (2005: 113). One of the parts of *The Bonniest Companie* is entitled 'Homespun', woven in the home, simple and homely, unpretentious, suggesting the interwoven fabric of poetry, foregrounding the phenomenological Being, tightly entwined with the world.

Dwelling

Jamie's writing is about Being in the world, to employ Heidegger's term, but also about being within and towards it. Immersed in the landscape, she experiences the world around, where 'to experience' means to face. In her poems and essays, Jamie powerfully foregrounds an embodied existence and a need to dwell wisely. The sense of perception in all its forms is predominant. It includes an emphasis on sight but also the sense of hearing and tactility. Observing and listening, Jamie carries on a silent dialogue with the world, attentive to its texture. She foregrounds a corporeal presence in the world, which is our carnal participation: the poet's subjectivity intermingles with the flesh of the world, 'this earthly cosmos that carnally enfolds us' (2007: 163). She moves through the palpable realm, directing herself through her senses, highlighting the fact that the earth is a corporeal place that provokes an embodied response: we are enmeshed with the natural world, we form part of a web of interdependent relations. Found afresh with a sensitive, sentient body, the world can be explored and experienced fully only through poetic language, which opens 'the luminous field', allowing us rare glimpses of its fabric. Lucid language is accompanied by its musicality, as in the poem 'The Whale-Watcher' from *The Tree House*: elliptical sentences and economical use of poetic devices are the main characteristics of Jamie's style. The music of her poems underlines an exchange, constituting a non-verbal way of communication, as Jamie maintains a dialogic relation with the natural world. Highlighting the importance of musicality in Jamie's poetry, Rachel Falconer devotes an essay to that aspect, where music is understood as a 'rhythmic organisation of sound, the patterns of repetition and fracture, and also the sonority of these patterns, the way they amplify in the recurrence' (2015b: 157). The constellated musical aspects of auditory perception are as important as the ocular in her sensual relations with the world, emphasising the phenomenology of sound in particular, and aural phenomena in general. 'Ethics begins in listening,' as Adam Potkay argues (2012: 13), positing that a formal condition for ethics may be the 'phenomenology of hearing, which involves responsiveness (a step toward responsibility) and vulnerability (a sense of which underscores our obligation to care for others)' (2012: 13). The faculty of hearing brings with it a responsibility, as Gerald Bruns writes, explaining a passage from Heidegger's *Logos* (*Heraklit, fragment 50*): 'The ear puts us in the mode of being summoned, of being answerable and having to appear. It situates us. It brings us into the open, puts us at risk, whereas the eye allows us to stand or hang back, seeing but unseen' (qtd in Potkay 2012: 13). In 'A Poetics of Listening', Faith Lawrence engagingly discusses the insistence on and persistence of aurality in Jamie's poetry (2015: 11). Yet the song of the earth cannot be subsumed into poetic language, which Jamie realises. Citing the final lines of *The Tree House*, in which the speaker concludes that birdsong 'isn't mine to give' (Jamie 2004b: 49), Gairn points out that 'while Jamie ardently believes in language's capacity to bring us closer to the natural world, she is forced to admit there are limitations' (2008: 162).

Negotiations of our place in the world constitute an important theme in Jamie's writing. As Gairn writes, 'Jamie's idea of reconciliation with the natural world involves recognising the evidence of dwelling, rejecting the notion of certain landscapes as untouched wildernesses' (2015: 135). The poet considers contemporary people's attempts to dwell, as well as what remains from the ancient habitations (Jamie 2005: 115). Dwelling is often described in terms of settlement in permanent villages, but from a temporal or historical perspective the word 'permanent' may seem ironic in the face of their destruction and disappearance. They cannot be said to be lasting or continuing without interruption, intended to remain unchanged indefinitely. Yet, those settlements – in whatever form – come to be embedded in the natural landscape. They leave traces in and on the land: their material, fragmented remains become the remainder (and reminder) of human absence. As we inhabit or pass through a place, we experience the transience of our experience, its flitting nature. Moving through a landscape, we notice its impermanence, which, because of the changeability, foregrounds its flickering presence. We sense it with and through our bodies. As David Abram suggests, 'The landscape as I directly experience it is hardly a determinate object; it is an ambiguous realm that responds to my emotions and calls forth feelings from me in turn' (1996: 33). The act of facing the world makes us realise that we share dwelling in a Heideggerian sense; we are intertwined in the world, our entanglement creating a mesh, an interconnected network. Yet, as we make our dwelling, we may become entangled in the minutiae of the everyday, in a perpetual search for something, thus unconscious or unreflective, oblivious of dwelling – something better, else, different. Jamie's poems remind us that everything is here, enclosed in the landscape, steadily emanating from it, as in 'Even the raven' (2012d: 49), which echoes what Merleau-Ponty has said about our need to 'rediscover the world in which we live, yet which we are always prone to forget' (2008: 32). It is a recurrent theme in Jamie's writing. At times, such rediscovery takes a form of winding paths, which leads to clearings. In his discussion of 'The Bower' (2004b: 17), Wheatley suggests that it might be seen 'as a poem of Heideggerian *Holzwege*, forest trails in search of an epiphanic clearing' (2015: 57).[7] Literally 'timber tracks' (Young and Haynes 2002: ix), *Holzwege* are pathways, trails in the forest leading to clearings, but they may also cul-de-sacs, as discussed in the chapter on Kenneth White. This ambivalence is rendered in the final Jamie poem:

But when song, cast
from such frail enclaves
meets the forest's edge,
it returns in waves. (ll. 18–22)

In a poem entitled 'Blossom' from *The Bonniest Companie* (2015: 24), the 'laggard soul' does not notice 'the world's touch', neglecting its contact, blind to 'the trees courageous with blossom' (l. 8). Instead of seeing that 'it's here, everything' ('Even the raven', l. 9) we wanted or would want, we seem to be obsessed with the question: what will we leave behind? Some hints are enclosed in 'Reliquary' (2004b: 37), its title suggesting the landscape as a receptacle in which relics are held; ancient hamlets 'stain' (l. 2) the land, while our modern interventions – 'our fibre-optic cables' (l. 4) – criss-cross it smugly. These are intrusions into landscape: intrusions that promise remote communication, teletechnologically, while interrupting communal communication and communion between self and world. And so we need to 'witness these brittle' (l. 5) bluebells, 'like tiny hearts in caskets / tossed onto a battle ground' (ll. 7–8). The image of tiny hearts in caskets emphasises a pointless sacrifice. The ephemerality of flowers contrasts with the lasting stains of villages. Traces remain, whether visible or invisible, organic (matter) or inorganic (information transferred through the cables). The natural world is sacrificed in the fight for land ownership, foregrounding the contrast between (im)permanent settlements and vegetation. Foregrounding the ephemerality of things and the fleetingness of various phenomena might offer a response to people's need to transform landscape in order to leave a trace. The infamous residue of human presence described by Jamie includes littered beaches with 'plastic floats and turquoise rope . . . a baby's yellow bathtime duck . . . the severed head of doll' (2005: 60).

Jamie brings to our attention the dominance of the human, who demonstrates an exploitative approach to the natural world, where nature is merely a resource. The eponymous poem from the 2004 collection, *The Tree House* (2004b: 41–3), describes a degree of affinity we share with the world, which we none the less destroy. The third stanza echoes evoke the unity of the subject with the tree:

> I lay to sleep,
> beside me neither man
> nor child, but a lichened branch
> wound through the wooden chamber,
> pulling it close; a complicity. (ll. 11–15)

Physical closeness brings an affinity of sorts, 'a complicity', camaraderie. The tree and the woman are folded together; they are companions, partners. The last stanza describes the act of furnishing the earth, which is an egocentric human act, detrimental in its effects, leaving

> planks and packing chests
> a dwelling of sorts; a gall
> we've asked the tree to carry
> of its own dead, and every spring
> to drape in leaf and blossom, like a pall. (ll. 41–5)

A gall, or something bitter to endure, is a burden imposed on the tree, something that 'we've asked the tree to carry'. The tree goes through the process of mourning 'its own dead'. The final line contains a powerful equivocation: a pall is a cloud of smoke that covers a place and makes it dark, but also a heavy cloth that is used for covering a coffin, hearse or tomb, a gall. The latter meaning is strengthened by the use of the verb 'drape' that opens that line, which is ambiguous, as it may suggest that it is adorned, covered as if with folds of cloth, a shroud being drawn. Similarly, in the poem 'The Wishing Tree' (2004b: 3), nature is treated as currency, a matter of value, something material, calculated to bring profit. The tree is suffocated by human dreams and demands, becoming a symbol of the natural world treated as a human resource. As Lynn Davidson argues, 'The ideas of wilderness, with its implications of an unknown, unpeopled land, and fairyland, with its ephemeral almost-people in magical almost-places, are called to account by the wishing tree, who has suffered for both conceits' (2015: 94). The speaker suggests how we tend to impose meanings on the natural world, seeing it through the lens of utility, which leads to our ignorance as 'the world of perception is, to a great extent, unknown territory as long as we remain in the practical or utilitarian attitude' (Merleau-Ponty 2008: 31). We treat nature as amusement, as diversion, a source of a mixture of fear and wonder, and yet we invariably intrude on and exploit it. Insisting on a rigid hierarchy, subsuming nature into well-defined categories, considering everything as a 'resource' belittle the natural world, enable its instrumentalisation. As Tim Ingold writes in his Preface to the re-issue of *The Perception of the Environment: Essays on Livelihood, Dwelling and Skill*, we often perceive landscape in terms of its pragmatic purpose, not as a thing-in-itself but a 'taskscape' (2011b: xviii). He argues for the use of a less 'snug' term to replace dwelling, suggesting the more neutral 'habitation',[8] which allows for movement rather than a sense of being bound to one place. Jamie's writing foregrounds the need to be in the landscape without doing, without perceiving it pragmatically. It is also a powerful reminder that places we inhabit are transient, and so are we together with them.

We are reminded too that the landscape is not (should not be) subjugated to human needs. Jamie's speakers often communicate with the natural world, listening and demonstrating an openness, as in the poem 'The Glen' (2015: 19), in which she addresses heather and a bird, asking to share a stone, seeking their permission: 'if you don't mind, heather of the hillside, / and it's alright by you, small invincible bird' (ll. 7–8). By drawing on the phenomenological heritage, particularly the Husserlian understanding of analogical apperception – the moment when the consciousness connects with the body (Husserl 2012: 105) – Jamie proposes an approach to dwelling that is not instrumental but one that is empathetic, respectful, based on listening to other beings and things. However, every being's *Umwelt* delineates the boundaries of empathy. As Abram argues,

> Our experience may indeed be a variant of these other modes of sensitivity; nevertheless, we cannot, as humans, precisely experience the living sensations of another form. We do not know, with full clarity, their desires or motivations; we cannot know, or can never be sure that we know, what they know. (1996: 14)

Thus, the ecologist and philosopher approach the question of knowing the world. The negative statements – 'we cannot' repeated twice, 'we do not know' and we 'can never be sure' – underline a certain impossibility, uncertainty, the limits of understanding that are there in the natural world, things we cannot know or experience. Other life forms have other experiences, which remain impenetrable. Jamie is well aware of the limitations. Her writing is about listening to the world and engaging in a quiet conversation with it. Quietly and closely observant, she admires the wisdom of daisies, which yield to the natural cycle, saying, 'We are flowers of the common / sward, that much we understand' ('Daisies', 2004b: 32, ll. 1–2). The poem celebrates the wisdom of small flowers that comprehend their own limits – 'Evening / means sleep, and surely it's better / to renew ourselves than die / of all that openness?' – and finitude – 'die we will . . . die / never knowing what we miss'. Their un-self-aware existence may, indeed, seem enviable. Similarly, animals dwell in an unreflective manner. In 'Merle' (2015: 5), the blackbird 'doesn't know he's born / doesn't know he's praise and part' (ll. 3–4) of human culture. The word 'thon' in the first line, '[t]hon blackbird in the briar' (l. 1), a Scottish word, grounds the poem, emphasising its locality as does the title. The use of Scottish, an older speech, is rooted in the land, singing with a more authentic being before the growing separation from the world. The blackbird's selfhood is stressed. Further, 'haar' (l. 11) spread over the Scottish landscape, Rum Cuillin, makes a reference to the weather-world. The tension between 'soon' and 'now' emphasises temporality, the latter turning swiftly into the former, as the final lines indicate: 'but for now the blackie's / the centre of the world's eye / – till there! He's flown' (ll. 14–16). The poem registers the dynamic changes in the world, the flying away of the blackbird, the observation, a mere glimpse that is granted if we are lucky. In the Introduction to *The World of Perception*, Thomas Baldwin writes how an animal 'gives shape' to its world (2008: 21). As Merleau-Ponty notices, 'We are rediscovering our interest in the space in which we are situated. Though we see it only from a limited perspective – our perspective – this space is nevertheless where we reside and we relate to it through our bodies' (2008: 53). Citing the German psychologist Wolfgang Köhler, Merleau-Ponty writes about 'the originality of the animal world', which 'will remain hidden to us for as long as we continue . . . to set it tasks that are not its own' (2008: 58). Jamie's writing demonstrates that being in the world is corporeal, and that a direct engagement enables experience and knowledge to be gathered if we are sufficiently watchful. Such a bodily immersion is essential as we orient ourselves in the world through our senses. The world contains a multitude of voices and Jamie listens closely to the non-verbal language, translating it into poetic speech.

In 'Crex-Crex', Jamie ponders on the human–bird intertwining.[9] In being onomatopoeic, the name may be said to constitute a form of bridging, whereby the human crosses into the animal world or otherwise voices it. The eponymous corncrakes, called 'little gods of the field'

(2005: 98), have always been surrounded by mystery. This shy bird hides in tall vegetation, its rasping call – from which it was given its onomatopoeic name – can be heard, though the bird remains but rarely seen. When it can no longer be heard in winter, people try to find an explanation for its disappearance. The warden on the island of Coll states that it is good that we do not know, 'good that there is still some mystery in the world' (2005: 94). The mystery of the natural world remains impervious to the human mind. Thanks to analogical apperception, we may only intuit the kinship of other beings, and experience the chiasm in a corporeal manner.

As a result of taking no notice of, or being cut off from, intuitive connections, people often ignore the kinship between them and overlook the nature of things, introducing their own flawed order. As Jamie demonstrates, human impact concerns all spheres. In her essay, 'Darkness and Light', she writes about light pollution and the importance of darkness in our world is foregrounded: 'Pity the dark: we're so concerned to overcome and banish it, it's crammed full of all that's devilish, like some grim cupboard under the stair. But dark is good. We are conceived and carried in the darkness, are we not?' (2005: 3). Language influences the manner in which we approach the natural world, the way we perceive it: 'Our vocabulary ebbs with the daylight, closes down with the cones of our retinas' (2005: 3). Together with all phenomena of our civilisation – culture, religion, urban development, technological advances – language shapes the world, making it more and more synthetic, banishing those of its elements deemed inconvenient to us, inconsiderate of other beings.

Temporality

Yet we forget that the separation between us and the world is an artificial one (as is the notion of the 'natural'). The sensing body sustains change as itself and as part of the body-world. Human consciousness is immersed in temporality; it acutely experiences transience. According to a phenomenological understanding, time is space: either the observer moves or time does. In *Phenomenology of Perception*, Merleau-Ponty reflects on 'our primordial experience' of time, possible because of the human embodiment in the world, and this gives rise to his ontology of the flesh. As he argues – and as has already been expanded on in the Introduction – we are not placed 'in' the world, but we are 'of' the world, which enabled him to form a theory of time as depth. Our intertwining with the world, or, as Westling puts it, 'the body's chiasmic relations to its *Umwelt*' (2013: 41), results from an interdependence of time and self, inflecting our experience of the world around.

The sense of temporality is a marked feature of Jamie's writing. As one of her essays, 'The Woman in the Field', concludes, 'You are placed in landscape, you are placed in time' (2012c: 71). The above quotation equates landscape with a sense of temporality. What is change for people, animals? What is the difference in perception? The cycles of nature are observed in migrating birds or the changing light. Landscape appears as necessarily mutable. As John Stilgoe writes, landscape is something inherently impermanent (2015: 4–5). Temporality is inscribed in landscape. Being part of the weather-world, landscapes inevitably undergo change. The passive form of the verb in the above statement, 'You are placed in landscape, you are placed in time,' is significant: we are situated, lodged, settled in landscape – this is our plight, as Heidegger writes. We have to learn how to dwell, as our being in the world depends on dwelling. One of Jamie's main concerns lies in dwelling, which takes place in time, and many of her poems and essays represent a moment suspended in time, thus underlining an awareness of temporality, which intensifies our self-awareness of this very world. She writes about home and dwelling in their ontological and temporal dimensions.

Our perception of place, often affected by an awareness of the passage of time, depends on the changes we notice in familiar surroundings: how something we thought we knew so well, the familiar, newly perceived, suddenly becomes unfamiliar, *Unheimlich*. It is through time that we gain a dwelling perspective, as inhabiting a place means co-existing with the landscape and being attuned to its transformations. Offering a reflection on temporality as embedded in the land, Jamie points to the necessity of negotiating our own dwelling place within a temporal framework. She focuses on recording ongoing transformations in the landscape stretched over time, simultaneously recognising value in impermanence. She records the ephemeral and transitory in order to bear witness to its temporality. Temporality is thus represented in past, present and future considerations of change.

Jamie's work deepens the understanding of the social, environmental, cultural and affective change going on in the natural world, such as cycles of nature, as observed in changing light and variable weather patterns. Human time is measured according to the cycles of the natural world: northern lights, seasonal changes, nesting birds and migrating salmon among others. Change takes place – it passes over space and time. Markings in caves that date back to Palaeolithic times are contrasted with the plastic litter produced in our own age ('Markings' and 'Findings', both from the collection *Findings*). Jamie's poems and essays are a form of testimonial mapping between past, present and future. She approaches the changes in landscape calmly. She does not write in the vein of elegiac literature typical of many nature writers who bemoan the ongoing change, recognising the sense of continuity that may be experienced, carved as it is in the landscape. Employing Richard Kerridge's concept of 'crowded environments' (2001: 126), Lilley argues that landscapes in Jamie's writing may be understood in a similar way, and additionally, their '"crowded" states are given an historical consciousness through her archaeologically inflected considerations of the "marks" left behind, and the interrelationship between human and non-human forces by which they are shaped' (2013: 24).

As dwelling takes place in time, it involves change, transformation and disruption of environments. We may talk about a phenomenology of time as things appear to us as temporal, including such elements as perception, memory, expectation, imagination, habituation, self-awareness and self-identity over time. Time consciousness involves the living present, as 'Time forms a chiasm, past and present are *Ineinander*, each enveloping-enveloped – and that itself is the flesh' (1968: 267). Many poems and essays represent a moment suspended in time, thus underlining an awareness of temporality, which intensifies self-awareness in this very world. For instance, in 'Water Day' (2004b: 8–9), the thawing of snow becomes an event, 'the water's / urgency' (ll. 7–8) and 'the beauty / of its governance' (ll. 8–9) offer a chance to reflect on 'the tenancy of our short lives' (l. 31). Jamie describes the repercussions of landscape change, the land undergoing processes of transformation. We walk the same earth as wild aurochs ('The Woman in the Field', 2012c: 71). Such continuity within mutability astounds. Jamie reminds us that we are inhabiting the same earth as the Neolithic people; we are roaming the same areas as animals now extinct. This is the same landscape the peoples who lived here thousands of years ago understood, as she writes. The same topography – the surface shape and features of the land – still remains as it was then, despite the changes that the landscape has undergone over time. The thousands of years that have passed since the Neolithic people dwelled here indicate a degree of continuity, yet this permanence, inscribed in the land, is intermingled with a sense of transience: everything shall pass, only the wind and the sea will remain, and in themselves they are constantly inconstant, as Jamie concludes. Even 'a plain of stones', 'even grey / stones one can walk across' (ll. 8–10), is a sea, although it 'left' (l. 7) many thousand years ago ('A Raised Beach', 2012a: 18). By alluding to Hugh MacDiarmid's well-known poem 'On a Raised Beach', Jamie places the poem 'self-consciously in the shadow' of the Scottish poet, as David Wheatley suggests. In his discussion,

Wheatley foreground's the 'non-communication' occurring in the poem, arguing that 'the poem questions its own motives in trying to make this mute force speak' (2015: 56). For Wheatley, the speaker's 'acceptance' of 'nature's indifference' further demonstrates that Jamie's is not 'the poetry of dwelling', thus agreeing with Peter Mackay whom he cites. Yet, it is possible to argue that 'A Raised Beach' expresses the Heideggerian 'dwelling plight', a moment when a mortal, faced with the other elements of the four-fold – the stones, the sea and the sky – attempts to find her place in the world. We cannot talk of 'non-communication' where the exchange occurs between the speaker and the moon, and the speaker and the sea: the exchange is transformation, it takes time – it has a sense of time – becoming an interchange, an intertwining. Paradoxically, perhaps, permanence is found in the weather-world, in its cycles, even if they are irregular. At the same time, the land is subject to aeolian and fluvial change, where the process of formation of landscape is a trans-formation.

Jamie is careful to retain a sense of time and narrative in relation to space and place. She is a witness of change, where the verb 'witness' (related to 'wit') means 'see or know by personal presence, observe'. There is, as Lucy Collins puts it, 'the sense of watchful responsibility that marks Jamie's engagement with the environment' (2011: 151). Her writing bears testimony to the changes. Jamie's second essay collection, *Sightlines*, opens with 'Aurora' and ends with 'Wind', beginning with light (with a brief essay entitled simply 'Light' inserted in the middle) and closing with wind.[10] The unchangeable changeability of things is embodied in weather, dynamic and unpredictable by its nature. As Ingold argues, we inhabit 'a world of earth and sky – a weather-world', filled with 'movements, occurrences, growths, swellings and protuberances' (2011a: 117).[11] The essay 'Wind' ends with a phrase that brings to mind fairy tales, mythifying the landscape: 'Once upon a time, and not so long ago, it was a forest with trees, but the sea rose and covered it over. The wind and the sea.[12] Everything else is provisional. A wing's beat and it's gone' (2012c: 242).[13] The only two elements that are lasting are water and the atmosphere. The wind and water are known for their ability to shape the surface of the earth, the two forces shaping the face of our planet and causing its erosion, landform and deposit. The sea was once land, as 'There are myths and fragments which suggest that the sea that we were flying over was once land' ('Wind', 2012c: 242). The land will be under the sea one day, as the future will bring erasure of the world we know, of us, as '[e]verything will fall into the sea' ('Sabbath', 2005: 178). Only traces will remain. The statement cited above – 'everything else is provisional' – is repeated in *The Bonniest*

Companie in the poem entitled 'Fianuis' (2015: 38). Fianuis is the name of the Isle of Rona, or 'Island at the edge of the world', meaning 'testimony' or 'witness' (2006: n.p.). It used to be inhabited but 'now the island is returned to birds and seals' ('On Rona', 2012c: 182). At 'the land's frayed end' (l. 2) the swiftly moving clouds and the changing wind remained and will remain, with the terns screaming '[c]hange, change' (l. 8). The mutability is contained in the natural world; it is the natural world, reminding us that we constantly witness provisionality and impermanence, and that we are part of that provisionality and impermanence. As we are subjects or beings-in-the-world, we are its flesh, we are also of and in the world (I see the world, I am the world). Therefore, because we witness mutability we come to gain a sense of our own impermanence.

The poem entitled 'Glacial' (2015: 4) offers a perspective on the Scottish landscape, which is rather forbidding, as the first line suggests. From the point of view of the Romans, the landscape is characterised by excess but it is excess of the wrong kind. The words 'too many' and 'too much' are repeated: 'too many mountains, too many / wanchancy[14] tribes ... too much grim north, too much faraway snow' (ll. 7–8, l. 11). Temporality is once again foregrounded with a look at the past (the Romans) and the present ('Let's bide here a moment', l. 12), and in the last lines directing us towards the future ('and see for miles, all the way hence / to the lynx's return, the re-established wolf's', ll. 15–16). The landscapes of Scotland create a sense of familiarity. Citing Tacitus, Peter Davidson describes the impression Scotland made on Romans with its secret hills: 'a culture almost invisible from mainstream Britain, almost forgotten, but at one with the culture of continental Europe. A culture of exile and correspondence, of remoteness and biding your time' (2013: 11–12). The Romans moved from the South up to the grim North, where there are snows and the weather is inclement. Their perception of the landscape was thus shaped by the weather-world. The title of the poem may refer to the weather, the icy wind and air, but also to the past of the landscape, to a geological phenomenon, to glacial movement, stretched over time. As the lines of the poem suggest, being in the moment comes from inhaling the world, an acute sense of perception, the ability to stand still. The reference to looking ahead at the end of the poem suggests hope for the return of wild Being.

The tension between the temporary and the permanent is a recurrent theme. The title essay from the collection, 'Findings', is preceded by a citation from George Mackay Brown, 'Bone is subtle and lasting' (2005: 49). The opening sentence proves that: 'I hacked off the gannet's head with my penknife, which turned into one of those jobs you wish you'd never started' (2005: 49). Gannets have strong necks from diving, we learn. Found washed up on Arran, an Ailsa Craig gannet becomes part of the landscape Jamie encounters there, next to plastic rubbish. Subtle and lasting: lasting, or existing, continuing, remaining for a long time. The bones of the gannet last, but how long do they last? How about shielings, how about grass in 'Markings', another essay from *Findings*, where Jamie describes huts that

> were never meant to be permanent, always would have been the subject of running repairs and rebuilding. What was more lasting, a stronger mark on the landscape of the glen, were the green knolls each hut had had created around itself. . . . Whatever it was, it has lasted to this day. Two centuries on, the shieling huts were ruins but the grass still remembered to be green. (2005: 124)

The problem of permanence is thus challenged and futurity becomes problematised, as the future will bring erasure of our world and eventually 'everything will fall into the sea'.

In one of her earliest poems, 'View from the Cliffs' (1979; re-published in *Mr and Mrs Scotland Are Dead*, 2002b: 11), Jamie depicts a landscape that seems timeless. Published when Jamie was seventeen, the poem demonstrates a high level of poetic skill characterised by a pared-down style, sparse lines, and lucid language accompanied by its musicality; elliptical sentences and an economical use of poetic devices are the main features of Jamie's style. She frequently focuses on being in a wild place[15] and forming part of it. The language of the poem is spare, but very rich for all its sparsity and taciturnity, suggesting the unmediated perception of the world, the phenomenological *epochē*, a suspension of judgement, a transcendental reduction on the way to comprehension. It allows for common beliefs to be put in 'brackets', as Husserl says (2012: 57), and the appearance of things to be highlighted.

The title, 'View from the Cliffs', offers a vantage point, 'a consciousness which embraces and constitutes the world' (2008: 8), in the words of Merleau-Ponty. There is 'nothing' (l. 4) apart from birds and water. The elements of the natural world in the poem include the ocean, seabirds, rocks and lobsters (two, the ocean and rocks, pertaining to the inanimate world, permanent elements of the landscape, and the other two, seabirds and marine crustaceans, part of the animate world, both these groups being part of the sea). The human beings on the beach – the fishermen – rely on the sea. They find wisdom in direct contact with the natural world. The view contains no mechanical, man-made elements: even the machine becomes a walnut. The human Man blends with, is inmixed in, the landscape.

The poem emphasises musicality by its phonetic orchestration: 'walnut lifts / lobsters for London' (ll. 7–8). The alliteration – 'seabirds / stirring a storm' (ll. 5–6) – foregrounds the sound: vowels include a long 'e' in seabirds, juxtaposed with a short one in stirring; there is an open vowel at the end in storm, also an 'r', the sibilant foregrounding the hissing sound. There is no regular rhyme scheme, but an internal rhythm is achieved in the first line where final diphthong in the name of the archipelago echoes in the fourth letter of the alphabet: Orkney – D. Enjambments are combined with alliterations, creating an effect of flowing lines. The word play (l. 6) – 'stirring a storm in a teapot' – introduces gentle humour. The answer provided (l. 10) – the word ending with a question mark is a subversive device – to an unasked question is a 'walking-pace world' (l. 11). There are two verbs in the first stanza – 'rise' (l. 1) and 'roll' (l. 2) – and just one verb, 'lifts' (l. 7), in the second stanza. It creates an impression of a static, permanent, unchangeable order of the world: being situated in the world, the chiasmus, being inextricably connected with it. The poem is about the incarnate existence, a bodily presence, being immersed in the landscape, here and now, but at the same time it foregrounds the sense of timelessness.

The theme is continued in Jamie's latest collection, *The Bonniest Companie*, as the opening poem, 'The Shrew' (2015: 3), focuses on death and the fragility of life. The speaker addresses geese in a tone suggesting envy that they have their place on earth: 'Arctic-hatched, comfy-looking geese / occupying our fields' (ll. 5–6). As opposed to earth-bound creatures like the dead shrew or the speaker, acutely aware of her own mortality, geese are comfortable in their element. The last four lines of the poem stress the creatures' vulnerability as well as the unexpectedness of death, foregrounded in the expression 'caught mid-thought, mid-dash' (l. 13). The poem demonstrates how intertwined our lives are with other creatures, as when we witness the death of an animal, we can imagine our own. What links us to animals is the incarnate existence: 'As humans, we are well acquainted with the needs and capacities of the human body – we *live* our own bodies and so know, from within, the possibilities of our form' (Abram 1996: 13). We realise our finite incarnate being more acutely – we are perhaps reminded of it – in the presence of animals and their vulnerability. Given the phenomenological perspective and the intertwining, the chiasmic relation of self to world, it may be said that the formal devices of poetry are the material embodiment in the trace of writing of one's being intertwined in the world.

The Unseen Landscape Within

Never a mere spectator, Jamie always takes part in the world, garnering knowledge by watching and listening to it, corporeally immersed. In the collection *This Weird Estate*, comprising six poems published in a limited edition in 2007, the poet reaches for the invisible, looking at the body from the inside. Lucy Collins attempts to place the poems gathered in the volume 'at the interface of the poet's engagement with generational change and ecological responsibility' (2015: 112), suggesting that Jamie 'dwells on both the experiential reality of embodied life and its metaphorical power' (2015: 120). The poem opening the collection, from which the title comes, is in Scots. The heart, 'laird o this weird estate' (l. 12), the strange body kingdom, contains 'briars and thorns' (l. 5). In the third poem, a sonnet, starting with the words, 'little man, homunculus' (l. 1), the images foreground interconnectedness. For instance, the foetus, 'tissue-wrapped in nature's layers and folds' (l. 10), is compared to a nut or a seed – 'a nut tucked in its shell, seed in a pod' (l. 6). Connections equally occur on the phonetic level, as demonstrated in the alliteration 'curled in the coracle / which carries' (l. 7). The alliteration links the body with its receptacle and its function. The word 'coracle' signifies a round boat of wicker, coated with skins, the name perhaps derived from the hides that cover; it is a fitting metaphor for the womb. As Hannah Arendt argues, 'Metaphors are the means by which the oneness of the world is brought about' (1999: 20). The powerful sense of intertwining is continued: 'precious cargoes, nourished through a cord'. The expression 'carries you downriver to your birth' (l. 8) introduces a parallel between a body and the earth, which is further developed in the final stanza. The word 'downriver' is once more suggestive of a corporeal landscape. The final stanza emphasises the similarity between the birth of a human being and the birth of the earth. Connecting the human body with the flesh of the world, Jamie foregrounds our corporeal immersion in it.

In other poems, similar images abound. For instance, in the fourth poem printed on the page opposite Richard Quain's *The Anatomy of the Arteries of the Human Body*, vol. 1 (1841), the open belly of a model, a boy, is compared to 'an animal's // lair' (ll. 6–7). In 'World Tree' (2015: 37), the speaker addresses a tree; the final stanza, the sap of the world, its lifeblood courses in our bodies, akin to consciousness that rises in us. Thus, the human and plant come to life analogously. The question 'what kind' turns into 'why'; a botanical enquiry becomes an existential anxiety, an ontological problem. We are all connected with a form of mycorrhiza; there is no world that is not the separate, disconnected self. Collins posits that these poems 'remind us of the moral obligation to be attentive to our own lives as well as to the greater materiality of the earth' (2015: 120). Materiality involves plurality, enacted in the poem by the enumeration 'elder or hawthorn, bour or may', and the recognition of these aspects of the world brings the speaker closer to the 'world tree', inmixing the sap with blood. As Abram writes,

> cycling of the human back into the larger world ensures that the other forms of experience that we encounter – whether ants, or willow trees, or clouds – are never absolutely alien to ourselves. Despite the obvious differences in shape, and ability, and style of being, they remain at least distantly familiar, even familial. It is, paradoxically, this perceived kinship or consanguinity that renders the difference, or otherness, so eerily potent. (1996: 16)

Growing together, we are linked in a form of a 'mycelial network'.[16] Jamie presents the *Lebenswelt*,[17] how hers is an all-embracing consciousness, having bodily perspective, and thereby the manner in which the self, the living body is stitched into the world. Our whole selves are immersed in the world, tuned with it, its sap rising in our bodies. The insertion of the world between the leaves of the body means that I experience the world sensually, I exist in the world through my body. I perceive the world outside my body as well as its 'nature within' (Jamie 2012c: 36). There is no separation between the self and the world, I see all the world there is, I am involved, or enveloped in this world; therefore, there is no separation between the self and the world.

Gifts of the Wild

Yet Cartesian perspective still seems to dominate human actions. The penultimate untitled poem in the collection *This Weird Estate* is an address to human beings. It is composed of two stanzas, each seven lines long. Printed opposite Richard Quain's *The Anatomy of the Arteries of the Body*, vol. 2 (1844), it refers to the human curiosity to see what lies under the skin, 'seized / with the need to know' (ll. 1–2). The long vowel in 'need' prolongs the force of 'seized', emphasising the meaning of the verb 'to seize', or to take possession of, forcibly, take by force. The exact etymology is uncertain but one of the possible origins is Old English *secan* 'to seek', which here expresses the urge to seek answers. One may read such forces, rhymes, echoes, alliterations and connecting threads in the poetry as enacting, performing for the reader the intertwining, the linguistic stitching of the embodied experience of being in the world;

hence your drawing your reader's attention to such devices. The poem both maps and performs, enacts as it makes the connection, recording as well as presenting. The first stanza is about the God-like behaviour of humans, the arrogance that comes with the assumption that things are knowable. The 'you' is addressed to a collective 'human' who, obsessed with the need to find answers, 'opened each other' (l. 7). The expression emphasises the violence of the act. There is a single category, 'human', abstract, 'you' as opposed to 'we', liberated, intertwined with other beings. The freedom is the freedom that knowledge brings of the self, self-consciousness. But that freedom to think also includes a desire for the freedom to renounce the knowingness, and so release from the ambivalence of realisation that knowledge comes at the price of human imprisonment to the 'God-like' condition of intellect. There is a connection between heart and head, the former 'shattered' (l. 4) or 'ablaze' (l. 5), the latter 'calculating' (l. 6). The search for a link is suggested by the word 'couple', meaning to join, connect, associate. The stereotypical division is between the heart, the locus of the emotions, and the head, responsible for reason. This dualistic image of the separation between body and mind is in stark contrast to the image of the world's mind from the poem 'Pipistrelles' (2004b: 30), discussed below, in which it is represented as single, all-embracing. To return to the penultimate poem from *This Weird Estate*, the opening line of the second stanza is a plea for a life in the world, for lives spent 'decently among animals' / – as corals, perhaps, or shy deer – ' (ll. 9–10). The adverb 'decently', which could perhaps mean fittingly, suitably, appropriately, suggests a preferable life choice. It is not a life 'buried in your dark machine' (l. 13), but spent among other beings: thus decently. The preposition is important here: not 'in' but 'among'. Not buried deep or opening each other but living 'as corals . . . or shy deer', in an attempt to come close to wild Being. It is a move away from anthropocentrism and solipsism. The final lines evoke an image pertaining to modernity – that of 'a dark machine', never ceasing its action – thus addressing the Cartesian legacy of the human body as a machine. This mechanistic vision is refuted in the poem, together with a belief that the invisible can be grasped merely by turning it inside out, when the urge to know becomes a form of arrogance. The body is filled with secrets, 'no more buried', but laid out, exposed, which does not yield all the answers. The poetic subject suggests embracing the not knowing, making an appeal to people to cease this dual existence, abandon the split, reunite with the natural world, offering a plea for reconnection.[18] What we have is a choice between a life spent peering inside oneself and other beings in search of answers, as opposed to a life outside, among animals, immersed in the world rather than oneself: living in openness on to the world, dehiscent, accepting 'silent knowing' (Merleau-Ponty 1968: 178) as the essence of Being. We 'open each other' but we remain closed to the world, largely oblivious to its wonders, out of touch with our selves. Merleau-Ponty illustrates this opening, writing, as he does, that reception of the world 'is consciousness of the world because it reveals that world as strange and paradoxical' (1962: xv), a constant source of enchantment and wonder. Jamie captures that strangeness in demonstrating ways in which the self responds to the sublime in the landscape. The responses are not about the imposition of the ego or attempts to achieve mastery over the natural world. The subject is not at the centre but mingles with the flesh of the world. Jamie returns to a Kantian subject that restores the order of subject and world, finding a manner of bringing Kant and Merleau-Ponty together in a form of reconciliation through the poetry.

Thus, this strange world remains wild for us. Referring to Jamie's review of Robert Macfarlane's *The Wild Places*, Alan Riach comments, 'The wild places evoke not only open, expansive, uninhabited land, but locations in time,' where 'the language of place names offers a history far from serene' (2015: 21). The landscape reverberates with the past, yet 'To visit the wilderness is to cross, out of history and into a perpetual present,' as Gary Snyder says. It is 'a way of life attuned to the slower and steadier processes of nature' (1990: 15). In Jamie's writing, wilderness is reversible, placed both outside and inside.[19] The weird estate of our bodies preserves its own mysteries and secrets, hidden in the realm of the invisible, despite being cut open and dissected. The inner landscape remains as inscrutable as the outer one, abounding in unknown, unknowable forms. In 'Pathologies', an essay from *Sightlines*, Jamie explores the wilderness hidden in the body. Nature is 'not all primroses and otters'; 'There's our own intimate, inner natural world, the body's weird shapes and forms, and they sometimes go awry' (2012c: 24). Among the various creatures, there are bacteria 'that can pull the rug from under us' (2012c: 24), and seen through a microscope, create landscapes: 'River deltas and marshes, peninsulas and atolls' (2012c: 34). Jamie suggests that our hunter–gatherer eyes turn the sight into a pastoral scene, and so the bacteria seem to be 'grazing' (2012c: 34), as her husband notices. It is a wildness imbued with wonder. After Jamie witnesses a post-mortem, she sees how 'flesh, bodily substance, colons and livers and hearts, had taken on a new wonder' (2012c: 40), pushing away the thought that 'we are just meat'. As she admits, 'If you had to design a pump or gas-exchange system or device for absorbing nutrients, you would never, ever, think of using meat' (2012c: 40). Jamie returns to the motif of health and sickness in 'Healings 2' (Jamie and Collins

2013: 7), in which she states that 'To be healed is not to be saved from mortality but rather, released back into it: we are returned to the wild, into possibility for ageing, and change,' once more confirming that Being involves undergoing constant change, that, in effect, change is its inherent feature.

The final poem in *This Weird Estate*, printed opposite an X-ray presenting a foetus, opens with an image in which the speaker seeks succour in the natural world, walking into the wood, 'and she, in her kindness / gave what she could' (ll. 3–4), thus personifying the wood, endowing it with a female form and a human feature that is kindness. There are names relating to human body parts: beard and lungwort, or pulmonaria, which received its name because it resembled lungs. Twelve lines, three stanzas, short lines, regular rhymes of one-syllable words ('wood' / 'could', 'sprigs' / 'twigs', 'wild' / 'child'). The 'gifts of the wild' brought home by the speaker include beard lichen, lungwort, 'blaeberry sprigs' (l. 6), 'birch twigs' (l. 8) and 'tendrils of cold moss' (l. 7), the list taking up all of the second stanza, thus creating a sense of the abundance of the natural world. One word – 'blaeberry' – indicates that the speaker of the poem is Scottish. As Robert Crawford puts it, in Jamie's poems, English is 'very lightly caressed by a grace of Scots' (2015: 37). The verb in the expression 'bore home' (l. 9), in its double meaning of to give birth and to carry a burden, is particularly resonant in the context of the final line, as it alludes to a miscarriage. Alliterations in lines 2 and 8 link the words phonetically, reinforcing the connection between the speaker and the wood, which is strongly expressed throughout the poem. Wilderness brought home undergoes a process of domestication: arranged repeatedly, endlessly. Yet the wood's generosity – the natural world's generosity – is not sufficient to help console the speaker, to comfort after loss, to fill the gap.

The above poem may be said to constitute a continuation of Jamie's collection *Jizzen* ('childbed' in Scots), in which she explores the theme of birth and motherhood, which Juliet Simpson sees as conveying

> a gravity of connectedness generated by birth, yet through it, a grace of possible new centring in the rescuing of belonging and land from cliché, and in the rich textures, materials and sublimated voices, making the very weft of what becomes cultural being. (2015: 81)

Here the mother's body is home, our first accommodation: an originary home, following the Old English name for it, *banhus*, bone house: as Carol Bigwood argues, the pregnancy of our home with regard to the sensitivity and rhythms of flesh (2007: 111). The body becomes a 'primal ecological home' (Cataldi and Harrick 2007: 8), a site of touch that, in Merleau-Pontyan understanding, is reversible as we touch and are touched.

Incorrigibly Plural

Knowledge as presented in Jamie's poems and essays is not a knowledge of scientific enquiry, but a knowledge of gentle observation, engendering wonder at what is 'strange and paradoxical' (Merleau-Ponty 1962: 11). It is a representation of the 'incorrigibly plural' world, as Louis MacNeice puts it (cited by Jamie in one of her essays, 2005: 44). This plurality, multiplicity, profusion is contained in Jamie's quiet poems and compact essays. Thus, in this part of the chapter, I would like to examine the engagement with the natural world as demonstrated in Jamie's poems, in order to see how these negotiations are related to diverse ways of knowing, demonstrating a longing for unity and wholeness, which I recognise in Jamie's work as participating in the world here and now, her work stressing that the knowledge of self and the world comes from 'the body's silent conversation with things' (Abram 1996: 49).

As has already been mentioned, we know the world through corporeal participation, through our senses and our whole body. Despite its claims, science does not penetrate 'to the heart of things, to the object as it is in itself' (Merleau-Ponty 2008: 31); it does not reveal things 'as they are' by dismantling everything, taking it to pieces to uncover a structure or pattern. What science in fact offers are merely 'approximate expressions' of physical events (Merleau-Ponty 2008: 14). In order to acquire knowledge, scientific investigation focuses on measuring, counting, collecting data, making hypotheses, inferring, often as a result of a total disengagement from the world. We need to remind ourselves that science should be rooted in the world, and, as with the other poets in this volume, Kathleen Jamie reminds us constantly. 'Forgetting the truth of being in favor of the pressing throng of beings unthought in their essence is . . . "falling"', a failure to realise 'an essential relationship of humans to being' (Heidegger 1998a: 253). The poetry of the *oikos* is a more truthful and ethical[20] dis-covering of the world as it is.

If we cannot remind ourselves, we suffer as a result of estrangement from the world, becoming cut off, trying desperately to apprehend the meaning. In reaction to this state, Jamie advocates rootedness, immediacy and corporeal participation that enables an affinity with the world. Employing the senses, she enters in a direct dialogue with the natural world ('Alder', 'Roses' and 'An Avowal'), listening to its sounds and whispers. In 'Alder' (2004b: 7), the poetic subject turns to the tree with empathy, mildly enquiring, 'won't you teach me // a way to live / on this damp ambiguous earth?' (ll. 10–12). The imploring tone of the appeal, 'won't you', carries a degree of despair. Being 'ambiguous', the earth cannot be understood directly or clearly; a certain kind of mediation is necessary. The attempts to communicate happen through the act of listening, thus lending priority to auditory perception, then conveying it on to the language of poetry. The perception of sounds belongs to other perceptual modalities, at times eclipsed by the dominating sense of sight. In Jamie's poems it is given an important place, as they repeatedly demonstrate a dialogic relation with the natural world: swifts (2012a: 19), spiders (2012a: 20), daisies (2012a: 32) and deer (2015: 25) are given a voice to communicate their belonging. Their utterances foreground the problem of our sharing dwelling with other creatures, as proper dwelling equals co-existence on earth. Once again, we are reminded that our dwelling is necessarily marked with impermanence, something we are made to realise as we watch and listen to the world.

These are merely passing glimpses as we gain brief access to this knowledge, transient or, as Jamie has it, 'flitting' in its nature. The word 'flitting', coming from Norse and common in Scotland and northern England, seems particularly apt in the context of Jamie's writing as regards its various meanings: to depart or die, to move lightly and swiftly; to fly, dart, or skim along; to flutter, as a bird; to pass quickly, as time. The pervading sense of provisionality, or fleetingness, captured and conveyed by the poems is foregrounded by the recurrent use of air-borne figures (swallows, ospreys, pipistrelles, blackbirds, hawks, fulmars, hermit thrushes, a fox- and swamp-sparrow, a starling), not grounded but inhabiting spaces in between. 'A dwelling of sorts' ('The Tree House', 2004b: 41) suggests an indeterminacy, the impossibility of defining or characterising being. This uncertainty – and precariousness – mark our air-borne negotiations. As suggested by the expression cited above, 'A wing's beat and it's gone' (2012c: 242), time may be counted by animal movement.

This provisionality, or indeed elusiveness of knowledge, is foregrounded in poems like 'Pipistrelles' (2004b: 30–1). A longing for unity and wholeness pervades the poem. The word 'interstices', in the lines 'the world's / mind is such interstices' (ll. 17–18), suggests places in between, gaps in time, niches, crevices, a small space that lies between things. The space will never be filled; we will always be left with the inability to understand. They remain unfilled but come to be occupied by perception, and the consciousness of perception as a self-reflective awareness appears and rises. 'The new form' tested by bats endowed with 'a single / edgy intelligence' (ll. 13–14) cannot be comprehended. The world's single mind unfolds before us, allowing us a glimpse of fragments of a luminous field. The word 'mind' makes a frequent appearance in Jamie's poems – for instance, in 'Migratory I', 'The Berries' and 'Deliverance', all from *The Bonniest Companie* – in the function of a verb, suggesting we should be aware, notice the natural world, and consider it important, and also remember, remind ourselves of it.

The sense of sight provides mere flickers and glimmers; full access is never granted and thus we need to rely on what Husserl calls analogical apperception. Understanding is elusive, indirect, knowledge not gained (although, in effect, it is), a different kind of knowledge perhaps, a self-realisation of things unknown, of the ineffable, of the unknowability of things, of some elusive mystery. Pipistrelles provide a momentary glimpse into some other realm, usually inaccessible to people. Their appearance, sudden as it is, offers a chance for an epiphanic moment, a brief glimpse of the unknowable.

Similarly, in 'The Dipper' (2004b: 49), limits of knowledge are foregrounded as the speaker, looking at a bird, realises the unbridgeable gap, an abyss that remains a mystery. There is no access to the world of other beings. Existential questions return in 'Rhododendrons' (2004b: 33), in which the poetic subject imagines what it is like to 'exist / so bright and fateless' (ll. 11–12) in the form of a flower. The words ending the poem reflect the unyielding nature of things, delineating the limits of knowledge, as the speaker's musings are interrupted by the hasty friends and as 'darkness was weighing / the flowers and birds' backs' (ll. 16–17). 'But we are not creatures of the wind' (2005: 240), Jamie notes, and we are bound to earth, enfolded in the *Umwelt*, bound in a dwelling that comes to be disclosed to us. As the above poems demonstrate, our knowledge comes from making our dwelling with other beings, which inform us of fundamental things.

In 'The Buddleia' (2004b: 27), Jamie emphasises the apparent randomness of the natural laws, defying rigid scientific categorisation. Divinity is hidden in the plurality of 'lupins' (l. 15) and not in 'the masculine / God of my youth' (ll. 12–13); the efficiency of buddleia's self-sufficiency is highlighted by the enjambment, splitting the word 'self- / seeded' (ll. 15–16) in half, thus emphasising the flowers' intertwined relation with pollinators. The world in all its incorrigible plurality renounces the monotheistic idea with its rigid patriarchal vertical hierarchy. In a detailed analysis, Davidson suggests that the poetic repetition occurring in the poem caused the repeated word to be 'released from a site-specific context' and enter a new context, as a result of which 'it is infused by the words around it', thus 'ensuring that meaning remains open, fluid and capable of change within an evolving environment' (2015: 96). In her reading of 'The Buddleia', Gairn suggests that, together with other poems from the collection, it 'speak[s] of the need to find or construct spaces for reverie as a way of attending to and living with nature' (2008: 177), even if the attempts to collapse binaries are sometimes 'frustrated' (2008: 177). This lack of vertical power relations and binary oppositions is also emphasised in 'Roses' (2012a: 27), where the flowers are 'without leadership' (l. 9); each flower is 'equal, in the scented mass' (l. 14) in a non-hierarchical world. Roses exclaim: *'The world is ours too!'* (l. 7); they reclaim the world for themselves, unsupported, as there is no spokesperson in sight but each flower is endowed with agency, as the first-person pronouns 'ours' (l. 7) and 'my' (l. 12) emphasise. And so they 'haggle' (l. 12) (quite vigorously) for *'my little / portion of happiness'* (ll. 12–13), as they say.

In 'The Beach', the poem opening *The Overhaul* (2012d: 3), the final lines evoke a certain detachment. The poem's brevity, its compact lines composed of four tercets with trimeter and dimeter lines, and the final couplet with weak tetrameter lines, allude to a sonnet form. It is a landscape after the 'big westerly', the storm beach almost empty save for driftwood, 'a few brave souls' and 'frayed / blue polyprop rope' (ll. 7–8), the latter a reminder of synthetic plastic floating in the seas, which they sometimes throw 'back at us' (l. 9). The penultimate stanza opens with a statement, as if cut mid-sentence by a dash. The clause 'what a species' (l. 10) seems to express disbelief, further enhanced by the lack of an exclamation mark. The distance is diminished in the third line with the words 'all of us' (l. 12); the 'species' two lines down becomes 'us'. The gerunds 'working', 'hoping' and 'hankering' indicate a suspension, a never-ending cycle. As in another poem from the same collection, 'Even the raven', cited above, these lines seem to prompt us to realise that everything is here, now.

Lines of Landscape

Is there an alternative to the suspended existence? Art, argues Merleau-Ponty, is close to capturing the essence, by offering a 'gaze at infinity' (2008: 40). For Heidegger, art embodies the world (2013b: 17–79) and thus maintains that gaze into the infinite.[21] Jamie's poetry, like that of Burnside, White and Robertson, is the bridge between self and world in the grasping of sensuousness but also the feeling embodied in the self, translated as feeling embodied in words, poetry being the sensuousness analogous to logic in the philosophical thought of Husserl, Heidegger and Merleau-Ponty.

Poetry proposes knowing that is not mechanical or measured, but intuitive; it is not certain, but nebulous and instantaneous. The source of this profound, intimate knowledge is direct, preconceptual experience that is not quantifiable or measurable. In her work, Jamie confirms that demonstrating that knowledge of the world requires our deep and direct involvement. We are involved in the places we inhabit, 'involved' meaning enveloped or surrounded; the word comes from the Latin *involvere*, literally 'roll into', from 'in' and *volvere* 'to roll', originally 'envelop, surround', with the sense of 'take in, include'. This carnal resonance is part of 'our difficult / chthonic anchorage / in the apple-sweetened earth' ('The Tree House', 2004b: 41). We may add here what Merleau-Ponty says: 'the body is our anchorage in the world' (1962: 146).

Language provides a link. As Jamie says in an interview,

> I used to believe that language was what got in the way, and that if only we could stop thinking in language we'd have more direct access to the world. ... I've learned now ... that language is what we do as human beings, that it is where we're at home, that's our means of negotiating with the world. So, it doesn't get in the way, it enables. We do language like spiders do webs. (2012a: n.p.)

In another interview, Jamie confesses again that she used to consider language as an obstacle to understanding the world. As she admits,

> I used to think that language was what got in the way, that it was a screen, a dark glass. That you could not get at the world because you were stuck with language, but now I think that's wrong. Now I think language is what connects us with the world. (McGuire 2009: 147)

The expression 'a dark glass' brings to mind the Biblical phrase from Paul's Letter to the Corinthians: 'For now we see through a glass, darkly' (1 Corinthians 13: 12). It foregrounds the limited capacity, a narrow vision or an obstructed view. However, this perception has changed. Language does not separate but unites, as demonstrated by the quotation from the beginning of the chapter – poetry is a 'connective tissue where [the writer] meets the world, and it rises out of that, that liminal place'. In this place where the poet meets the world, poetic language negotiates external factors that impact upon it, and in doing so, the poet can begin to negotiate a place in the world and illuminate this different kind of experience for the reader. For Jamie, this means time and human experience. These are attempts at minimising the ego in search of true speech, and opening the self to the world in order that the world speaks through you. In the process of writing a temporary or perhaps even an extemporary self, it comes to being for a moment. It always arises in relation and in response to the world. As Jamie says, 'writing a book is an exchange between an ad hoc self and its world' (2012b: n.p.).

To end this chapter, I would like to return to *Frissure*, a collection of Jamie's prose poems combined with artwork by Brigid Collins, a book coupling image and text. In a poem entitled 'Line' (2013: 17), Jamie makes associations between poetry and landscape. The poem opens with a question: 'What is a line but landscape?' (l. 1). The wandering eye takes the reader over the distant hills and the river, the perspective shifting to the non-human: 'as seen by a migrating bird' (l. 2). From the physical environment, the speaker moves to its representation as a line, which may also be a map of that river, 'etched on parchment' (l. 3). The next part of the poem dwells on lines of poetry: a line is something 'half-remembered' (l. 4), a fragment of something, 'a scrap of an auld song' (l. 5). It may also be an opening, 'a beginning' (l. 5), first written down 'when an artist first acts on her page' (l. 5). Thus, a line is an act of memory and creation. The final part repeats the initial question in a shortened form. The reduction of the sentence serves as a way to expand the term. The answer is 'A border, a symbol of defence, of defiance' (l. 6): a border line, a line of defence. By employing the near-homonym, Jamie combines defence with defiance. This gesture foregrounds the force of a single line (of poetry) to oppose, express a disagreement. From lines of landscape we move through poetry and other forms of art to opposition, to drawing a line. Lines of poetry translate the lines of landscape. As Merleau-Ponty points out, language forms itself (1968: 137). It already pre-exists in the world, assuming a form once we attempt to express our Being. We negotiate the world through language, our home, as Jamie puts it, creating a rich interwoven fabric.

> Language is the house of being. In its home human beings dwell. Those who think and those who create with words are the guardians of this home. Their guardianship accomplishes the manifestation of being insofar as they bring this manifestation to language and preserve it in language through their saying. (Heidegger 1998a: 239)[22]

Spiders make webs, which make Jamie think of ears, 'or those satellite dishes attuned to every nuance of the universe' (2005: 101). Poetic language, this connective tissue attuned to the world, creates a line of defence against the separation of the self and the world.

Notes

1. In an interview, Jamie said, 'I have a horror of [my writing] being filed under Scottish and the publisher has a horror of it being filed under Mind, Body and Spirit' (Scott 2005: n.p.). She refutes labels such as a 'woman writer' or a 'Scottish writer', as her work focuses on 'redefining and refreshing what these categories mean' (Scott 2005: n.p.).
2. In his scathing critique of Heidegger (and, in effect, of all ontologies), Levinas observes that 'Heidegger, with the whole of Western history, takes the relation with the Other as enacted in the destiny of sedentary peoples, the possessors and builders of the earth. ... Ontology becomes ontology of nature, impersonal fecundity, faceless generous mother, matrix of particular beings, inexhaustible matter for things' (1969: 46). And further: 'Even though it opposes the technological passion issued forth from the forgetting of Being hidden by existents, Heideggerian ontology, which subordinates the relationship with the Other to the relation with Being in general, remains under obedience to the anonymous, and leads inevitably to another power, to imperialist domination, to tyranny. Tyranny is not the pure and simple extension of technology to reified men. Its origin lies back in the pagan "moods", in the enrootedness in the earth, in the adoration that enslaved men can devote to their masters. *Being* before the *existent*, ontology before metaphysics, is freedom (be it the freedom of theory) before justice. It is a movement within the same before obligation to the other' (1969: 46–7). While the concept of dwelling may indeed imagine a sedentary, rural lifestyle, in the above passage Levinas seems to ignore that it also entails an ethical responsibility, *Mitsein*, or being-with, a possibility of being with others, ontology expounded by Heidegger in *Being and Time*. In reference to Jamie's writing, Levinasian faciality poses a problem. As Rachel Falconer points out, Levinas writes mostly of the human face while Jamie's poetry 'has habitually engaged with the non-human other (2015b: 158). For a discussion of faciality see Benso (2000).
3. On the limitations of Bate's discussion see Rigby (2004a: 427–42).
4. Mackay also argues that Jamie is more focused on travelling and thus is not concerned with dwelling. It is important to note that her travel writing forms a significant yet not exclusive part of her œuvre. There are also many poems and essays that centre around home.
5. Anthropocene has become a very catchy, 'fashionable' term since it was coined in 2001, quickly turning into a hyperobject, to employ Morton's term. For the most recent discussions on Anthropocene see *Ecocriticism on the Edge: The Anthropocene as a Threshold Concept* (2015) by Timothy Clark, *Twilight of the Anthropocene Idols* (2016) by Tom Cohen, Claire Colebrook and J. Hillis Miller, and *Dark Ecology: For a Logic of Future Coexistence* (2016) by Timothy Morton. See the note on the Anthropocene in the chapter on John Burnside.
6. Jamie uses the phrase in her essay 'Wind' from *Sightlines* (2012c: 242) and a poem, 'Fianuis' (2015: 38), from *The Bonniest Companie*. I will return to the sense of transience in her work, as I consider it to be one of her main preoccupations.

7. As Wheatley notes, the fact that Jamie includes her own translations of Hölderlin into Scots underlines links between her and Heidegger, for whose thought Hölderlin was fundamental (2015: 57). Crawford argues that the fact that Jamie's 'admired Hölderlin speaks in an intimate lyrical vernacular ... is an indication of how central to her sense of language this mode of utterance is' (2015: 40).
8. In the Preface to the 2011 re-issue of *The Perception of the Environment: Essays on Livelihood, Dwelling and Skill*, Tim Ingold admits that he regrets having coined the expression 'the dwelling perspective', as it is too 'facile' (2011b: xviii). As he writes, 'despite my insistence both that dwelling goes on along paths of movement rather than in bounded places, and that such movement may involve pain and discomfort, there seemed to be no way of avoiding the connotations of snug, well-wrapped localism that come to mind whenever the word "dwelling" is used. For this reason, I have opted in more recent work for the more neutral notion of "habitation", and prefer to speak of "inhabiting" rather than "dwelling". Another word that figures prominently in *Perception*, but with which I am no longer entirely comfortable, is "taskscape"' (2011b: xviii). It is important to note here that habitation comes from the Latin 'habitare', meaning 'to dwell' and 'to have, hold, possess'. Related to the word 'habit', it suggests that of which we no longer are mindful. To 'dwell' in Old High German means 'to tarry, delay, stay' without the sense of ownership; thus it suggests being in the land without possessing it.
9. John Clare's poem 'The Landrail', to which Jamie refers in her essay, addresses the difficulty of seeing corncrakes: ''Tis like a fancy everywhere / A sort of living doubt.'
10. Interestingly, the previous collection, *Findings*, opens with the essay 'Darkness and Light'.
11. The weather-world receives considerable attention from various authors, explored by Tim Ingold (2011a), Richard Mabey (2013), Peter Davidson (2015), and Alexandra Harris (2015), among others.
12. Cf. John Brannigan, 'The Poetry of the Shipping Forecast' (n.d.), and Seamus Heaney, *Field Work* (1979).
13. The lines echo Iain Crichton Smith's poem 'Aberdeen', expressing a similar sentiment:

    > Riches are what we find
    > in what is transient, perilous and oblique,
    > the random glitter of the sun and wind. (Crichton Smith 2011: 416)

14. The word means ill-fated, mischievous, uncanny, weird, unlucky or dangerous.
15. Jamie herself challenges the notion of 'wilderness'. See *Findings* (2005: 126).
16. In his paper, 'Mycorrhizal Links Between Plants: Their Functioning and Ecological Significance', published in 1988, the plant scientist E. I. Newman argues for the existence of a network of plants.
17. *Lebenswelt*, or the intersubjective lifeworld experienced pre-cognitively, is a collective dimension that is always there but is easily overlooked (1996: 40). For Merleau-Ponty, consciousness is all-embracing: 'I am consciousness which embraces and constitutes the world' (2008: 8). Merleau-Ponty

compares the placement of the body in the world to 'the heart ... in the organism' (1962: 209). We have a bodily perspective, 'the body's point of view' (1962: 209), as Merleau-Ponty calls it, limited spatially and temporally. As Ingold points out 'since the living body is primordially and irrevocably stitched into the fabric of the world, our perception of the world is no more, and no less, than the world's perception of itself – in and through us' (2011a: 12).

18. It is reminiscent of John Burnside's poem, from the collection *The Good Neighbour*, entitled '*De Humani Corporis Fabrica* (after Vesalius)', in which the poet writes about our urge to 'peer into the dark machinery' and 'hydraulics for a soul' (2005a: 4–7).
19. Eleanor Bell links Jamie's work with that of Nan Shepherd, arguing that 'for Jamie, the mixture of mediating the natural world and the wild through the body, domesticating the wild in small, ordinary ways ... make it at least partially comprehensible' (2015: 132). Nan Shepherd's *The Living Mountain* (2011; first published in 1977), as well as her embodied poems about the Cairngorms, explore intimate ways of being in the landscape, reconsidering terms like 'nature' and 'wilderness'. In its recent critical reassessment, Shepherd's writing has been brought to wider attention, demonstrating the ways in which it explores ways of embodied being in the world. Robert Macfarlane suggests that Shepherd's work displays 'affinities' with Merleau-Ponty's thought (2011: xxx).
20. Ethical in J. Hillis Miller's sense of the ethics of reading (1987: 181–91).
21. What connects Heidegger to Jamie and to Merleau-Ponty is that, in its modern sense, aesthetics is feeling, *aisthēsis*, emerging from a realisation 'in the field of sensuousness [analogous to] what logic is in the domain of thinking' (Heidegger 1979: 83).
22. I agree with Rigby, who writes about Heidegger's troubling insistence on the privileging of human language. As she argues, a claim that the world needs us to be named might sound like a return to 'the hubris of anthropocentrism' (2004a: 433), as it is not the world that needs us but we who 'need to name things so that we can share understandings about what we perceive and value, what we fear and desire, how we should live and how we should die. It is not for us to claim sole rights to the song of the earth, but rather to use our specifically human capacity for song in the widest sense' (2004a: 434). Both Jamie and Burnside realise this and express it in their work.

Chapter 4

'A word will set the seed / of life and death': Robin Robertson's Protean Lyric

Wonder, Landscape, Legend

'In the face of a god-shaped hole, we are all surely looking for patterns and rhythms of beauty and significance that may help us to make sense of what we experience' (Vincenz 2010: n.p.). Robin Robertson's words explain why many of his poems express secular wonder, set in a search for meaning in the experiential world, which in Robertson's case often involves the encounter between human perception and what we call 'the natural' environment. It is not child-like wonder but distanced, often crepuscular wonder, as he blends dark and at times terrifying images with glimpses of wonder and beauty.[1] Robertson creates access to an aesthetic sublime. Proposing wonder as a mode of engagement with the world, his poetry stands in opposition to a teleological vision of things, as 'a world capable of enchanting need not be designed, or predisposed towards human happiness, or expressive of intrinsic purpose or meaning' (Bennett 2001: 11). Stretched between the mythical and the philosophical, the literary and the metaphysical, the existential and the material, Robertson's poetry constantly oscillates around liminality: edges, junctures and transitions. 'Besieged by symmetries, condemned to these patterns of love and loss' (Wroe 2008: n.p.), it is preoccupied with passion and death. Lined with tenebrosity and focused on temporality and transience, the poems offer a grim view of nature and habitat, often filled with a sense of the uncanny. Within the poetry of the *oikos*, it presents uneasy dwelling, dwelling that is painful and even, more often than not, impossible. From Heidegger's expression the 'dwelling plight' (2013a: 159), Robertson takes the last word, centring most of his poetry around it. The word dark comes to mind in reference to many poems, both taking on the sense of pessimistic, bleak or grim and also demonstrating the inherent order of the world, governed by chaos and change.

The need for the re-enchantment of place is present in these poems, which at times attempt to decipher signs in the landscape in search of signification for the subject who is unaware of wonder and enchantment. Robertson brings back what is immanent in the text of the landscape, in such a way that the poet-subject acts as a kind of reader or medium. There are echoes of Kantian immanence in Robertson's lyric, whereby '[t]he beyond is by definition inaccessible to the senses; that is why our access to it must have something of the magical about it' (Bennett 2001: 46). The natural world features prominently, as landscape has left a lasting impression on his work. Images of the world – both beautiful and menacing – abound in his poems, which have a wide range of settings: Scotland, Greece, Ireland, Italy, India. Yet he invariably returns to northeast Scotland. As he says, 'I grew up with a very strong sense of place, in a landscape that seemed freighted with significance, mystery and power. Everything since has seemed a displacement: a deracination' (Vincenz 2010: n.p.). Described by Alan Riach as a 'London Scot' (2009: 16), Robertson draws 'particular strengths . . . from the caustic distance from specific locations in and around Aberdeen' (2009: 16).

History, legend and myth forged in the Scottish landscape are combined with classical myths and folk tales, which merge in his work. 'Robertson's use of the mythically "freighted" landscapes of Scotland makes manifest the profound interrelationship between landscape and the myths and tales which inform our relationship with it' (Borthwick 2011: 136). Having grown up in a place where Pictish and Celtic cultures intertwine, where landscape is filled with standing stones and culture is rich in folklore and superstition, Robertson is steeped in Scottish folk tales, the Greek myths and the brothers Grimm. His is a poetry immersed in local culture yet also drawing from the sources of European literature. References to classical texts, particularly to Ovid's *Metamorphoses*, are frequent. There are poems 'after' other poets, such as Nonnus, Rainer Maria Rilke, Eugenio Montale, Pablo Neruda, Charles Baudelaire and Thomas Tranströmer. Apart from the literary intertexts, there are visual referents such as Goya, Fra Angelico, Chardin and Tiepolo, all forming a mesh of intertexts that enrich Robertson's manifold body of poetry.

Thematically different, each collection is dominated by a running thread. As Robertson reveals, he gives his books 'thematic labels'. For instance, the theme of *Slow Air* (2002) is grief and mourning, that of *Swithering* (2006) is stasis and paralysis, and *Hill of Doors* (2013) concerns itself with houses and homes (Naomi 2015: n.p.). *The Wrecking Light* (2010) is 'steeped in myths, from Ovid to the folklore of Scotland', as he takes a lot of inspiration from myths, trying to give something back to such a nourishing tradition. I take some of the imagery and vocabulary from that mythic word-hoard of Celtic stories. The themes are the usual cheery ones: murder, rape, revenge, a kick in the genitals, diseases, witchcraft. . . .' (Anon. 2010: n.p.)

Through his finely chiselled verse and vivid, striking imagery, Robertson foregrounds the wonder and fragility of being, against the disturbance and violence inscribed in the Scottish landscape. As he says,

> Where I'm from, violence is inherent in the landscape – the natural, elemental violence of the north-east coast of Scotland. . . . That unease, that anxiety, the sense of threat, that's certainly something I'm interested in. It tends not to be the threat of physical violence, though, but of something that's otherworldly, beyond my ken. (Naomi 2015: n.p.)

As David Borthwick argues, Robertson's

> concerns are environmental as much as cultural, because the poet employs the elements of almost lost communal culture in order to emphasise the essential communion between human and nonhuman worlds, confronting the reader with a poetry that is sometimes uncanny, unsettling in a range of ways, making use of folklore and the supernatural. . . . Uncanny references to folk tradition and supernatural phenomena are used to highlight contemporary relationships with the natural or nonhuman world, foregrounding a form of connective estrangement; that is, connection to nature is often expressed through its apparent failure: in terms of estrangement, loss, or the inability to found a relationship with the non-human world. (2011: 135–6)

One of the most pronounced characteristics of Robertson's style is a highly controlled manner, marked by one-syllable, chant-like words creating an incantatory effect, redolent of spells. In spite of rarely introducing rhymes, he maintains a rhythm through rigorously organised lines. He occasionally uses the sonnet form and the imagery of ballads.

Enchantment

Despite the darkness underlying Robertson's writing, many of his poems express a sense of wonderment. As he admits, he hopes that there is some 'celebration of the wonders of the world' in his poetry (Anon. 2010: n.p.). The use of the word 'wonder' indicates Robertson's propensity to perceive things through the prism of enchantment, which may arise at the realisation of human embeddedness in the world, as in a haiku titled 'Natural History' (2002: 61). It is indicated that the poem was written 'after Pliny', thus directing us to Pliny's *Naturae historiae*, the subject of which is 'a barren one – the world of nature, or in other words life' (1967: 9). This pithy description of his book suggests how the haiku might be understood. The world of nature is life; they cannot be divided; the subject of life lies *within* the non-human world. Encompassing a wide range of subjects that includes a study of organic plants, animals and inorganic matter, *Natural History* demonstrates that all the animal, vegetal and mineral elements of the world form a coherent, entwined whole. In Robertson's poem, the curtain 'cannot be pulled' (l. 2), there is no separation of the self from things, yet what is required is careful observation, as 'it is the brute being of perception that permits understanding' (Merleau-Ponty 2003: 224). Watching brings a dehiscence, an opening, a disclosure of things, uncovering what is hidden or what, for Heidegger, is unconcealedness, *aletheia*, *alētheuein*, which is the ability 'to take the being which is intended, and which is intended as such, as uncovered in truthful safe-keeping' (1992: 378). And further, what poetry, *poïesis*, is in its becoming, is also a revealing, an instant *alētheuein*, the unconcealment of *aletheia*, which involves 'the realm of revealing'.

If it appears, the divine is not concentrated but rather dispersed, rooted in natural phenomena. Such a vision of things often appears in Robertson's poetry, as 'a secularised reverence is part of this writing from the beginning' (Nicholson 2009: 82). This reverence in the face of the world is indeed behind many poems and its secular aspect prevails. Robertson's poetry is never overtly religious, yet divinity hides in plain sight as God appears in a form of micro and macro elements of the non-human world. In 'Three Ways of Looking at God' (1997: 4), the title is possibly an allusion to Wallace Stevens, 'Thirteen Ways of Looking at a Blackbird', but also makes it known that there is a tripartite appointment here – father, son and holy spirit – and three is, moreover, a mystical cosmic number. The elusive weather-world in the first stanza is rendered in the materiality of language in the assonance and alliteration: 'sand and stone' (l. 1), 'chirr of crickets' (l. 3), 'seed-pods detonating' (l. 3) – the accretion of the dental consonant /d/, in the compound word 'seed-pods', and the exchange of s and d bringing forth the physicality of heat and light. The stanza is filled with sound amplified by the still air: the short vibrant trills of insects, the popping of pods likened to explosions, the song of the earth transposed through the intertwining of vowels and consonants, breaking a sense of stasis in the trapped light, and 'a walled heat' (l. 1) causing 'a claustrophobia of sand and stone' (l. 1). The sound effects are diminished in the second stanza, where the alliteration '[t]he sky is slashed like a sail' (l. 7) ends the waiting of the valley for a storm. A community of witnesses listen to the distant sounds in the valley, attentive to the 'rumours': 'goats' voices, gear-changes, the stirrings of dogs' (l. 10). A religious reference appears towards the end of the stanza in the figure of lambs who, in a joyful, child-like manner, 'skitter from their first communion' (l. 12), suggesting a thin, perhaps inevitable Christian filter over this world, implied directly by the title. In a way, broadly speaking, a Judeo-Christian paradigm or inheritance is there in that place, at that time, and the poet inevitably is inside this discourse. It enchants in its diversity as the third stanza marks a shift from the first stanza, which contains one bird, to a plurality of birds. Against romantic expectations, these birds do not sing but 'flinch / and scatter' (ll. 14–15). The whole third stanza depicts an image that is mute yet imbued with the violence of movement: the trees 'bend to the grain of the gale' (l. 16), while the final line – 'All night: thunder, torn leaves; a sheathing of wings' (l. 18) – mirroring the first line, introduces a syntactic separation. It contains no verb to join the elements, five nouns, the colon standing in for a verb, the only verbal form being the past participle 'torn' (l. 18), thus returning to the impression of stasis from the first stanza in a circular motion, the sameness in difference of the natural laws.

The Protean Nature of the Sea

In constant movement, the sea, a major theme in Robertson's poetry, is the embodiment of a changeable world, shimmering with light and the possibilities of permanent alteration. It is also part of the visible horizon, and allows for that registration in the human subject in Robertson's part of Scotland of the liminal nature of the subject's felt world. The first collection, *The Wrecking Light*, is filled not only with the sea but with water in all its forms: oceans, lakes, rivers, streams, creeks. As the poet himself admits, it is 'a very watery book' (Anon. 2010: n.p.). The volume is divided into three parts, each bearing water in its title: 'Silvered Water', 'Broken Water', 'Unspoken Water', associated with traditional Scottish culture, as Robertson explains in the notes. For example, the expression 'silvered water' signifies 'placing a silver coin in a bowl of water or throwing it into a well', which is 'a traditional Scottish blessing, or a preparation for a wish' (2010: 93). 'Unspoken water' denotes 'running water taken from under a bridge (over which the living pass and the dead are carried) and collected in a vessel that should not be allowed to touch the ground'. The water is then used to cure a sick or bewitched person, which involves a complex ritual, regarded in Scotland as 'a powerful charm against the Evil Eye and for healing the sick' (2010: 95).

In 'Diving' (2010: 84–5), Robertson places the sea at the centre.

Even though the title announces an activity, the poem focuses on an evocation of 'the sudden sea', proclaimed in the first line. The depiction is dynamic, dominated by light and movement in a powerful intertwining. The alliterations create sound effects through an accumulation of sibilant consonants and alliteration, enhancing the unifying the work of the poem: the sea is 'sudden' (l. 1) and 'soundless' (l. 2), while the diver plunges through 'a changed channel' (l. 2). The sound effects 'dive' through the poem, alliteration and sibilance passing through the text as a motion that 'dives' into the depths of the imagery. The self becomes entirely entangled in the world, as the sole possible suggestion of a human presence lies in the title and another non-finite verb, which opens the third and last stanza: 'dreaming', a gerund without a subject, thus indicating the action, not the person partaking.

> The only sound
> is the sea's mouth and the ticking
> of the many mouths
> that feed within in, sipping the light. (ll. 19–22)

The self's perception is dominated by visuality and aurality, the former with a particular attention to colour and movement. In the first stanza the colour is 'dashed' (l. 3), there is 'something / slow and grey' (ll. 5–6), 'cobalt blue' (l. 8), and 'silver fish' (l. 9) are seen. The emphasis on perceiving and capturing colour continues in the second stanza, where there is 'the rock-weed's rust and green' (l. 14), 'one red / twist' (ll. 15–16) and 'a million tiny shocks of white' (l. 17). Finally, in the third stanza, we have 'the sea-bed green' and 'the columns of gold'. The movement is underlined by words such as 'scrolling' (l. 3), 'sashaying' (l. 7) and 'spill and flicker away' (l. 10). The motion is also underlined by the 'something slow and grey' (l. 6) and 'slowly, silently' (l. 30). The phenomenological aspect of the experience is emphasised by this minute attention to hue and intensity. The compound nouns, in which hyphens retain in the anastomotic gap the words in their singularity, unexpectedly force new images on our consciousness and so re-enchant the world for us; nouns such as 'sea-darts' (l. 4), 'water-light' (l. 12), 'rock-weed' (l. 14), 'sea-wavering' (l. 15) and 'sea-forest' (l. 23) tie the words together as the sea water envelops and engulfs things, but also, in doing so, transform the perception. The sea's overpowering presence keeps 'a world in thrall' (l. 27). In a recurrent trope typical of Robertson's work, the poem fuses two landscapes, chiasmically entwined: the sea and the forest. In the final stanza, the expressions 'the sea-forest' (l. 23) and 'the sea-bed green as a forest floor' (l. 24) call up a different landscape in an imaginative leap. '[C]harting by light' (l. 28), the self maps the unknown territory, unconcealing it. Light plays an essential part in the poem, appearing throughout in various forms and expressions: 'water-light' (l. 12), 'sunlight' (l. 13), 'sipping the light' (l. 22), 'charting by light' (l. 28). The strong masculine rhyme 'light / glide' enhances the pervasive presence of the former penetrating the sea. As Derrida writes, 'the prevalence given to the *phenomenological* metaphor, to all the varieties of *phainesthai*, of shining, lightning, clearing . . . opens onto the space of presence and the presence of space, understood within the opposition of the near and the far' (1982: 132). We feel this opposition in the poem through the diving motion. We are in the diving motion as we read, placed in it by sound and sense, while we are also always at a remove because we are reading a poem; we remind ourselves that we are reading a poem, and so we are not 'in' the water.

To the subject who experiences 'diving', the occurrence is in effect enthralling, as the sea dissolves the self's identitarian boundaries: writing as diving, reading as diving, allowing for the experience of the motion of fluidity in the fluid, of responding to a fluidity of phenomenal perception. There are no personal pronouns in the poem that would be indicative of the human presence, and the only words suggesting a subject are three non-finite verb forms: 'diving' in the title, 'dreaming' and 'charting'. In being gerunds, they maintain a constantly present tense, a present without presence, making the poem the experience of diving, dreaming, charting. These three terms are keywords for reading Robertson's poetry. In the moment of immersion, the self sheds its features, becoming engulfed by the element, intertwined with it. As David Wills observes, water 'rewrites boundaries and bears us far from home' (2008: 20), arguing that there is 'something of the paradox of how the fluid element holds us without housing us' (2008: 20). Water offers no home but in that instant of immersion, the self experiences a welding with the underwater world, immersing itself in 'plankton, sea-darts' (l. 4), 'through a school / of cobalt blue, / thin chains of silver fish' (ll. 8–10), being part of it. There occurs an intertwining of the elements, which 'imitate each other': fire and water, the light and the sea. The reference to the elements is redolent of the flesh, best compared to an 'element' in the same sense that we

> speak of water, air, earth, and fire, that is, in the sense of a *general thing*, midway between the spatio-temporal individual and the idea, a sort of incarnate principle that brings a style of being wherever there is a fragment of being that presents an alethic modality of the truth of being wherever the fragment is figured. The flesh is in this sense an 'element' of Being. (Merleau-Ponty 1968: 139)

Thus flesh with flesh, the diver is one in the intermingled elements of water and light. Reversible, the flesh of the world returns to itself (Merleau-Ponty 1968: 146). The result of this entanglement is a refreshed perception, as if washed anew, allowing for a renewed, re-enchanted poetic language that returns to the reader/diver enchantment. Merleau-Ponty's first description of the flesh combines images of the sea meeting the beach. For Irigaray, such an image is a recreation of an originary force, 'a reality in intra-uterine nesting' (Irigaray 1993: 152). As she says, 'Enveloping things with his look, the seer would give birth to them, and/yet the mystery of his own birth would subsist in them. For now they contain this mystery of the prenatal night where he was palpated without seeing' (Irigaray 1993: 154). Similarly, David Wills employs the image of the amniotic fluid when writing about the element of water:

> Water, among all the four elements, bears the human in a type of passive and symbiotic relation from the time of our amniotic buoyancy in the womb, as a form of originary prosthesis. Fire, by contrast, is something our bodies cannot touch; air, similarly, is approachable only by means of complex contrivances; earth is closer to water in supporting or cradling the body; but only water itself both offers the particular supine repose of flotation and works as a medium of propulsion. We recline in the oceanic element as if in a fluid machine, one moulded to our body and minutely tuned to the lunar clockwork, moving cyclically forward even as we lie back. (Wills 2008: 20)

In Robertson's poem entitled 'The Translator' from his 1997 collection, *A Painted Field* (46), the translator disappears in the landscape of language, immersing her-/himself, finding a common rhythm, and adjusting to it. Translating is represented as submerging oneself in the landscape. By his/her complete corporeal immersion, the translator possesses the world of the text as 'the body is our general medium for having a world' (Merleau-Ponty 1962: 146). The entire poem is composed mostly of strong, one-syllable words, with only two three-syllable words in the last two lines of the poem: 'turbulence' (l. 8) and 'undertow' (l. 9). The repetitive nature of the translator's task is foregrounded in the first two lines, in the words 'west / and west again' (ll. 1–2). The verb 'strike out' (l. 3) plays on its two meanings: to begin to move with energy or determination, but also cross out, cancel or erase, a common practice probably of every translator. The expression 'on his own' (l. 3) emphasises the solitary nature of the profession, the loneliness of a long-distance translator. The next line, 'in open water', suggests that it is a brave, daring task, a leap into the unknown. The alliteration in the fifth line, 'sewing the surface' (l. 5), performatively demonstrates how the translator works to mend the rip on the surface of the text. The state of confusion without any order that arises, the 'turbulence' (l. 8), recreates sudden, perhaps violent movements. The word 'undertow' (l. 9) emphasises an underlying current of another language beneath the surface, but also something that is in opposition to what is apparent, a certain unfathomable depth of the poetic language, something abyssal. In an intriguing image, the translator is almost consumed by language, becoming 'one quarter man, / three quarters verb' (ll. 6–7), where 'verb' (from Latin *verbum*, word) represents all language, expressing an act, or a mode of being. There is one verb in the poem, and that is 'go' in the first line, as the translator is gearing up for action. It is modified by the auxiliary 'will', an expression of intention, the best intentions. The three gerunds – 'striking out' (l. 3), 'sewing' (5) and 'fitting' (8) (just like 'diving' in the title, 'dreaming' and 'charting') – stress the continuous form that characterises the task. They abandon the active force of an indicative verb in favour of the suspensive passivity of the gerund. Merleau-Ponty has this to say on the human body that is apropos Robertson's grasp of the human enfolded and finding itself in the non-human world: 'Its *Umwelt* . . . is not subjected, received: it moves; it defines the action itself. Moreover, it is open, transformable' (2003: 221). Taking this further, David Wills writes

> The world as other is experienced not as a world of represented objects but as what Levinas calls the 'element', an enjoyed and lived-in world that as it were precedes the known world. The lived-in world is an interior, a milieu that one basks or bathes in, and whose constituents, unlike movable objects (*meubles*, 'furniture'), cannot be possessed; it exists as a sort of natural or amniotic commonwealth, with explicit connotations of liquidity. (Wills 2008: 53)

Wills cites Levinas's *Totality and Infinity*: 'the wave that engulfs and submerges and drowns – an incessant movement of afflux without respite' (1969: 135). The sea is represented as a sublime unstoppable force, inevitably inspiring awe, a violent movement of a mass of water. The implacable nature of the sea is frequently represented as a corporeal force. For instance, 'Corryvreckan' (2013: 10–11) offers an image of the protean flesh of the world. The word *corryvreckan* in Gaelic means 'cauldron of the speckled seas' or 'cauldron of the plaid', and is the name of a strait between the islands of Jura and Scarba off the west coast of Scotland. The gulf features in Scottish mythology as the Goddess of Winter, Cailleach (creator, weather deity), a powerful weather kelpie who washes her plait in the waters there, which marks the moment when autumn turns into winter (McNeill 1959: 20–1). Whirlpools develop, hazardous for navigation, producing an intense tidal race. The sea comes alive in the poem; it becomes a figure of Cailleach. The epigraph to the poem, 'a depe horlepoole quhairin if schippis do enter their in so refuge but death onlie' (2013: 10), comes from *A Rutter of the*

Scottish Seas by Alexander Lindsay, published around 1540, containing maps and descriptions of the coast of Scotland. The cited lines leave no hope: once a ship enters the gulf, there is only death. This is a warning for the sailor but also the reader of this poem, which powerfully evokes the magnanimous nature of the element through the use of lexis, sound and rhythm. In the line 'The opened body of water that today we rode across' (l. 36), the self is placed precariously between the two leaves, to use a Merleau-Pontyan image. The words 'gullet' (l. 34), 'throat' (l. 35) and 'body' (l. 36) in the final lines endow the sea with a corporeal form, as if the speaker were witnessing the making/birth of a living organism whose elemental force is not mythical but very real, wild, unharnessed. The cyclical nature of the sea, 'each wave swallowing its own form / and returning, remaking itself' (ll. 14–15) is awe-inspiring, sublime, an 'awful wonder' as Blake put it, the uncanny rising to the surface as the sea 'gets stranger' (l. 17). The movement of the sea is underlined by the reverberation of the alliterative sounds in 'ringer and raging' (l. 19) and 'boils that bulge and blister, burst' (l. 23). The immanent force of the sea is foregrounded by likening it to a monumental building: the passage is called Great Door, Dorus Mhor (l. 2) – Dorus Mhor (or Mor) is one of the tidal gates, a narrow strait of standing waves, where the sea is very violent, the inflow of water pushing through the strait – and each wave is 'as tall as a church door' (l. 12). The poem is characterised by long, irregular lines and the lack of a regular rhyme scheme. The verbal effect is achieved by an accumulation of words, separated by commas, which intensifies the sense of the unharnessed force of the sea. One could argue that such 'building up' is both architectural and also part of the poetic architectonic, so that the poem 'constructs'; it is not merely a representation but a performative speech act that brings the reader into a perilous intimacy with the force the text seeks to convey. Similarly, a number of non-verbal sentences – 'a sluice through a bottleneck' (l. 4), 'a great seething' (l. 5), 'the frenzy of water feeding on water' (l. 5), 'the long throat of Corryvreckan' – create the impression of rushing. In being 'unverbed', they are fragments, indicating a kind of urgent violence. At the same time, they build as much as they break up, they create a motion of building–unbuilding, suggestive of a world in tumult. The one-word statements, such as the 'maelstrom' (l. 35), offer an attempt to grasp the implacable nature of the element: a mighty whirlpool, the maelstrom is a body of swirling water. The poet presents a powerful image that does not stand alone, but he also indicates how the poem is itself a maelstrom because it breaks up conventional syntax and grammar. There is a concentration of verbal nouns in the first stanza – 'thickening' (l. 1), 'seething' (l. 5) – and gerunds – 'squeezing' (l. 2), 'climbing over' (l. 3), 'feeding' (l. 5). The accumulation of strong one-syllable words, such as in the line 'the great black gullet of loss' (l. 34), create a pounding effect; gerunds and alliterations create a sonic storm of sorts. The whole poem conjures up an image of the power of the sea focused around the sense of sight, as perception dominates; there are no other senses involved, the poem reading as if, like the visible world, it were engulfed by the immense waves.

Images of the natural world governed by movement are also evoked in 'Fluid' (2002: 60). The expression 'shape-changing' (l. 3) foregrounds the protean nature of the world, orchestrated into 'one whole thing' (l. 5). The form of the poem – lines scattered on the page without any punctuation marks, running in a flowing motion, all combined by enjambments – emphasises this theme. Characterised by 'the integrity and tension' (l. 1), the shoal is likened to a swarm, 'that net of birds' (l. 7), 'insect-mist' (l. 11). The collective nouns 'shoal' and 'swarm', as well as words like 'net', 'mist' and 'mesh', foreground the intertwining of various forms, their interpenetration. The verb 'fish' (l. 11), applied in reference to birds, creates a further link between species. The flock moves 'unloosened' (l. 9) and the myriad of insects 'forms / and unforms' (ll. 12–13), the repeated negative neologisms reinforcing the impossibility of describing or even apprehending the rhythms. Even the shadows create a 'mesh' (l. 14). The poem reveals an interweaving system of things, one linked with the other, all resembling one another as '[a]ll things swim and glitter' (Emerson 1950: 342). As in 'Diving', 'The Translator' and 'Corryvreckan', discussed above, 'Fluid' focuses on the shimmering world, the protean nature of the sea, its originary force or 'amniotic commonwealth', whereby liquidity enables the self to be 'open, transformable'.

Liminality, Edges, Hauntings

Imbued with a strange power, the sea in Robertson's poetry is also a site of powerful hauntings, reminding us that 'ghostlike we glide through nature' (Emerson 1950: 342). Ghosts drift on the tide, and conversely, always returning, the tide is a revenant. In the poem discussed above, 'Diving', among plankton and shoals of fish there appears 'the slope and loom of ghosts' (ll. 4–5). Spectres are embedded in the world, even if they are not of its fabric; the land and sea are inhabited by ghosts. As in Kantian philosophy, in Robertson's poetic world, 'encounters with nature retain a fascinating but also unsettling power to throw us a tenuous line to an other-world' (Bennett 2001: 44). In 'Fugue of Phantoms' (1997:

34), haunting is captured by the sound of the sea, its insistent nature appearing oppressive. The sound gives phantoms an aural embodiment. The double fricative of the title, together with numerous alliterations, foregrounds the reverberative nature of memories and the interweaving, repetitive elements of the fugue, the fleeing and chasing in a tidal movement, its intricate dance. The repetition is also there on a lexical level, emphasised further by the word 'keen', which is repeated twice, its gerund form stressing the persistence of the lamentation and strengthening the word that precedes it: namely, 'coronach'. The latter means 'a funeral dirge sung or played on the bagpipes' and comes from Scottish Gaelic. There is an anaphora in each stanza: 'this is', then 'these are'. The four quatrains are followed by a rhyming couplet in which, suddenly, the speaking I makes this emphatic, expressive presence, 'where nothing is anywhere simply present or absent' (Derrida 1981: 26). As Julian Wolfreys observes,

> The identification of spectrality appears in a gap between the limits of two ontological categories. The definition escapes any positivist or constructivist logic by emerging between, and yet not as part of, two negations: *neither, nor*. A third term, the spectral, speaks of the limits of determination, while arriving beyond the terminal both in and of identification in either case (alive/dead) and not as an oppositional or dialectical term itself defined as part of some logical economy. (2002: x)

Ghosts inhabit cross-spaces, shifting in form, occupying a great number of poems. One such example is 'The Ghost of Actaeon' (2013: 38), in which the hero's ghost, in a doubly transformed form and 'much changed' (l. 2), visits his sleeping mother, explaining what happened to him. Ghosts appear, crossing the threshold of form in multiple ways: from human to non-human animal, from life to death, from material to spectral. In 'The God Who Disappears', Dionysus is 'born to a life of dying', a paradox that makes him both present and absent, as in another ontological paradox; he is a '[g]host of abandon, and abandoning, / he shatters us to make us whole'. In 'Ghost of a Garden', through uncovering and revealing, the speaker 'discovers' (l. 1) that he 'found' (l. 2) himself, 'in here'. 'Here' is in effect 'there': a realm where his father can be seen. The movement resembles what Jessica Dubow calls 'negative phenomenology', a 'perceptual capacity that answers not to the appearance of anything or enfolds any passage from the unknown to the known, but which demands a constant dispersion, a temporal abyss into which immediate visibilities slip the moment they are glimpsed' (2011: 191). In Robertson's poems, disturbed dreams and returning family presences often recur, as in this short, evocative poem with 'a garden run to seed', a man sleepwalking out to a toolshed to find his father 'weeping / and I cannot help him because he is dead' (2006: 20). As Julian Wolfreys observes, 'Robertson's "selves" . . . are *phantasma* and *spectral*: figures become visible through the *poïesis*, the making of the visible motions and phenomena' of the world (2019: 308).

Changeability imprinted in the world marks this poetry, frequently manifested in states in between – moments caught on the cusp – which feature prominently. Robertson explains his preference for liminality, associating this with his place of origin:

> I was brought up in a liminal world, on the north-east coast, and have always been interested in borders – 'drawn to edges' – where there always seems to be friction and instability and change: all useful for what I'm trying to do. I like flux, but don't care too much for utter desolation – particularly the West Texas version, which is desolation with fences. (Robertson 2015: n.p.)

Borders and edges of both a spatial and a temporal kind return in many poems.

For instance, liminal junctures constitute a dominant feature in 'The Lake at Dusk' (2006: 46–7), in which the speaker witnesses a transition from day into night unfolding in front of his eyes and along the lines of the poem, revealing 'fissures and gaps into which subjectivities slip and lodge themselves' (Merleau-Ponty 1962: 389). A crepuscular moment, twilight has a liminal dimension in terms of a temporal dimension. The poem is a phenomenal recording of the movement of light and wind spread against the trees, seeping through. The lake surface forms the tain of the mirror, a site of displaced light that endows water with visibility as the setting sun leaves an alliterative 'red-raking' (l. 10) print on the surface of the lake. The forest is filled with sound, constantly stirring: a bird call breaks the silence, 'the ditches churn with frogs' (l. 19), 'the reed-pool trembles' (l. 27). The lake surface as the tain of the mirror also serves as a substrate on which the image of the world comes to be inversely represented or figured. It is thus a figure for the poem itself, which, in being constructed from the phenomenal reality, is both what is reflected, what is atop the substrate, and also, in a double chiasmic fold, becomes or performs the subject's perception of the world. In performing this, the poem becomes a substrate in reflecting, like the surface of a lake, the tain that it itself becomes. This is a world filled with language: the wind leaves 'paw-prints on the water / for the water-witch to read' (ll. 4–5), the frogs 'let a cloudy scribble' (l. 23) and 'all of them carry the same rubric, / legible and bright' (ll. 25–6), suggestive of a boundless text of the non-human world filled with signs that are at times impossible to decipher. Signification is everywhere; it is endless, abyssal. While the former inscription has an addressee inhabiting the mythical realm, the latter may be read by the passer-by. The self is inscribed in the text – the opening words, 'I watch' (l. 1), foreground subjective perception, while 'I pause' (l. 14) mark the speaker's embodied movement. The self's visual immersion in the landscape expands the lived world as 'My point of view is for me not so much a limitation of my experience as a way I have of infiltrating into the world in its entirety' (Merleau-Ponty 1962: 384). The transition from the sun setting in stanzas one and two to darkness in the final stanza calls the speaker's sense of sight into question, in the epistemological certainty it is supposed to offer and introducing uncertainty, traced by the move from a firm statement 'I watch' in the first line to the two questions at the end, 'Is this a way through the forest, / this path? Is this the way I came?' (ll. 34–5). The two questions evoke rising panic, perhaps even horror at being lost, a horror of nothingness. Two contradictory statements that follow one another – 'the tracks are bloodied; / the tracks are washed clean' (ll. 31–2) – introduce a confusing state of unknowability, all sense of direction disoriented, as in darkness 'all maps are useless' (l. 30). The speaker finds 'the forest is triggered and tripwired' (l. 13), in the invisible thicket of threats. These are the ambivalent Heideggerian *Holzwege*, pathmarks, which may lead to a clearing, which will unconceal things but which may also end in a cul-de-sac, leading to a dead end, a thickening, darkening, suggestive of Dante's *erronea selva*, meandering forest. As those quotations that are phrased as questions, more knowledge – going further into the forest – only lead to further uncertainty and doubt.

Two other poems that employ liminal moments of the day – 'At Dusk' (1997: 28) and 'At Dawn' (2006: 5) – form a matching pair, not only because of their temporal setting. The transitional points create oneiric images, redolent of the world of grim folk tales and an uncanny atmosphere. Both include a list of objects, resembling tokens charged with an unknown meaning, which the speaker finds, including a photograph of himself 'looking slightly younger, / stretched out, on a trestle table' ('At Dawn', l. 25), 'a urine sample / with my name and date of birth' (ll. 8–9), and a bone with his name 'carved on it, mis-spelt' ('At Dusk', l. 11): a spectral, photographic image and traces of bodily matter. The self is inscribed in a site and transported into the past and future, respectively, rooting him in the present, as 'Through my perceptual field with its temporal horizons I am present to my present, to all the preceding past and to a future' (Merleau-Ponty 1962: 386). Even if the setting of those poems differs – in 'At Dusk' the speaker walks through the woods, in 'At Dawn' he takes 'a new path off the mountain' (l. 1) – what connects them is the assemblage of objects, an unlikely medley of things that the speaker sees. In 'At Dawn', the speaker finds a ruined croft, 'in each corner something else' (l. 10), the place filled with discarded objects, some of which are menacing, like 'a biscuit-tin of human hair' (l. 7). The things are a mixture of old and new: for instance, 'a blade-bone of a sheep' (l. 15) and 'five elder twigs, freshly cut' (l. 12). Both poems include unsettling animal presences that involve the gaze: 'the lopped head of a roe deer, / its throat full of wire' ('At Dawn', ll. 20–1), 'a mackerel / . . . one eye / looking up at me' ('At Dawn', ll. 16–18), 'a cat, lying, looking at me' ('At Dusk', l. 3) and 'the white grin of a snared fox' ('At Dusk', l. 6), all creating a sense of another order, distinct and incomprehensible but violently tainted with human acts, as the wire and snare suggest.

Liminality and transition form the theme of the poem 'Primavera', focused mainly on the change of seasons but also addressing climate change.[2] As we learn from the note,

> Some licence has been allowed with the phenomenological facts, but the poem is, in essence, accurate. If measured over flat ground, seasonal change moves at something close to walking speed. If global temperatures are allowed to increase at the current rate, in forty years Spring will arrive a fortnight earlier than it does today. (Robertson 2006: 82)

Set in Vallombrosa, Tuscany, it lists plants 'passing the word' (l. 3), which appear one by one in spring, such as brimstone, a flowering deciduous ornamental growing with a ground-covering habit, speedwell, violet, wood anemone and celandine. The expression 'passing the word' underlines the interconnectedness of things, where information is spread quickly. In botany, 'budburst' (l. 16) is the emergence of new leaves on a plant at the beginning of each growing season, the word stressing the motion of 'the lights of the flowers / coming on in waves' (ll. 14–15) and 'the flushing of trees' (l. 17). The accumulation of participles – 'coming on' (l. 15), 'flushing' (l. 17), 'moving' (l. 15) and 'rising' (l. 11) – further underlines dynamic movement. The word 'flushing', meaning a sudden flow, an increase or abundant growth, but also a surge of emotion, combines the vegetal and the human. This fusion is further signalled in the expression 'the sap moving with me' (l. 10), suggesting the adherence of the self to the world. Yet, as Robertson suggests, the glimpse of brute being in which the self is entwined with the world may last but a moment.

The forest, a site of strange occurrences, is a recurrent liminal setting suggestive of an ancient world, a locus of secrets. This motif constitutes a link with fairy and folk tales, where forests are often sites of threat, presenting sylvan terrors. Entering the forest is crossing a threshold, stepping into the unknown, daring to uncover the obscured, hidden secrets of the living world. The forest is a treacherous site, as in 'A Gift' (2010: 19), where all plants are poisonous, suggestive of a deadly danger lurking in the woods, where what may appear to be innocent – foxgloves, cherry-laurel, herb bennet, clematis, laburnum and 'dwayberries' (l. 7) – turn out to be deadly nightshade. As in many folk tales, the forest represents a near-impenetrable world, a habitat of animals and other creatures, where protagonists must lose themselves to find the way to become who they truly are. They cross the border from civilisation to the realm of wilderness, from a familiar to a dark, unknown world. For didactic purposes, these stories often depict them as they emerge transformed – transmogrified – with a much more developed sense of self and the world, altered by the experience. As we come to understand, Robertson's poems offer endings that are far from happy, focusing on the experience of the uncanny. 'Nature', apprehended as near as possible on its own terms, is, to recall Robertson's own words, 'beyond [the subject's] ken'. There are direct references to folklore, such as a citation coming from a folk song, 'The False Bride', which appears in both *Swithering* and *A Painted Field*, serving as the title of the volume of selected poems, *Sailing the Forest*. Offering an enquiry into the possibilities of a chiasmatic reversal, there is the intertwining of sea and land, already mentioned above. The trope is used again in 'Swimming in the Woods', 'The Wood of Lost Things' (2010: 67–9) and 'Web' (2010: 60). The woods are thus perpetually a site of darkness, another of Dante's figures, the *selva oscura*, the dark forest (*Inferno*, 1.2), an entrance to the underworld, a primordial world full of unnamed matter, bringing disorientation, where the protagonist is lost and must extricate him-/herself. 'A tangle of thorn and bitter leaves' (ll. 2–3), 'The Wood of the Suicides' (2002: 26–7) – after Dante's *Inferno*, Canto XIII – is 'another dark wood' (l. 2), 'the ruined wood' (ll. 6–7), in which the speaker is an intertwining of human and tree, their flesh chiasmatically joined ('the twig of my finger', ll. 10–11), sap and blood mixed. Paradoxically, perhaps, in this poem, embeddedness in the world – the speaker's soul trapped in a seed – becomes 'a third term, the spectral' (Wolfreys 2002: x).

Change and Metamorphosis

Transformation and metamorphosis dominate the world of Robertson's poetry. The phenomenal world is represented as powerfully protean, bringing about a change that is often violent, radical, irreversible. As Catherine Malabou argues, although in Western culture metamorphosis affects form, existentially and ontologically it does not change anything:

'it is only the external form of the being that changes, never its nature. Within change, being remains itself. The substantialist assumption is thus the travel companion of Western metamorphosis. Form transforms; substance remains' (2012: 7). This is captured in the title of Robertson's fourth volume, *Swithering*, a Scottish word meaning unsettled, unsure, wavering, turning, marked by a sense of flux and dynamic change. In its vernacular use, 'swithering' means a profound and violent uncertainty. Change and instability lie at the centre of this collection, foregrounding the elements of the world that remains redolent with dynamic processes of becoming. Often it is about becoming-authentic, a path that leads from the thread linking all three epigraphs, in which the word 'false' returns several times. As Malabou argues, transformation, or what she calls plasticity, has 'its own phenomenology that demands articulation' (Malabou 2012: 6); phenomenology as

> something *shows itself* when there is damage, a cut, something to which normal, creative plasticity gives neither access nor body: the deserting of subjectivity, the distancing of the individual who becomes a stranger to herself, who no longer recognizes anyone, who no longer recognizes herself, who no longer remembers her self. (Malabou 2012: 6)

A change occurs, something shows itself, another order is unconcealed through crevices, yet it remains outside the field of visibility, as metamorphoses often occur at night, when meaning is obscured. Images of crepuscularity abound in Robertson's work when the sense of self is affected by the lack of visibility and what it entails, lack of comprehension, 'the indeterminacy of nocturnal space, which is not empty, but a presence' (Vasseleu 1998: 84). Something emerges: 'types of beings impose a new form on their old form, without mediation or transition or glue or accountability' (Malabou 2012: 6).

Metamorphosis may be glimpsed but is frequently categorised as fantastical. Employing figures from Celtic folklore and setting his poems in a land inhabited by mythical creatures, which have the ability to move between elements, Robertson underlines the possibility of fusing worlds. Selkies, those shape-shifters from Scottish folklore, feature in 'Selkie' (2006: 21) and probably one of the best-known poems by Robertson, 'At Roane Head' (2010: 87). Extending his fascination with the shape-changing customary in myth and legend', as Colin Nicholson observes, Robertson's poem demonstrates a 'conversational familiarity . . . and Scoto-Irish idiom . . . [which] personalise an encounter with the folk-lore, fairy tale and popular beliefs that Edwin Muir warned all Scottish writers against' (McGuire and Nicholson 2009: 80). As Robertson writes in a note to 'Selkies', selkies have 'the ability to live in two elements' (2006: 82), as they take the form of seals in water but can shed their skin on land and assume a human form. A transgressive figure, the selkie travels between worlds, foregrounding the porousness of boundaries. In 'Selkie', after shedding his skin, the creature uses it to make music, 'stretching it / on the bodhrán's frame' (ll. 3–4). The skin that he 'shrugs' with ease is 'like a wet-suit' (l. 3), the one he puts on is 'the seal-skin' (l. 11), the change underlining the crossing from human to non-human animal, whereby the former is a simulacrum, the latter the real, becoming authentic. Bracketed by the selkie's words, the poem further enhances the transitional, passing nature of things. The nocturnal setting underlines the existence of the hidden side of things, which occasionally make themselves known to people.

Mythical figures such as Proteus, Menelaus, Dionysus, Marsyas and Actaeon, reappearing throughout Robertson's poetry, undergo material transformations, thus reminding us of the constant changeability of things, which occur in surprising ways, offering glimpses of 'enchanted materialism' (2001: 14), to use Bennett's term. Uncontrollable, liquid, ambivalent, they escape categorisation. In the final poem from *Swithering*, 'Holding Proteus' (2006: 80–1), the speaker is Menelaus, who describes his adventures to Telemachus in Book 4 of Homer's *Odyssey*. Marooned by the gods on Pharos off the coast of Egypt, he seeks to find a way off the island. The predicament, affording no obvious escape, appears to extend unbearably (according to Homer, it is twenty days), so much so that Menelaus claims that he has 'forgotten the sea's purpose / which is to change' (ll. 5–6). The imposed immobility makes him walk in circles:

I walk in my own footprints now
around this island,
around myself, waiting for wind, trying. (ll. 8–10)

The impasse that he experiences is foregrounded at the formal level with the introduction and repetition of the adverb 'around', thus enhancing the impression of being doubly trapped, caught in a loop: in a small space and inside oneself. The effect is further emphasised by the two participles, 'waiting' and 'trying', which give a sense of repeated inaction and action, bringing no solution. It is also achieved by the illusory present tense of the gerund form, as there is stasis in always being the same and the implication of that which is ongoing. His helplessness/paralysis is foregrounded at the corporeal level through the inefficacy of his body, in particular his hands, as the following lines demonstrate:

My hands have been still for so long
they can't tell what they hold. (ll. 13–14)

Similarly to 'The Lake at Dusk', there is a realisation, an understanding of an epistemological limit. The strong rhyme creates a chain-link between the two lines, tightening the connection between the one-syllable words, their decisiveness standing in contrast to the suspended sense of the previous lines based on participles. The two verbs 'tell' and 'hold' become entwined through their liquid consonants, 'l', their intertwining extended through the long vowel 'o'.

In Homer's epic poem, the daughter of Proteus, Eidothea, helps, advising 'you hold him there despite his striving and struggling to escape. For try he will, and will assume all manner of shapes of all things that move upon the earth, and of water, and of wondrous blazing fire' (*Odyssey*, Book IV: ll. 416–18). She warns, 'For hard is a god for a mortal man to master' (l. 397). Thus Menelaus grasps the god of sea change, 'mighty Proteus, the old man of the sea' (l. 365), 'the unerring old man of the sea, / immortal Proteus of Egypt, who knows the depths of every sea' (ll. 384–5), and holds him tight:

> the first he turned into a bearded lion, and then into a serpent, and a leopard, and a huge boar; then he turned into flowing water, and into a tree, high and leafy; but we held on unflinchingly with steadfast heart. (l. 460)

At last Menelaus, 'skilled in wizard arts' (l. 460), captures Proteus, herdsman of the sea-beasts, to make him reveal information that would help the stranded sailor leave the island. In Robertson's poem 'the sea is deadpan' (l. 23) and Menelaus admits, 'I have worshipped the wrong gods' (l. 24). The stasis is emphasised in the triple negative, which comes back as if it is an echo without the potential for a change: 'no breeze, no wind, no storm' (l. 22). This is another reference to Homer, as 'fair-haired Menelaus' (Homer: l. 265) tells Telemachus:

> the gods still held me back, because I offered not to them hecatombs that bring fulfilment, and the gods ever wished that men should be mindful of their commands. Now there is an island in the surging sea in front of Egypt, and men call it Pharos. (Homer: ll. 351–5)

In the next stanza, he dreams of assuming multifarious forms. This is a prelude to the enactment of the title in the next stanza, in which Menelaus addresses Proteus directly:

> You turn, in my arms, to a deer,
> a dolphin, shivering aspen, tiger, eel,
> lithe root of flame and broken water. (ll. 32–4)

The shape-shifting Proteus embodies the animal, vegetal and elemental world. By incorporating these components, Proteus comes to represent the abundance of the living world together with its endless potential to change, characterised by flexibility and grace ('lithe') and simultaneously irregular and disrupted ('broken'), thus combining mutually exclusive, contradictory aspects, fire and water. Menelaus holds him 'fast, / until you are flesh again, / seal-herder, seer, sea-guardian' (ll. 35–6). The root 'se-', recreated in all three words that take up the whole line, underline the god's original element, the sea. The changeable, mercurial – protean – nature of the sea is represented by the figure of Proteus. The sea's fluctuating, mutable character embodies the world in flux. As the truth-telling god, he can show Menelaus a safe way home. His truth-telling nature means that he is authentic in all forms he takes. Authenticity is therefore not reducible to a single identity, which is a powerfully counterintuitive realisation. Introducing those liminal places and moments where transformation and stasis or suspension take place, Robertson invites us to see anew and to think differently. In the course of the challenge, by accident, Menelaus also undergoes a change, as a metamorphosis is 'a vital hitch, a threatening detour that opens up another pathway, one that is unexpected, unpredictable, dark' (Malabou 2012: 6). The final two lines, 'I wake to sea-storm, sunstorm, bright waves; / the sea-wind tearing pages from my book' (ll. 40–1), foreground textuality, suggesting the protean nature of texts, which undergo various interpretations.

Robertson's fascination with metamorphoses makes him return to Ovid, adapting the stories to 'existential effect, so that classical metamorphosis is reterritorialised to generate local impact and contemporary resonance' (Nicholson 2009: 85). A recurrent figure, Actaeon is at the centre of 'The Ghost of Actaeon' (2013: 38), 'The Death of Actaeon' (2006: 12) and 'Actaeon: The Early Years' (2006: 52). Having committed an act of transgression by glimpsing Artemis, goddess of wild animals and vegetation, as she was bathing, he is transformed into a stag and killed by his own hounds. In Robertson's poems, his metamorphosis enhances the body's vulnerability, its susceptibility to harm and extreme pain, its finitude. Transformation, suffering and mortality are at the centre of 'The Flaying of Marsyas' (1997: 10), with a scene of torture from Ovid. After a deceptively idyllic first stanza, with 'sun among the leaves, / sifting down to dapple the soft ground' (ll. 1–2), and a gentle, rhythmical intertwining of sibilant, liquid and dental consonants, the poem quickly becomes dark and menacing, slowly unfolding the scene of torture. As Robertson says, 'I left out Ovid's "happy ending", with all the woodland creatures gathered round. That would have been much too Walt Disney' (Naomi 2015: n.p.). The skinning is carried out with butcher-like precision, to the accompaniment of expletives redolent of hate speech:

> coming down here with your dirty ways ...
> *Armpit to wrist, both sides.*
> Chasing our women ...
> Fine cuts round hoof and hand and neck.
> Can't even speak the language proper. (ll. 16–20)

The epidermal vulnerability takes a radical form when Marsyas, flayed, is separated from his exterior, 'the inner man revealed' (l. 34). This revealing – the unconcealedness – takes a radical form, in which, through reversibility, he touches the world as the world touches him. After the second section, evoking the crude brutality of the act, the next one, opening the third section, is strangely incongruous with its blend of flippancy and sophistication: 'Red Marsyas. Marsyas *écorché*' (l. 35). His outer layer, violently detached from him, resembles acts perpetrated on the non-human world, as 'the image of dead or thoroughly instrumentalised matter feeds human hubris and our earth-destroying fantasies of conquest and consumption' (Bennett 2010: ix). A being of nature, Marsyas is compared to a tree: 'live bark from the vascular tree' (l. 43), he possesses a 'trunk' (l. 47). His veins resemble plants: 'the tributaries tight as ivy or the livid vine' (l. 56); he 'hangs from a tree like a bad fruit' (l. 76). Finally, he is an animal: 'his heart like an animal breathing' (l. 61).

The figure of Dionysus, a nature god of fruitfulness and vegetation, a god of wine and ecstasy, reappears throughout Robertson's poetry.[3] He is a fundamental figure, recurring in a number of poems and translations.[4] Robertson comments on his fascination:

> Dionysus *is* destruction and rebirth. He is the only Classical god that dies. He is the god of many things – theatre, dance, wine, *ekstasis* – but also the god of transience: of vegetation and natural cycles. He is both the volatile Greek trickster – an Anansi, a Coyote, a Loki – but he is also the son of a mortal mother and a divine father, which may sound familiar: a god, murdered and resurrected [...] To me, he is the most interesting Greek god: Protean, shadowy, always *noir*, always other. He cannot be named, defined or contained and that liquid ambivalence and ambiguity is striking. (Robertson 2015: n.p.)

As he explains in the Introduction to *Bacchae*,

> With these attributes of ambiguity, risk and amorality, Dionysus feels strikingly modern. A *noir* god, he is the detached, disaffected, protean stranger that slips from the shadows: a barely contained power, moving from one identity to another, from this world to the next. (Robertson 2014: xxi)

Associated with wine, juice, sap and blood, the god embodies the lifeblood element in nature and its boundless, self-renewing energy, contrasted with death, aridity and sterility. As Nietzsche suggests, the Dionysian might also be a sign of 'endemic raptures, visions, and hallucinations which entire communities, entire cultural bodies, shared', associated with pain and 'the degree of ... sensitivity' (Nietzsche 2003: 4). Represented in a bestial shape, the god is identified with various animals in the belief that he incarnated the sacrificial beast, bearing such names as Thunderer, Bull-Horner and Bull-Faced. '[T]he god / of spark' ('Dionysus in Love', 2013: 14–20, ll. 23–4), Dionysus is believed to have originated the human race. According to the Orphic legend, the son of Zeus and his daughter Persephone, he is torn to pieces and eaten by Titans, but his heart is saved and resurrected by Zeus, who strikes the Titans with lightning, the first humans coming from the ashes. Associated with subjectivity, instincts and closeness of experience, Dionysus has the power to create and inspire ecstasy, which creates extreme emotions and chaos, destabilising social order. Having the power to remove the self from the body temporally, the ecstatic state is a reminder that we live through our bodies, that bodies are the means by which we experience the world. Dionysus embodies the protean elements of the natural world: wild, ambiguous, unstable. Volatile and transfiguring the material world, he stands against Cartesian thought, where matter is inert while the human mind is active and creative. God of wildness, originating from the earth, '[h]ardened by the hills of Phrygia, / quickened by its streams' (2013: 14, ll. 1–2), Dionysus releases feral energy, bringing 'fury' (2013: 52–4). His encounters with the Other, the boy Ampelos, are very close, 'flesh / on flesh' (2013: 14, ll. 15–16). His dead lover's body undergoes a transformation after Dionysus' tears fall on it:

> His feet taking root and the long legs
> thickening to stems, his belly twisting
> into a stalk that broke into branches
> and he shot up his own shape:
> leaves grew from his fingers, and up
> from the buds of his horns
> burst clusters of grapes, hard and green. (ll. 140–7)

Entwined with the earth, Ampelos is still alive and present for Dionysus, who tells him that he will 'wear your leaves in my hair instead of snakes / and wind your young shoots round my fennel wand. / I will let you soak through me' (ll. 158–61). The verb forms 'wind round' and 'soak through' foreground the intertwining of the two beings, a becoming other, enmeshed in the natural world. Seeking '*abandon, delirium*' (l. 166) and '*a brief forgetting*' (l. 168), Dionysus confronts being-towards-death that is a transformation of matter.

'That Endless Moment': Temporality, Fragility, Entropy

Mortality, vulnerability and the finitude of life constitute recurrent themes in Robertson's poetry, particularly contrasted with the impermanence of nature. As he says, 'There is, I think, a shared sense of awe at the implacable power of the natural world, and also the world of the machine, and nervousness about the fragility of the human in the face of both' (Robertson 2015: n.p.). These tropes are woven together through all of his work. For instance, *Slow Air* opens with two epigraphs that foreground the futility of all things. The first citation, which comes from Ecclesiastes (*vanitas vanitatum et omnia vanitas*), establishes the ground. The second is from Petrarch:

> and the fruit of my vanity is shame,
> and repentance, and the clear knowledge
> that whatever the world finds pleasing,
> is but a brief dream. (ll. 10–14)

The last stanza of the first poem in Petrarch's *Canzoniere* expresses futility, worthlessness, aimlessness. We project our life on to the horizon of death as 'The Dasein knows that it ends in death, that it exists with the anticipation of a being-toward-death, yet it cannot ever know that death in advance' (Wills 2008: 28). Death is the ultimate becoming, a becoming-unbecoming, a radical deterritorialisation, the loss of self into the world, into an absolute alterity. There is in Robertson's verse a discernible theological resonance, which I will explore in this section with explicit references to Biblical echoes that connect Robertson to a certain tradition in poetry.

In 'Annunciation' (2013: 1), Robertson combines these themes with a motif of the duality of existence. This ekphrastic poem is dominated by dichotomy, spread between life and death, 'or the end, where it all began', our Being governed by an eternal ebb and flow, 'everything streaming towards ... streaming away', the rhythm of things resembling the movement of water. The poem is filled with such dichotomous images, suggesting that two seemingly exclusive tendencies may co-exist. For instance, the line in the second stanza 'A word will set the seed / of life and death' carries Biblical overtones, echoing at least two quotations from the Book of Genesis: 'Then God said, 'Behold, I have given you every plant yielding seed that is on the surface of all the earth, and every tree which has fruit yielding seed; it shall be food for you' (Genesis 1: 29) and 'While the earth remains, Seedtime and harvest, And cold and heat, And summer and winter, And day and night Shall not cease' (Genesis

8: 22). The word becomes food, bearing fruit with a transmogrifying force. Such understanding leads to another Biblical reference, 'the *Word* became *flesh* and *made* His dwelling among us' (John 1: 14). The second citation from Genesis directs the reader to the sempiternal order of things, expressed also in the line from 'Annunciation'. The seed already contains its demise, the line reminding us Eliot's words 'In my beginning is my end,' which opens 'East Coker' and echoes throughout *Four Quartets*. The announcement of the Incarnation makes known, suggesting the power of language to alter the world, to reveal what is concealed.

The third stanza contains another dichotomy, being an allusion to the Seven Joys of Mary and the Seven Sorrows of Mary:

Or the end, when it all began –
the first seven joys
before the seven sorrows? (ll. 12–14)

The world is broken between the moment before and after, suspended in the moment, inducing wonder, this 'temporary suspension of chronological time and bodily movement' (Bennett 2001: 5). Silence precedes the word, which will bring 'the over-shadowing of this girl', spreading between life and death, light and shadow, beginning and end. That word, that seed, which follows that suspended moment, brings her an awareness of her fate. This is how Robertson depicts 'a world in which being is not given but rather emerges over time' (Merleau-Ponty 2008: 41). He – the angel Gabriel, unnamed in the poem, similarly to Mary, who is referred to simply as 'she' and 'this girl' – approaches from the garden to announce the miracle. The oxymoronic expression 'the endless moment' foregrounds the contradictory significance of the visit. A very brief portion of time, an instant, extends endlessly. From the Latin *momentum*, this momentary event suggests a moving power and change that arrives with it. This may involve such events as transubstantiation, epiphany, ecstasy, enchantment or metempsychosis. The fragile suspension of Being is captured in so many of Robertson's poems. On the formal level, the suspended moment is introduced through enjambments. In the third line of the first stanza, the enjambment emphasises the pause in the sentence: 'They hold each other's gaze at the point / of balance' (ll. 3–4). Separating the expression by a line break enhances the sense of a frozen instant. There are several versions of Fra Angelico's 'Annunciation', yet Robertson's epigraph does not state which one is alluded to in the poem. The best known is 'The Annunciation' at the Convent of San Marco in Florence, dating back to around 1450. The one displayed at the Museo Diocesano in Cortona depicts a scene in a decorative setting that highlights the importance of the visit. Another, which was painted at the monastery of San Marco in the north of Florence, more modest in its depiction of the scene, seems to match the one depicted in Robertson's poem, which focuses on the encounter between the angel and the future mother of God – 'But not yet: not quite yet' (l. 10). God is absent from the poem, just as he is absent from the painting, which emphasises the theme of immanence. If, according to the Gospel of St Luke, the mystery of the Incarnation is divine, 'for with God nothing will be impossible', this is not the moment for such elevated words. The moment is silent. 'Because she is only human' (l. 17), 'this girl' will remember 'the aftersong' (l. 16). The word perhaps echoes Nietzsche's 'Beyond Good and Evil: Prelude to a Philosophy of the Future. From High Mountains. Aftersong' (1886), with its final lines: 'Now the world laughs, the dread curtain is rent, / The wedding has come for light and darkness.' The words 'leaving' in the first line and 'gone' in the last one, bracketing the poem, announce the desertion of the known things.

A number of poems are devoted to the sense of a desired but unrealised change in pursuit of an authentic being. At times, the self experiences the desire to change but the impossibility of undergoing it in the face of an inexplicable paralysis. In 'Entropy', the sense of suspension is at the centre of the poem, the imagery constructed around it. The expressions 'Brownian motion' (l. 3), 'an emulsion of longing' (l. 6) and 'hesitation-marks' (l. 12) enhance the sensation of abeyance before the demise. The latter is explained in a note as 'preliminary shallow slashes to the wrist' (2006: 83). The city is 'the glare / of streets' (ll. 1–2). The figure at the end – 'Not praying, just on my knees in the dark' (l. 16) – 'existentialises the postlapsarian poetics that informs this work', as Nicholson argues (2009: 83). The degradation of matter and energy to an ultimate state of inert uniformity, entropy is a process of degradation or running down, or a trend towards disorder, chaos, disintegration. *Swithering* is 'a book of leaving or trying to leave' (Naomi 2015: n.p.). The latter dominates in the above poem, filled with quiet despair, foregrounding inertia and stasis, the impossibility of experiencing positive change, a dwelling that fails to bring even a momentary sense of belonging. This concern resides in Robertson's other collections, as, for instance, in a poem from *The Wrecking Light*, titled 'Tinsel'. The word denotes something that seems attractive and exciting, but also something of low quality and value, something trivial, or, as Robertson explains in a note, 'the losing of something; the sustaining of harm, damage or detriment; loss' (2010: 94). The worthlessness of tinsel, after the false promise it may initially give, stands in the poem for the loss of hope for a genuine, or wild, being.

A similar paralysis, if presented in a different setting, occurs in 'Easter, Liguria' (2010: 81). The poem evokes a self lost among the light and the sea. Through the sonnet form, Robertson challenges the Italian poetic tradition. The gerund forms – 'watching the ocean move' (l. 1), 'going home' (l. 6), 'Standing here, feeling nothing at all' (l. 12), 'leaving' (l. 13) – foreground the suspended state in which the subject finds himself. The immobility is further emphasised by the opening words, 'another day watching', introducing a sense of tedious repetition. The poem ends abruptly, with the line, 'I don't know', the shortest in the entire poem. It echoes the seventh line, 'I have no idea what that means.' In a dual world of light and darkness, the self lacks grounding: it is displaced, watching but unseeing, a sense of stasis pervading the lines. The poem evokes a yearning for a change that could 'emerge from apparently anodyne events, which ultimately prove to be veritable traumas inflecting the course of a life, producing the metamorphosis', which is unexpected, unforeseen (Malabou 2012: 6) but the speaker of the poem appears incapable of performing a leap, caught in the thrall of the self-same. The theme of epistemological limits recurs, foregrounding the liminal and placing the self on the cusp of not knowing, on the edge of an indirect, analogical apperception of the immanence of the wholly other, or God.[5]

Vitality of Matter

Intertwined with the self, others and the world, the body 'is one of the things, and in circuit with other things' (Merleau-Ponty 2003: 222). Some critics notice Robertson's tendency for 'intimate disclosure' (Nicholson 2009: 85), observing that 'self-disclosure predicates a continuing process of becoming, where the elaboration of Scottish senses of being in the world calls for serviceable compass-bearings on a never-ending journey' (Nicholson 2009: 85). Such disclosure may take a corporeal form, focusing on the body's fragility, as 'rather than a mind *and* a body, man is a mind *with* a body, a being who can only get to the truth of things because its body is, as it were, embedded in those things' (Merleau-Ponty 2008: 43). Sense arises from corporeal vulnerability, a being-open through crevices enabling communication. In 'A&E' (2013: 40), the speaker is forced to exhibit his vulnerability before the Other. Having woken to open sutures, he discovers the wetness of a living body that surprises, unprepared for such epidermal vulnerability. Bodily fluids – blood likened to urine – bring forth the subject's presencing, the Levinasian being-in-my-skin. At the A&E, the other's regard turns towards the gaping wound, the dehiscence of the skin communicating the singularity of the Other, 'the meaning (*sens*) of the skin is a direction (*sens*); it is a one-way street down which the Other approaches me and has a unique meaning (*sens unique*) for me' (Boothroyd 2013: 85). The gravity of the situation contrasts with the phrasing at the end of the poem:

> Unfashionable, but striking nonetheless:
> My chest undone like some rare waistcoat,
> With that lace-up front – a black *échelle* –
> Its red, wet-look leatherette,
> Those fancy, flapping lapels. (ll. 16–20)

The final, alliterative line, together with the penultimate line's internal rhyme, is almost – one feels compelled to say – frivolous and flippant. By comparing the open wound to a clothing item, the speaker attempts to hide defensively behind a joke, which helps bear the weight of radical vulnerability. As cloth means text, it might also be what, following Husserl, Derrida names 'the *interweaving* (*Verwebung*) of language, the interweaving of that which is purely language in language with the other threads of experience [that] constitutes a cloth' (Derrida 1982: 160).

In 'A Seagull Murmur' (2006: 48), during a medical intervention, the body is opened, its inner part touched. In the entwining with human and animal worlds, the poem introduces a conceit where 'the mewling sound of a leaking heart' (l. 4) is compared to the sound of 'a gull trapped in his chest' (l. 6), followed by a double metaphor 'a cut down his belly / like a fish, his open ribs // the ribs of a boat' (ll. 8–11). The opening yields an estrangement that is highlighted by the comparisons to a bird, a fish and a boat, following the movement from the belly to a fish to a boat, the word 'caulked' referring to the seams of wooden boats. This parallel is continued into the final stanza when the sound of the heart is likened to

> the dull clink
>   of a signal-buoy
> or a beak at the bars of a cage. (ll. 16–19)

In these metaphors, Robertson reveals hidden affinities and connections, making them visible through an uncovering, as the 'metaphor *comes back to physis*, to its truth and its presence. There, nature always refinds its own, proper analogy, its own resemblance to itself, takes increase only from itself. Nature gives itself in metaphor' (Derrida 1982: 244).

Median sternotomy is also depicted in 'The Halving' (2013: 36–7), two thirds of which is devoted to a detailed description of the medical procedure. The second part evokes the subject's alienated perception, summed up with a direct statement, 'I was out of my body,' a feeling of disconnection that foregrounds the vital need for embodiment: 'our relationship to space is not that of a pure disembodied subject to a distant object but rather that of a being which dwells in space relating to its natural habitat' (Merleau-Ponty 2008: 42). Merleau-Ponty's argument finds itself being given a disconcerting corporeal materiality in Robertson's poetic rendering of the anatomical intervention, as the poem becomes the corpus being opened, as well as being that form of text that opens the body to the strangeness, the estranging of an unfamiliar perception. As in other examples, Robertson's poetry is, simultaneously, commentary and act, representation and presentation or staging.

In 'Hanging Fire' (2002: 18), '[t]he impatience for summer' takes a form of desire, as the first lines attest, the feeling becoming 'ritual, imbedded / hard as a hinge / in the earth's mesh' (ll. 2–4). The depiction of a stalk pushing through the ground emphasises its fleshiness: at once vegetal and animal, 'flesh-green horn' (l. 6), a living body, 'cleft muscle'. Returning cyclically, desire is 'hard as hinge' (l. 3), its relentlessness contrasted with the earth's mesh. A hinge provides a firm hook but may also be a flexible ligamentous joint; a mesh makes reference to a fabric, a woven material or a web-like pattern. In this way, the simple construction of the hinge is contrasted with an intricate system of the mesh. The second stanza evokes the height of summer, its heat like 'hanging fire', akin to a diseased body, 'blighted' (l. 13), 'malformed' (l. 14). The word 'sarcoma' (l. 15) – from Greek *sarx*, 'flesh', meaning a malignant tumour, a mass of abnormal tissue – creates an ominous atmosphere. The impatience returns in the third stanza with dreams of rain and frost, and a cycle to bring back 'that familiar pulse' (l. 25) in the next spring, which is 'that stirring of old ground: / that ache we think is lust' (ll. 26–7). Each stanza is shorter by one line – 10, 9, 8, thereby resembling a countdown and also tracing that sense of impatience throughout the length of the poem. There is a vacillation between 'desire' (reverberating in words like 'impatience', 'ache', 'lust') for the summer to come and the urge to 'kill it back'. The co-existence with earthly seasonal cycles, an intimate intertwining, reappears every year without fail, and yet a shadow of equivocality is always there, marked by finitude; 'the ambiguity of being in the world', observes Merleau-Ponty, 'is expressed by the ambiguity of our body, and this latter is understood through the ambiguity of time' (Merleau-Ponty 1962: 87). This apprehension of the temporality of the body is captured in Robertson's enfolding of the subject into the seasonal cycle through the increasing impatience that is marked across the poem as the body desires the cycle of returns. This corporeal drive – an inevitable impulse buried in the body – is co-temporal with the rhythms of the non-human world. At times, cognitive skills dominate, obscuring corporeal experience: we 'think' that what we experience is lust. The description of the spring's vitality is dominated by verbs: the transformation from the bulb to the plant happens over six lines of the first stanza, when the 'spurred' stalk

> pushes, straining for air –
> flexes its distended,
> perfect, cleft muscle
> out and up through the crust. (ll. 7–10)

Words such as 'pushes', 'straining', 'flexes' and 'distended' stress the expansive nature of the flourishing vegetation, impatient to grow. The accumulation of prepositions in that final line of the first stanza – 'out and up through' – further foregrounds the force and the dynamic upward movement with which the plant appears. The individual self is absent from the poem; the collective noun 'we' appears in the final stanza ('we want it over', 'we think'). The image suggests material agency, vitality of matter, where things can grow 'not only to impede or block the will and designs of humans but also to act as quasi agents or forces with trajectories, propensities, or tendencies of their own' (Bennett 2010: viii), moving beyond the exclusively anthropocentric understanding of agency.

Vitality is often represented in highly erotic poems. Some depict the sexual act as a means of communication with the other and foreground the sensual aspect of our corporeal being. Eroticism is also expressed in the poems featuring plants; their bare sensuality is underlined in 'Hanging Fire', discussed above, 'Artichoke' (1997: 52) and 'Asparagus' (2006: 65). The plants' fleshiness, their vitality, highlights the imponderable change governing the world, which ceaselessly teems with life. The physicality of things is reflected in the physicality of language and in sensual, fleshy images. For instance, in the short, audacious 'Ludic' (1997: 35) the flesh is represented as raw and reversible: the inside appears outside, becoming both touching and touched, connecting the two people, as the flesh of the world 'functions as a general communications medium' (Harman 2005: 54). The poem follows the intertwined rhythm of the couple: the third-person pronoun in the opening line combines with the first-person pronoun at the end of the stanza, after which they both 'disappear' in the second stanza, only to emerge again at the beginning of the third and last stanza: 'We gape and we are healed: / her mouth on me' (ll. 7–8). They take a different form: she feels 'like liver', while the speaker becomes akin to a water-dwelling animal with his 'lucid milt' (l. 6). From the first line, the poem insists on a quick rhythm, with its predominantly one-syllable words and an intensive interchange of the liquid consonants 'l' and 'r'. Through these sounds, the poem further emphasises corporeality, forcing the tongue and the lips to perform the chant.

Corporeal intertwining also occurs on human–mineral level, as in the poem 'Sheela-na-gig' (1997: 9), the title of which refers to carvings of naked women displaying their vulva, found on castles, churches and other buildings, and said to ward off death and keep evil spirits away; the apotropaic figure is identified with a Celtic goddess present in Scottish and Irish mythology. The explorations of the sculpture are presented as an act of interpenetration. Through the interconnected communicative power of touch and imagination, parts of the body are represented as elements of the landscape – island, lake – rain, rainwater; '[w]ater' in the penultimate line is echoed in 'otter' in the next. Fixed elements of the landscape, such as the island and the lake, are contrasted in the final line with the rain, which makes the surface of water swell and gathers in the folds of the sculpture, and light, which 'deepens / at the lid of the lake' (ll. 7–8). The deepening of light, the crease on the surface is a trace left by an animal: 'an otter, body of a bird' (l. 9).

Robertson reminds us of (the absurdity of) the human need to elevate the self in the epigraph to *Hill of Doors*, citing Francis Picabia's words, 'let us not forget that the greatest man / is never more than an animal disguised as a god'.[6] In those simple words, Picabia – and, by citing the statement, Robertson – make us think of our animality, which we often conveniently forget, believing ourselves to be gods. As discussed in the second chapter of this study, we share with them the embodied life and, through this embodiment, the Levinasian 'epidermal' vulnerability, a passivity of the body (Bergo 2006: n.p.), which makes it subject to various forces. Vulnerability belongs to all living beings, as Anat Pick reminds us, citing Simone Weil's words, 'vulnerability is a mark of existence' (2011: 1). For Pick, the concept of 'vulnerability' resembles Agamben's concept of 'bare life' (Pick 2011: 15), or 'naked life', *nuda vita*, in which the sole prerogative is the biological fact of life and not the manner in which it is lived and its possibilities (Agamben 1998: 1–12). 'The creature, then, is first and foremost a living body – material, temporal, and vulnerable,' says Pick (2011: 5). Such an approach is represented in Robertson's poetry, as the material existence of animals recurs in many poems, particularly those included in *Swithering* (such as 'The Eel', 'Lizard', 'Trumpeter Swan' and 'Mar-Hawk'). Robertson returns to the experience of death brought closer by animal death in a number of poems, including 'A Quick Death' (2013: 12), 'The Language of Birds' (2002: 6), 'Dead Sheep in Co. Derry' (2002: 47) or 'Ode to a Large Tuna in the Market (*after Neruda*)' (2010: 53–5). In focusing on embodied being, corporeal fragility, and elements inextricably connected with vulnerability such as finitude and mortality, Robertson's lyric resembles Burnside's poetry.

There is no room for sentimental images of the natural world in this poetry that challenges romantic representations of nature. For instance, the poem 'What the Horses See at Night' (2006: 6–7)[7] should offer an equine nocturnal perspective on the world, as the title explicitly promises; yet, from the first lines, the images do not even strive to represent a non-human view, careful to consider a distinct *Umwelt*. 'Here is the problem – what is the animal of perceptions' (2003: 221), wonders Merleau-Ponty. The poem displays attempts to render animal alterity, yet anthropomorphisation dominates in the evocation of animal behaviour. Moreover, saying that the mink has a face problematises the concept, as in Levinasian philosophy a face entails an ethical responsibility that we have to the other, to whom we respond during encounters with 'the living presence' (Levinas 1969: 66) of the other, who is irreducible and infinite.[8] Following Levinas's claim that 'the face is present in its refusal to be contained' (1969: 194), that it 'resists possession' (1969: 197), the mink's face, 'already slippery with yolk' (l. 14), holds a mystery of the other, the encounter with whom 'opens the primordial discourse' (1969: 201). The poem evokes a yearning for such encounters, which is stressed in the final part, urging us to 'climb and walk / toward them [the horses] on the hill' (ll. 34–5), but also the enchantment of the natural world. The line '[t]he fox's call is red / and ribboned' (ll. 30–1) reveals a detail that is key to the whole poem: if, as in the title, this is what the horses supposedly see, these words betray the underlying theme – that is, a limited, Romantic, human perspective. Horses do indeed see during the night but, having dichromatic vision, they naturally see the blue and green colours of the spectrum and the colour variations based upon them, but cannot distinguish red. This detail highlights the fact that the images evoked in the poem are not what the horses see – how could they be? – but the poet's imagination; this seems like an obvious fact but nevertheless subtly stresses the inescapable fact of a human perspective, despite the claim made by the title of the poem. Assuming the horses' perspective, the poet imagines their *Umwelt*: a task made possible through the medium of poetry, but also one that may easily transform into a gesture of arrogance, as is the case with some Romantic poetry. In this poem, Robertson avoids this by withdrawing the ego, leaving light traces, which involve introducing the simile at the beginning, in which the forest is likened to a house, 'the doors' of which 'open / for the flitting / drift of deer' (ll. 3–5). Another trace is the participle 'crying' in the lines 'hear the vole / crying under the alder' (ll. 35–6), which further indicates a human perspective, present throughout but becoming explicit only in the penultimate line with the use of a pronoun 'our'. As the two final lines demonstrate, these are not horses who see at night: the perspective belongs to human animals, whose children sleep in beds.

From the first lines, the insistence on sound underlines the aural perception of the natural world: for instance, in the lines 'the bay's / tiny islands are drops / of solder / under a drogue moon' (ll. 15–18), with the interchange of dental 't' and 'd', plosive 'b' and sibilant 's'. The alliteration constitutes the poem's unifying principle, welding the words together with an alloy of sounds, fused to unite its elements. Sound effects return in the expression 'through the starting rain' (l. 26), with its resonating liquid consonant 'r'. In general, there is an abundance of water images, including the personifications in '[t]he sea's a heavy sleeper, / dreaming in and out with a catch / in each breath' (ll. 19–21); 'play of herring, a shoal / silvering open / the sheeted black skin of the sea' (ll. 23–5), as if the surface of water sheathed the flesh of the world; and finally, a Scots word, '*plowt*' (l. 22), meaning a heavy shower or a downpour. Natural elements are frequently the focus of Robertson's poetry, as they are also present in different forms in the poetry of Burnside, Jamie and White, and so the next part of this chapter is devoted to aspects of the weather-world.

Self in the Weather-World

In this the final section, I want to return to certain abiding themes and motifs in Robin Robertson's poetry, as a way of beginning to conclude this reading of the protean lyrical condition of his verse. In bringing back particular figures, I will be refocusing the reader's understanding, emphasising the weather-world in Robertson, and thus returning to the themes of temporality, fragility and entropy. The weather-world and the world of the sea-forest interchange; they are all aspects of becoming-unbecoming, of the self in suspension, vulnerable and fragile, in a state of decay and the abatement of energy. Impermanence and rootlessness may be the source of strength. The speaker of 'Beginning to Green' (2010: 75) confesses to finding 'a kind of hope' (l. 1) in homelessness. The pronoun 'they' (l. 6) vaguely points to the other. In a comparison to an over-wintering bird, the speaker's survival strategy either hibernation or migration, two ways to accomplish over-wintering. Unnoticed, disappearing for good, he has only birds for company. The speaker's uncertainty is contained in the pronouns 'a kind of' and 'some', which do not allow for enthusiasm. 'This' repeated four times – for instance, in the opening lines, 'here, in this / homelessness, in this place' (ll. 1–2) – suggests proximity and roundedness in the landscape, while the anaphora in lines 3 and 4 emphasises the location with the adverb 'where'. The self becomes immersed in a landscape, which opens under the sun, the world immaculate, 'mirror-less, flawless' (l. 10). The world is mirror-less because it is not specular, devoid of human presence and 'unmissed' (l. 13); the self may find itself again 'in this great unfurling' (l. 14), adhering to the flesh of the world. The sea and the skin, an entwining of corporeality and mutability, foreground the image of the self as world, the world as self, which is affected by plasticity, a momentary 'deserting of subjectivity', to use Malabou's term once again. The transition from grey to green brings self-reflection in the line 'I can see myself again' (l. 13), whereby 'the *phenomenological* metaphor', to return to Derrida's words, opens the subject 'onto the space of presence' (1982: 132), foregrounding the temporal and spatial embeddedness.

A number of poems place a solitary figure in the landscape, where the self, immersed in the world, contemplates its own solitariness, inscribed in a place, its identitarian boundaries dissolving, the self becoming engulfed in the natural elements, as in 'Diving'. In the poem 'In Memoriam David Jones' (1997: 26–7), Robertson employs a similar technique to that in 'Corryvreckan', discussed above, with a detailed description of the landscape, minutely recording undergoing changes. The speaking I remains unrevealed: all perception, fully immersed in the world. The landscape appears freed of human presence, and yet there is a wandering eye that registers the 'fleeing moorhens' and the disembodied self, reflecting on the movement of water in the river. The animals encountered are anthropomorphised: gulls are 'laughing like indulgent fathers', the seal is 'astonished'. The sameness in difference and the iterability of the world are highlighted in the final lines of the poem – 'a scene that stays the same ... has never tired, / will never tire of this' (ll. 27–30) – which suggest the never-ending cycle of the world, permanence in changeability. 'In Memoriam David Jones' belongs with poems that are evocations of the perceived world with the self withdrawn. The self retreats and becomes suspended, being the mere substrate on and from which the world projects. Atmospheric conditions pervade our being, seeping through in the form of metaphors, which manifests itself an interior weather-world, as in the poem 'Strindberg in Skovlyst' (2013: 43–7), where the speaker says, 'In my head, when the gales are running wild, / I steer towards catastrophe / then write about it' (ll. 62–3). Here the meteorological metaphor serves as a mark of reversibility, letting the landscape inside. There are also poems such as 'Easter, Liguria', discussed above, and 'Apart' (2002: 3), the title of which introduces an image of being separated by distance or time, *à part*, at the side, where the self is again withdrawn, at a remove. The collective subject of the poem creates a sense of community, a common plight even though experienced alone. The opening lines, '[w]e are drawn to edges, to our own / parapets and sea-walls' (ll. 1–2), suggest being placed on the periphery. A sense of loss pervades the poem, a realisation of incorrigible, repeated actions. The three gerunds opening stanzas two, three and four – 'returning' (l. 4), 'thinking' (l. 7), 'looking' (l. 9) – as well as 'finding' (l. 2) following a colon in the second line, create a sense of being suspended and futile repetition. The final line is composed entirely of one-syllable words: 'own' and 'fall' link the first line with the last one, as if accelerating the ending. Throughout Robertson's poetry, there is an insistence on aurality in the landscape, evoking the weather-world in poetic sound. As in the poems discussed above, 'Three Ways of Looking at God', 'Diving' and 'Corryvreckan,' sound effects such as alliteration and assonance foreground the sounds of the earth and simultaneously draw our attention to the materiality of language through complex patterning. In 'Storm' (1997: 14), silence opens and ends the poem, with the rain's brief tempestuous drumbeat; the evocation of the rain is aural, bracketed by the lack of sound. Through the first line – 'Faulted silence, dislocation' – liquid consonants roll off the tongue. The next line introduces an interplay of long and short vowels, and the consonantal rhythm of the aspirant 'h' and the dental 't'. The rain falls in line 6, the drumming of 't's and 'd's interchangeable with the liquid 'r's and 'l's, letting the reader hear the beat through the intricate sound patterning, which appears briefly, in a 'trembling life' of impressions (Merleau-Ponty 2008: 41), like the image itself.

The self's occasional retreat from the weather-world into the house and outside again brings together some of the major themes in Robertson's poetry that have discussed in this chapter, such as liminality, change, a vacillating movement, the motions of becoming, entropy and hauntings. This is the world, which

> exists in a chiasmatic relation with the domicile: the domicile holds back the flow of the liquid element, functioning as a form of resistance to it; but then it is from out of the domicile . . . that one plunges back into the element. (Wills 2008: 53)

As for Burnside and Jamie, the house functions as a significant motif for Robertson, emphasising a powerful, if uneasy, sense of place, indicative of a sense of displacement and deracination; often it is an attempt to make 'a home away from home', as in 'Strindberg in Skovlyst' (2013: 43). The house takes various, frequently highly ambivalent, forms. Robertson foregrounds its materiality, with doors, thresholds, keys, locks and passages recurring regularly, often in a state of dereliction, showing furniture abandoned in disuse, as in 'Retreat' (1997: 31). At times it is a living organism, as in 'The Oven Man' (2002: 11), where the house contains a 'skin of heat' (l. 2), emitting sounds that emphasise its vitality. The one-syllable verbs – 'rustles / and ticks, and clicks off' (ll. 9–10) – stress the living, dynamic nature of the house, together with other verbs, such as 're-inflates' (l. 1) and 'tightens it up' (l. 3). The poetic subject is 'inside, in expansive mood' (l. 12), making both the house and the self cohabit in a chiasmic entanglement. This places the non-Hibernian reader in a liminal place in relation to the culture, the lore, the world, as we are constantly being invited to accommodate estrangement. The house may also be an eerie, uncanny place of mystery, a locus of dark secrets, as in a much-analysed poem, 'At Roane Head' (2010: 87–9), mentioned above. The eeriness is carried into other poems, often without overt references to folk tales. For instance, the oneiric, surreal title of *Hill of Doors* merges landscape and a man-made structure. In many poems from this collection, such a dream-like atmosphere prevails, suggesting another order, constantly present on the peripheries of consciousness, as '[s]leep lingers all our lifetime about our eyes, as night hovers all day in the boughs of the fir tree' (Emerson 1950: 342). The work of experience takes place when the self returns to places, unexpectedly finding access, as in 'Finding the Keys' (2013: 68–9) and 'The Key' (2013: 77). The key recurs, opening up the possibility of communicating, as 'saying brings about an unlocking (*déverrouillement*) of communication that is also a "risky uncovering" of the self, a rupture in interiority and the "abandon of all shelter, exposure to traumas, vulnerability"' (Levinas, qtd in Wills 2008: 49). Some poems evoke the self's retreat from such an unlocking of communication, as in 'March, Lewisboro' (2002: 12–17), where daily dealings with things, or what Heidegger calls *Umgang*, appear impossible, unwanted, replaced by a dream of abandoning one's life and being born again. The house appears as something oppressive; the demands of another person and the inquisitive questions are rendered in shrill italics. This voice is contrasted with the outside, unconfined by demands, the world that just is. This is where the self feels at home, among the natural elements: the wind 'which breathes life into the leaves / till the trees are speaking' (ll. 71–2), 'a salting of snow, blown across the white table of the lake' (ll. 13–14), 'a sudden, exorbitant / flush of light' (ll. 74–5). In rhythmical couplets, the poet evokes the world in a series of glimpses, rendering moments of enchantment with its fauna and flora represented impressionistically.

Suspended between material and existential (a condition belonging to each of the poets in this study, in their own manner), the images privilege visual perception over aural: '[t]he frost's acoustic / futile against such silence' (ll. 47–8). The landscape is dotted with non-human beings, mainly birds, their names meticulously listed and including a rook, ducks, a swan, a Canada goose, crows, a hawk, a crow, a junco, a chickadee, grosbeaks, a crossbill, goldfinches, a sapsucker, a cardinal and white-tails. They appear flittingly, then return 'into their element, / which is breath' (ll. 113–14). The human world is markedly present in the gesture of naming, enacted on the world in the human belief that we are sovereign, which is vividly highlighted in the names of daffodils, narcissi and hydrangeas, which 'people the hollows' (l. 90): 'Manon Lescaut is here, / and Jules Verne // Rip Van Winkle bedded down / with Salome and Rosy Splendour / Burning Heart, Martinette, / Gigantic Star' (ll. 91–6). Yet the self is removed, the self-erasure of the speaker almost complete with the first-person possessive pronoun appearing in the penultimate line, '[m]y grey notebook' (l. 125), which at the same time introduces a self-conscious literary reference, the poem folding back on to itself. The poetic subject observes the natural world, attempting to put it into words, which will 'set the seed / of life and death'; this recalls the lines from 'Annunciation', as these fleeting observations are complemented by reminders of the fragility of matter, 'epidermal vulnerability' and entropy, leading towards death, disorder and change. Ever-present in this world, finitude is announced by '[s]tations of the necessary dead' (l. 53), marked by the images of the corpses of a rabbit, a crow and a roe deer. 'What life there is is felt and phantom' (l. 19): the words are suggestive of a site of powerful hauntings, a blend of phenomenological and metaphysical. In the end, what is left is 'glimpsed, half-heard beginnings; / the vestiges, and signs' (ll. 21–2). And this, we can say, is the condition of Scottish ecopoetics, as this is explored by White, Burnside, Jamie and Robertson.

Notes

1. Terror, wonder, sublime: there is in Robertson's poetry a Kantian sense of the sublime, which takes into account both terror and beauty, as aspects of wonder.
2. The poem was commissioned by John Burnside and Maurice Riordan for the anthology *Wild Reckoning* (2004). 'Primavera' was also published in *Swithering*.
3. 'Pentheus and Dionysus' and 'The Daughters of Minyas' (2010: 46–51); 'Dionysus and the Maiden' (after Nonnus) (2013: 52–4), 'The Coming God' (after Nonnus) (2013: 2–3), 'Dionysus in Love' (after Nonnus) (2013: 14–20).

4. Robertson has translated *Medea* (2008) and *Bacchae* (2014), both by Eurypides; *Bacchae* tells the story of the arrival of Dionysus in Thebes.
5. With an encrypted negative theology present in his poetry, Robertson may again be placed within the tradition of visionary poets, such as William Blake, Geoffrey Hill and David Jones.
6. The words are echoed in *Hamlet*: 'What a piece of work is a man! How noble in reason, how infinite in faculty! In form and moving how express and admirable! In action how like an angel, in apprehension how like a god! The beauty of the world. The paragon of animals!' (II, ii). Interestingly, Robertson points to his allegiance to a French avant-garde writer rather than an English author.
7. See Borthwick for an analysis of the poem through the notion of the uncanny (Borthwick 2011: 145).
8. It is important to remember that, for Levinas, '[r]esponsibility does not depend on reciprocity, in the asymmetrical encounter with the other,' as Cynthia D. Coe explains (2018: 196): 'When Levinas is asked about this in an interview, the question takes the form of whether animals have faces. He responds by affirming the "priority of the human face" over nonhuman animals, in whom "the face is not in its purest form". . . . Strangely, then, animals may have faces, but a comparatively weak form of that authority. . . . Unlike the response to the other, whose command is binding *not* because I recognize a shared characteristic, Levinas asserts that the obligation that I may feel toward the animal rests on the "transfer" of the experience of suffering from human to nonhuman animals' (Coe 2018: 196). According to Levinas, animal suffering has 'little moral standing' (Coe 2018: 197).

Bibliography

Abram, David (1996). *The Spell of the Sensuous: Perception and Language in a More-Than-Human World*. New York: Pantheon.
Abram, David (2010). *Becoming Animal: An Earthly Cosmology*. New York: Pantheon.
Agamben, Giorgio (1998). *Homo Sacer: Sovereign Power and Bare Life*. Trans. Daniel Heller-Roazen. Stanford: Stanford University Press.
Agamben, Giorgio (2003). *The Open: Man and Animal*. Trans. Kevin Attell. Stanford: Stanford University Press.
Alaimo, Stacey (2010). *Bodily Natures: Science, Environment, and the Material Self*. Bloomington and Indianapolis: Indiana University Press.
Arendt, Hannah (1999). 'Introduction'. In: Walter Benjamin, *Illuminations*. Trans. Harry Zohn. London: Pimlico, pp. 7–58.
Anon. (2010). 'Interview: Robin Robertson: Poet and Publisher'. *Scotland on Sunday*. 12 Feb., <http://www.scotsman.com/lifestyle/culture/books/interview-robin-robertson-poet-and-publisher-1-474043> (last accessed 26 Sep. 2018).
Ascherson, Neal (2002). *Stone Voices: The Search for Scotland*. London: Granta.
Baldwin, Thomas (2008). 'Introduction'. In: Maurice Merleau-Ponty, *The World of Perception*. Trans. Oliver Davis. London and New York: Routledge, pp. 1–28.
Bate, Jonathan (1991). *Romantic Ecology: Wordsworth and the Environmental Tradition*. London and New York: Routledge.
Bate, Jonathan (2000), *Song of the Earth*. London: Picador.
Bell, Eleanor (2015). 'Into the Centre of Things: Poetic Travel Narratives in the Work of Kathleen Jamie and Nan Shepherd'. In: Rachel Falconer, ed., *Kathleen Jamie: Essays and Poems on Her Work*. Edinburgh: Edinburgh University Press, pp. 126–33.
Bennett, Charles (2002). 'Current Literature 2000'. *English Studies*, 83: 149–63.
Bennett, Jane (2001). *The Enchantment of Modern Life: Attachments, Crossings, and Ethics*. Princeton, NJ: Princeton University Press.
Bennett, Jane (2010). *Vibrant Matter: A Political Ecology of Things*. Durham, NC: Duke University Press.
Benso, Silvia (2000). *The Face of Things: A Different Side of Ethics*. New York: SUNY Press.

Bergo, Bettina (2017). 'Emmanuel Levinas'. In: Edward N. Zalta, ed., *The Stanford Encyclopedia of Philosophy*, Fall, <https://plato.stanford.edu/archives/fall2017/entries/levinas/> (last accessed 28 Jan. 2018).

Bigwood, Carol (2007). 'Logos of Our Eco in the Feminine: An Approach Through Heidegger, Irigaray and Merleau-Ponty'. In: Suzanne L. Cataldi and William S. Harrick, eds, *Merleau-Ponty and Environmental Philosophy: Dwelling on the Landscapes of Thought*. Albany: SUNY Press, pp. 93–117.

Bloch, Felix (1976). 'Heisenberg and the Early Days of Quantum Mechanics'. *Physics Today* 29 (12): 27.

Boothroyd, Dave (2013). *Ethical Subjects in Contemporary Culture*. Edinburgh: Edinburgh University Press.

Borthwick, David (2011). '"The tilt from one parish / into another': Estrangement, Continuity and Connection in the Poetry of John Burnside, Kathleen Jamie and Robin Robertson'. *Scottish Literary Review* 3 (2): 133–48.

Bowd, Gavin, Charles Forsdick and Norman Bissell, eds (2005). *Grounding a World: Essays on the Work of Kenneth White*. Glasgow: Alba.

Brakoniecki, Kazimierz (2010). *Poeta kosmograf*. Olsztyn: Centrum Polsko-Francuskie.

Brannigan, John (n.d.). '"Dreaming of the Islands": The Poetry of the Shipping Forecast', <http://www.ucd.ie/scholarcast/scholarcast25.html> (last accessed 29 Jan. 2018).

Brewster, Scott (2006). 'Beating, Retreating: Violence and Withdrawal in Ian Banks and John Burnside'. In: James McGonigal and Kirsten Stirling, eds, *Ethically Speaking: Voice and Values in Modern Scottish Writing*. Amsterdam and New York: Rodopi, pp. 179–98.

Bristow, Tom (2009). 'Negative Poetics and Immanence: Reading John Burnside's "Homage to Henri Bergson"'. *Green Letters: Studies in Ecocriticism* 10 (1): 50–69.

Bristow, Tom (2011). 'Environment, History, Literature: Materialism as Cultural Ecology in John Burnside's "Four Quartets"'. *Scottish Literary Review* 3 (2): 149–70.

Bristow, Tom (2012). 'Ideas of Dwelling: Residence and Transport in Scottish Geography, German Folk Culture and the American Post-Romantic Hinterland of John Burnside's "Epithalamium"'. *Australian Folklore* 27: 108–20.

Bristow, Tom (2015). *The Anthropocene Lyric: An Affective Geography of Poetry, Person, Place*. London: Palgrave Macmillan.

Brown, Ian, and Colin Nicholson (2009). 'Arcades – The 1960s and 1970s'. In: Ian Brown and Alan Riach, eds, *The Edinburgh Companion to Twentieth-Century Scottish Literature*. Edinburgh: Edinburgh University Press, pp. 133–44.

Bsaithi, Omar (2008). *Kenneth White's Geopoetics in the Arabian Context*. Newcastle: Cambridge Scholars.

Buchanan, Brett (2008). *Onto-Ethologies: The Animal Environments of Uexküll, Heidegger, Merleau-Ponty and Deleuze*. New York: SUNY Press.

Buell, Lawrence (1995). *The Environmental Imagination: Thoreau, Nature Writing, and the Formation of American Culture*. Cambridge, MA, and London: Belknap Press of Harvard University Press.

Buell, Lawrence (2005). *The Future of Environmental Criticism: Environmental Crisis and Literary Imagination*. Malden: Blackwell.

Burnside, John (1988). *The Hoop*. Manchester: Carcanet.

Burnside, John (1992). *Feast Days*. London: Martin Secker and Warburg.
Burnside, John (1994). *The Myth of the Twin*. London: Cape.
Burnside, John (1997). *A Normal Skin*. London: Cape.
Burnside, John (2000). *The Asylum Dance*. London: Cape.
Burnside, John (2002). *The Light Trap*. London: Cape.
Burnside, John (2003). *Otro Mundo es Posible: Poetry, Dissidence and Reality TV. A Poet's Polemic*. Edinburgh: Scottish Book Trust.
Burnside, John (2005a). *The Good Neighbour*. London: Cape.
Burnside, John (2005b). 'Travelling into the Quotidian: Some Notes on Allison Funk's "Heartland" Poems'. *Poetry Review* 95: 59–70.
Burnside, John (2006). 'A Science of Belonging: Poetry as Ecology'. In: Robert Crawford, ed., *Contemporary Poetry and Contemporary Science*. Oxford: Oxford University Press, pp. 91–106.
Burnside, John (2007). *Gift Songs*. London: Cape.
Burnside, John (2009). *The Hunt in the Forest*. London: Cape.
Burnside, John (2011a). *Black Cat Bone*. London: Cape.
Burnside, John (2011b). Interview. Patricia McCarthy. *AGENDA Dwelling Places: An Appreciation of John Burnside* (45: 4/ 46: 1): 22–38.
Burnside, John (2013). *I Put a Spell on You: Seven Digressions on Love and Glamour*. London: Cape.
Burnside, John (2014). *All One Breath*. London: Cape.
Burnside, John (2017). *Still Life with Feeding Snake*. London: Cape.
Burnside, John, and Will Maclean (2014). *A Catechism of the Laws of Storms*. London: Art First.
Burnside, John, and Maurice Riordan, eds (2004). 'Introduction'. In: *Wild Reckoning: An Anthology Provoked by Rachel Carson's Silent Spring*. London: Calouste Gulbenkian Foundation, pp. 13–21.
Carman, Taylor (1999). 'The Body in Husserl and Merleau-Ponty'. *Philosophical Topics* 27: 2.
Carman, Taylor (2014). 'Foreword'. In: Maurice Merleau-Ponty, *Phenomenology of Perception*. Trans. Donald A. Landes. London: Routledge and Kegan Paul, pp. vii–xvi.
Cataldi, Suzanne L., and William S. Harrick, eds (2007). 'Introduction'. In: *Merleau-Ponty and Environmental Philosophy*. Albany: SUNY Press.
Clark, Timothy (2011). *The Cambridge Introduction to Literature and Environment*. Cambridge: Cambridge University Press.
Clark, Timothy (2015). *Ecocriticism on the Edge: The Anthropocene as a Threshold Concept*. London: Bloomsbury.
Coe, Cynthia D. (2018). *Levinas and the Trauma of Responsibility*. Bloomington: Indiana University Press.
Cohen, Jeffrey Jerome (2014). 'Introduction: Ecostitial'. In: *Inhuman Nature*. Washington, DC: Oliphaunt, pp. i–x.
Cohen, Jeffrey Jerome (2015). *Stone: An Ecology of the Inhuman*. Minneapolis and London: Minnesota University Press.
Cohen, Tom, Claire Colebrook and J. Hillis Miller (2016). *Twilight of the Anthropocene Idols*. London: Open Humanities Press.
Collins, Lucy (2011). '"Toward a Brink": The Poetry of Kathleen Jamie and the Environmental Crisis'. In: A. Karhio, S. Crosson, C. I. Armstrong, eds, *Crisis and Contemporary Poetry*. London: Palgrave Macmillan.

Collins, Lucy (2015). 'Nature and Embodiment in *This Weird Estate*'. In: Rachel Falconer, ed., *Kathleen Jamie: Essays and Poems on Her Work*. Edinburgh: Edinburgh University Press, pp. 112–22.

Craig, Cairns (2009). 'Kenneth White'. In: Matt McGuire and Colin Nicholson, eds, *Edinburgh Companion to Contemporary Scottish Poetry*. Edinburgh: Edinburgh University Press, pp. 154–71.

Craig, Cairns (2013). 'Intellectual Nomad'. *Scottish Review of Books*. 28 Jun., <https://www.scottishreviewofbooks.org/2013/06/intellectual-nomad> (last accessed 30 Aug. 2018).

Crawford, Robert, ed. (2006). *Contemporary Poetry and Contemporary Science*. Oxford: Oxford University Press.

Crawford, Robert (2015). 'Kathleen's Scots'. In: Rachel Falconer, ed., *Kathleen Jamie: Essays and Poems on Her Work*. Edinburgh: Edinburgh University Press, pp. 33–41.

Crichton Smith, Iain (2011). *New Collected Poems*. Ed. Matthew McGuire. Manchester: Carcanet Press.

Davidson, Lynn (2015). 'Repetition, Return and the Negotiation of Place in The Tree House'. In: Rachel Falconer, ed., *Kathleen Jamie: Essays and Poems on Her Work*. Edinburgh: Edinburgh University Press, pp. 93–9.

Davidson, Peter (2005). *The Idea of North*. London: Reaktion.

Davidson, Peter (2013). *Distance and Memory*. Manchester: Carcanet.

Davidson, Peter (2015). *The Last of the Light: About Twilight*. London: Reaktion.

Deleuze, Gilles, and Félix Guattari (1987). *A Thousand Plateaus: Capitalism and Schizophrenia*. Trans. Brian Massumi. London and Minneapolis: University of Minnesota Press.

Derrida, Jacques (1973). *Speech and Phenomena: And Other Essays on Husserl's Theory of Signs*. Trans. David Allison. Evanston: Northwestern University Press.

Derrida, Jacques (1979). 'Living On: *Border Lines*'. Trans. James Hulbert. In: Harold Bloom, Paul de Man, Jacques Derrida, Geoffrey Hartman and J. Hillis Miller, *Deconstruction and Criticism*. London and Henley: Routledge and Kegan Paul, pp. 75–176.

Derrida, Jacques (1981). *Positions*. Trans. Alan Bass. Chicago: University of Chicago Press.

Derrida, Jacques (1982). *Margins of Philosophy*. Trans. Alan Bass. Brighton: Harvester Press.

Derrida, Jacques (1988). *Limited Inc*. Evanston: Northwestern University Press.

Derrida, Jacques (1995a). 'Che cos'è poesia'. Trans. Peggy Kamuf. In: Elisabeth Weber, ed., *Points: Interviews, 1974–1994*. Stanford: Stanford University Press.

Derrida, Jacques (1995b), with Elisabeth Weber. 'Passages – From Traumatism to Promise'. In: Elisabeth Weber, ed., *Points: Interviews, 1974–1994*. Stanford: Stanford University Press, pp. 394–5.

Derrida, Jacques (1997). *Of Grammatology*. Trans. Gayatri Chakravorty Spivak. Baltimore and London: Johns Hopkins University Press.

Derrida, Jacques (2006). *Specters of Marx: The State of the Debt, the Work of Mourning, & the New International*. Trans. Peggy Kamuf. New York and London: Bernd Magnus and Stephen Cullenberg.

Derrida, Jacques (2008). *The Animal That Therefore I Am*. Trans. David Wills. New York: Fordham University Press.
Derrida, Jacques (2013). *Signature Derrida*. Ed. and Preface Jay Williams. Introduction Françoise Meltzer. Trans. Geoffrey Bennington, Rachel Bowlby, Pascale-Anne Brault, Peggy Kamuf, Michael Naas, Avital Ronell, Lawrence Venuti and David Wills. Chicago: University of Chicago Press.
Dósa, Attila (2009a). 'John Burnside: Poets and Other Animals'. In: *Beyond Identity: New Horizons in Modern Scottish Poetry*. Amsterdam and New York: Rodopi, pp. 113–34.
Dósa, Attila (2009b). 'Kathleen Jamie: More than Human'. In: *Beyond Identity: New Horizons in Modern Scottish Poetry*. Amsterdam and New York: Rodopi, pp. 135–45.
Dósa, Attila (2009c). 'Kenneth White: A Strategist of Mutation'. In: *Beyond Identity: New Horizons in Modern Scottish Poetry*. Amsterdam and New York: Rodopi, pp. 259–79.
Dreyfus, Hubert L. (1991). *Being-in-the-World: A Commentary on Heidegger's Being and Time, Division I*. Cambridge, MA: MIT.
Dubow, Jessica (2011). 'Still-Life, After-Life, Nature Morte: W. G. Sebald and the Demands of Landscape'. In: Stephen Daniels, Dydia DeLyser, J. Nicholas Entrikin and Doug Richardson, eds, *Envisioning Landscapes, Making Worlds: Geography and the Humanities*. London: Routledge, pp. 188–97.
Dunne, Sean (1990). 'Traveller in the Diamond Country: Notes on the Poetry of Kenneth White'. *The Poetry Ireland Review* 29: 111–17.
Elder, John (1985). *Imagining the Earth: Poetry and the Vision of Nature*. Urbana and Chicago: University of Illinois Press.
Emerson, Ralph Waldo (1950). 'Experience'. In: *The Complete Essays and Other Writings*. Ed. Brooks Atkinson. Foreword Tremaine McDowell. New York: Modern Library, pp. 342–65.
Eurypides (2008). *Medea*. Trans. Robin Robertson. London: Vintage.
Eurypides (2014). *Bacchae*. Trans. Robin Robertson. London: Vintage.
Falconer, Rachel (2015a). 'Introduction'. In: *Kathleen Jamie: Essays and Poems on Her Work*. Edinburgh: Edinburgh University Press.
Falconer, Rachel (2015b). 'Midlife Music: The Overhaul and Frissure'. In: *Kathleen Jamie: Essays and Poems on Her Work*. Edinburgh: Edinburgh University Press, pp. 156–67.
Fazzini, Marco (2009). 'Kenneth White and John Burnside'. In: Matt McGuire and Colin Nicholson, eds, *The Edinburgh Companion to Contemporary Scottish Poetry*. Edinburgh: Edinburgh University Press.
Fraser, Lilias (2001). 'Interview with Kathleen Jamie'. *Scottish Studies Review*, Spring, 2 (1): 15–23.
Fritsch, Matthias, Philippe Lynes and David Wood (2018). *Eco-Deconstruction: Derrida and Environmental Philosophy*. New York: Fordham University Press.
Gairn, Louisa (2008). *Ecology and Modern Scottish Literature*. Edinburgh: Edinburgh University Press.
Gairn, Louisa (2015). 'Connective Leaps: *Sightlines* and *The Overhaul*'. In: Rachel Falconer, ed., *Kathleen Jamie: Essays and Poems on Her Work*. Edinburgh: Edinburgh University Press, pp. 134–45.

Gardiner, Michael (2009). 'Arcades – the 1980s and 1990s'. In: Ian Brown and Alan Riach, eds, *The Edinburgh Companion to Twentieth-Century Scottish Literature*. Edinburgh: Edinburgh University Press, pp. 181–92.
Gasché, Rodolphe (1987). 'Reading Chiasms: An Introduction'. In: Andrzej Warminski. *Readings in Interpretation: Hölderlin, Hegel, Heidegger*. Minneapolis: University of Minnesota Press, pp. ix–xxvi.
Gasché, Rodolphe (1999). *Of Minimal Things: Studies on the Notion of Relation*. New York: Stanford University Press.
Gifford, Douglas, Sarah Dunnigan and Alan MacGillivray, eds (2002). *Scottish Literature*. Edinburgh: Edinburgh University Press.
Glotfelty, Cheryll, and Harold Fromm (1996). *The Ecocriticism Reader: Landmarks in Literary Ecology*. Athens: University of Georgia Press.
Goodbody, Axel, and Kate Rigby, eds (2011). 'Introduction'. In: *Ecocritical Theory: New European Approaches*. Charlottesville: University of Virginia Press, pp. 1–14.
Goodyear, Dana (2008). 'Zen Master: Gary Snyder and the Art of Life'. *New Yorker*. 20 Oct., <https://www.newyorker.com/magazine/2008/10/20/zen-master> (last accessed 29 Jan 2018).
Graham, Lesley (2011). 'Kenneth White's Essays: Cartography Grounded in Self'. *Études écossaises* 14.
Hall, Dewey W., ed. (2016a). *Romantic Ecocriticism: Origins and Legacies*. Lanham, MD: Rowman and Littlefield.
Hall, Dewey W. (2016b). *Romantic Naturalists, Early Environmentalists: An Ecocritical Study, 1789–1912*. London and New York: Routledge.
Harman, Graham (2005). *Guerrilla Metaphysics: Phenomenology and the Carpentry of Things*. Chicago and LaSalle, IL: Open Court.
Harris, Alexandra (2015). *Weatherland: Writers and Artists under English Skies*. London: Thames and Hudson.
Hashas, Mohammed (2017). *Intercultural Geopoetics in Kenneth White's Open World*. Newcastle: Cambridge Scholars.
Heaney, Seamus (1979). *Field Work*. London: Faber and Faber.
Heidegger, Martin (1979). *Nietzsche: The Will to Power as Art*. Ed. and trans. David Farrell Krell. New York: Harper and Row.
Heidegger, Martin (1992). 'Phänomenologische Interpretationen zu Aristoteles (Anzeige der hermeneutischen Situation)'. Trans. Michael Bauer. *Man and World* 25: 358–93. [First published in *Dilthey Jahrbuch für Philosophie und Geschichte der Geisteswissenschaften* 6 (1989), pp. 228–74.]
Heidegger, Martin (1993). *Basic Writings*. Ed. David Farrell Krell. San Francisco: HarperCollins.
Heidegger, Martin (1998a). 'Letter on "Humanism"'. In: *Pathmarks*. Trans. Frank A. Capuzzi. Ed. William McNeill. Cambridge: Cambridge University Press, pp. 239–77.
Heidegger, Martin (1998b). *Pathmarks*. Trans. Frank A. Capuzzi. Ed. William McNeill. Cambridge: Cambridge University Press.
Heidegger, Martin (2010). *Being and Time*. Trans. Joan Stambaugh. Albany, NY: SUNY Press.
Heidegger, Martin (2013a). 'Building Dwelling Thinking'. In: *Poetry Language Thought*. Trans. Albert Hofstadter. New York: Harper and Row, pp. 145–61.

Heidegger, Martin (2013b). 'Origin of the Work of Art'. In: *Poetry Language Thought*. Trans. Albert Hofstadter. New York: Harper and Row, pp. 17–79.
Heidegger, Martin (2013c). *Poetry Language Thought*. Trans. Albert Hofstadter. New York: Harper and Row.
Heise, Ursula K. (2008). *Sense of Place, Sense of the Planet: The Environmental Imagination of the Global*. Oxford: Oxford University Press.
Homer (1996). *The Odyssey*. Trans. Robert Fagles. Int. and Notes Bernard Knox. New York: Viking.
Husserl, Edmund (2012). *Ideas: General Introduction to Pure Phenomenology*. Trans. W. R. Boyce Gibson. London and New York: Routledge.
Hutchings, Kevin (2007). 'Ecocriticism in British Romantic Studies'. *Literature Compass* 4 (1): 172–202.
Hutchings, Kevin, and John Miller, eds (2016). *Transatlantic Literary Ecologies: Nature and Culture in the Nineteenth-Century Anglophone Atlantic World*. Ashgate Series in Nineteenth-Century Transatlantic Studies. London and New York: Routledge.
Ingold, Tim (2011a). *Being Alive: Essays on Movement, Knowledge and Description*. New York and London: Routledge.
Ingold, Tim (2011b). *The Perception of the Environment: Essays on Livelihood, Dwelling and Skill*. London and New York: Routledge, pp. xv–xix.
Irigaray, Luce (1983). *The Forgetting of Air in Martin Heidegger*. London: Athlone Press.
Irigaray, Luce (1993). *An Ethics of Sexual Difference*. Trans. Carolyn Burke and Gillian C. Gill. Ithaca, NY: Cornell University Press.
Irigaray, Luce, and Michael Marder (2016). *Through Vegetal Being*. New York: Columbia University Press.
Jamet, Pierre (2005). 'Kenneth White and Religion'. In: Gavin Bowd, Charles Forsdick and Norman Bissell, eds, *Grounding a World: Essays on the Work of Kenneth White*. Glasgow: Alba, pp. 96–108.
Jamet, Pierre (2009). 'The Poetry and Ideas of Kenneth White: A Perspective from France'. *Scottish Literary Review* 1: 103–24.
Jamie, Kathleen. *Kathleen Jamie* website, <http://www.kathleenjamie.com/about/> (last accessed 12 Feb. 2019).
Jamie, Kathleen (2002a). *Among Muslims: Meetings at the Frontiers of Pakistan*. London: Sort of Books.
Jamie, Kathleen (2002b). *Mr and Mrs Scotland are Dead: Poems 1980–1994*. Tarset: Bloodaxe.
Jamie, Kathleen (2004a). 'Relative Values'. *PBS Bulletin*, August, 202: 5–7.
Jamie, Kathleen (2004b). *The Tree House*. London: Picador.
Jamie, Kathleen (2005). *Findings*. London: Sort of Books.
Jamie, Kathleen (2006). 'Island at the Edge of the World'. *The Guardian*. 26 Aug., <https://www.theguardian.com/books/2006/aug/26/featuresreviews.guardianreview4> (last accessed 15 Mar. 2018).
Jamie, Kathleen (2007). *This Weird Estate*. Edinburgh: Scotland&Medicine.
Jamie, Kathleen (2008). 'A Lone Enraptured Male: Review of *The Wild Places* by Robert Macfarlane'. *London Review of Books* 30 (5): 25–7.
Jamie, Kathleen (2012a). Interview. *Scottish Review of Books*, 8 June, 8 (2), <https://www.scottishreviewofbooks.org/2012/06/the-srb-interview-kathleen-jamie/> (last accessed 26 Dec. 2017).

Jamie, Kathleen (2012b). 'Kathleen Jamie on Writing a Book'. *The Guardian*. 16 Apr., <https://www.theguardian.com/books/2012/aug/17/kathleen-jamie-writing-book-self> (last accessed 14 Dec. 2017).
Jamie, Kathleen (2012c). *Sightlines*. London: Sort of Books.
Jamie, Kathleen (2012d). *The Overhaul*. London: Picador.
Jamie, Kathleen (2015). *The Bonniest Companie*. London: Picador.
Jamie, Kathleen, and Brigid Collins (2013). *Frissure*. Edinburgh: Polygon.
Kant, Immanuel (1987). *Critique of Judgment*. Trans. Werner S. Pluhar. Indianapolis and Cambridge, MA: Hackett.
Kelman, James (2002). *And the Judges Said . . . : Essays*. Edinburgh, Polygon.
Kennedy, Innes (2007). 'Nomad in Atopia: The Geopoetic Ethics of Kenneth White'. In: Gilles Leydier, ed., *Scotland and Europe, Scotland in Europe*. Newcastle: Cambridge Scholars, pp. 170–83.
Kerridge, Richard (2001). 'Ecological Hardy'. In: Karla M. Armbruster and Kathleen. R. Wallace, eds, *Beyond Nature Writing: Expanding the Boundaries of Ecocriticism*. Charlottesville: University Press of Virginia.
Kerridge, Richard, and Neil Sammells (1998). *Writing the Environment: Ecocriticism and Literature*. London and New York: Zed Books.
Kroeber, Karl (1974). '"Home at Grasmere": Ecological Holiness'. *PMLA* 89: 132–41.
Kroeber, Karl (1995). *Ecological Literary Criticism: Romantic Imagining and the Biology of Mind*. New York: Columbia University Press.
Kronenberg, Anna (2014). *Geopoetyka: Związki literatury i środowiska*. Łódź: Wydawnictwo Uniwersytetu Łódzkiego.
Latour, Bruno (1993). *We Have Never Been Modern*. Trans. Catherine Porter. Cambridge, MA: Harvard University Press.
Lawrence, Faith (2015). 'A Poetics of Listening'. In: Rachel Falconer, ed., *Kathleen Jamie: Essays and Poems on Her Work*. Edinburgh: Edinburgh University Press, pp. 10–20.
Leopold, Aldo (1949). *A Sand County Almanac and Sketches Here and There*. London: Oxford University Press.
Levinas, Emmanuel (1969). *Totality and Infinity: An Essay on Exteriority*. Trans. Alphonso Lingis. Pittsburgh: Duquesne University Press.
Levinas, Emmanuel (1978). *Otherwise than Being or Beyond Essence*. Trans. Alphonso Lingis. Dordrecht and Boston: Kluwer Academic.
Lilley, Deborah (2013). 'Kathleen Jamie: Rethinking the Externality and Idealisation of Nature'. *Green Letters: Studies in Ecocriticism* 17 (1): 16–26.
Logan, William (2007). 'The World Is Too Much With Us'. *The New Criterion*. Dec., pp. 61–8.
Mabey, Richard (2013). *Turned Out Nice Again*. London: Profile.
McCaig, Norman (1969). *A Man in My Position*. London: Chatto and Windus.
Macfarlane, Robert (2011). 'Introduction'. In: Nan Shepherd, *The Living Mountain*. Edinburgh: Canongate, pp. ix–xxxiv.
McGonigal, James (2006). 'Translating God: Negative Theology and Two Scottish Poets'. In: James McGonigal and Kirsten Stirling, eds, *Ethically Speaking: Voice and Values in Modern Scottish Writing*. Amsterdam and New York: Rodopi, pp. 223–46.

McGuire, Matt (2009). 'Kathleen Jamie'. In: Matt McGuire and Colin Nicholson, eds, *The Edinburgh Companion to Contemporary Scottish Poetry*. Edinburgh: Edinburgh University Press, pp. 141–53.
McGuire, Matt, and Colin Nicholson (2009). *The Edinburgh Companion to Contemporary Scottish Poetry*. Edinburgh: Edinburgh University Press.
Mackay, Peter (2015). 'The Tilt from One Parish to Another': *The Tree House* and *Findings*'. In: Rachel Falconer, ed., *Kathleen Jamie: Essays and Poems on Her Work*. Edinburgh: Edinburgh University Press, pp. 84–92.
McKusick, James C. (2000). *Green Writing: Romanticism and Ecology*. New York and London: Palgrave.
MacLachlan, Christopher (1998). 'Nature in Scottish Literature'. In: Patrick D. Murphy, Terry Gifford and Katsunori Yamazato, eds, *Literature of Nature: An International Sourcebook*. London and New York: Routledge, pp. 184–90.
McManus, Tony (2005). 'Kenneth White: A Transcendental Scot'. In: Gavin Bowd, Charles Forsdick and Norman Bissell, eds, *Grounding a World: Essays on the Work of Kenneth White*. Glasgow: Alba.
McNeill, Marian F. (1959). *The Silver Bough*. Glasgow: William MacLellan.
Malabou, Catherine (2012). *Ontology of Accident: An Essay on Destructive Plasticity*. Trans. Carolyn Shread. Cambridge: Polity Press.
Malpas, Jeff (2006). *Heidegger's Topology: Being, Place, World*. Cambridge, MA, and London: MIT Press.
Malpas, Jess (2018). *Place and Experience: A Philosophical Topography*. Second edn. London and New York: Routledge.
Marratto, Scott L. (2012). *The Intercorporeal Self: Merleau-Ponty on Subjectivity*. Albany, NY: SUNY Press.
Marsack, Robyn (2009). 'The Seven Poets Generation'. In: Ian Brown and Alan Riach, eds, *The Edinburgh Companion to Twentieth-Century Scottish Literature*. Edinburgh: Edinburgh University Press, pp. 156–67.
Marx, Leo (1964). *The Machine in the Garden: Technology and the Pastoral Ideal in American Culture*. Oxford: Oxford University Press.
Matthews, Steven (2010). 'Bodies of Work'. *Poetry Review* 100 (1): 90–2.
Meeker, Joseph W. ([1974] 1997). *The Comedy of Survival: Literary Ecology and a Play Ethic*. Tucson: University of Arizona Press.
Merleau-Ponty, Maurice (1962). *Phenomenology of Perception*. Trans. Donald A. Landes. London: Routledge and Kegan Paul.
Merleau-Ponty, Maurice (1964). *The Primacy of Perception*. Trans. William Cobb. Ed. James Edie. Evanston: Northern University Press.
Merleau-Ponty, Maurice (1967). *The Structure of Behaviour*. Trans. Alden L. Fisher. Foreword John Wild. Evanston: Northern University Press.
Merleau-Ponty, Maurice (1968). *The Visible and the Invisible. Followed by Working Notes*. Ed. Claude Lefort. Trans. Alphonso Lingis. Evanston: Northwestern University Press.
Merleau-Ponty, Maurice (1973). *The Prose of the World*. Trans. John O'Neill. Ed. Claude Lefort. Evanston: Northwestern University Press.
Merleau-Ponty, Maurice (2003). *Nature*. Compiled by Dominique Seglard. Trans. Robert Vallier. Evanston: Northwestern University Press.
Merleau-Ponty, Maurice (2008). *The World of Perception*. Trans. Oliver Davis. London and New York: Routledge.

Michaelis, Amanda G. (2010). 'The Mystic and the Poet: Identity Formation, Deformation, and Reformation in Elizabeth Jennings' "Teresa of Avila" and Kathleen Jamie's "Julian of Norwich"'. *Christianity and Literature* 59 (4): 665–81.
Miller, J. Hillis (1987). 'The Ethics of Reading'. *Style* 21 (2): 181–91.
Miller, J. Hillis (1995). *Topographies*. Stanford: Stanford University Press.
Mitchell, Andrew J. (2015). *The Fourfold: Reading the Late Heidegger*. Evanston: Northwestern University Press.
Morton, Timothy (2007). *Ecology without Nature: Rethinking Environmental Aesthetics*. Cambridge, MA, and London: Harvard University Press.
Morton, Timothy (2010). *The Ecological Thought*. Cambridge, MA, and London: Harvard University Press.
Morton, Timothy (2011). 'Mesh'. In: Stephanie LeMenager, Teresa Shewry and Ken Hiltner, eds, *Environmental Criticism for the Twenty-First Century*. London and New York: Routledge, pp. 19–30.
Morton, Timothy (2013). *Hyperobjects: Philosophy and Ecology after the End of the World*. Minneapolis and London: Minnesota University Press.
Morton, Timothy (2016). *Dark Ecology: For a Logic of Future Coexistence*. New York: Columbia University Press.
Murphy, Patrick D., Terry Gifford and Katsunori Yamazato, eds (1998). *Literature of Nature: An International Sourcebook*. London and New York: Routledge.
Naomi, Katrina (2015). Interview with Robin Robertson. *Writers in Conversation* 2 (1), Feb.
Newell, J. Philip (2003). *The Book of Creation: The Practice of Celtic Spirituality*. Norwich: Canterbury Press/Hymns Ancient and Modern.
Newman, E. I. (1988). 'Mycorrhizal Links Between Plants: Their Functioning and Ecological Significance'. *Advances in Ecological Research* 18: 243–70.
Nicholson, Colin (2009). 'Nomadic Subjects in Recent Poetry'. In: Matt McGuire and Colin Nicholson, eds, *The Edinburgh Companion to Contemporary Scottish Poetry*. Edinburgh: Edinburgh University Press, pp. 80–96.
Nietzsche, Friedrich (2003). *The Birth of Tragedy*. Trans. Ian C. Johnston. Blackmask Online, <https://archive.org/stream/BirthOfTragedy/bitrad_djvu.txt> (last accessed 14 Feb. 2019).
Oerlemans, Onno (2002). *Romanticism and the Materiality of Nature*. Toronto: University of Toronto Press.
Palgrave, Francis T. (1897). *Landscape and Poetry: From Homer to Tennyson*. London: Macmillan.
Paterson, Don (2018). *The Poem: Lyric, Sign, Metre*. London: Faber and Faber.
Paterson, Don, and Charles Simic, eds (2004). *New British Poetry*. Saint Paul: Graywolf Press.
Philipse, Herman (1998). *Heidegger's Philosophy of Being: A Critical Interpretation*. Princeton, NJ: Princeton University Press.
Pick, Anat (2011). *Creaturely Poetics: Animality and Vulnerability in Literature and Film*. New York: Columbia University Press.
Pliny the Elder (1967). *Natural History*. Trans. H. Rackham. Cambridge, MA: Harvard University Press.
Potkay, Adam (2012). *Wordsworth's Ethics*. Baltimore: Johns Hopkins University Press.

Reynolds, Jack (2004). *Merleau-Ponty and Derrida: Intertwining Embodiment and Alterity*. Athens: Ohio University Press.
Riach, Alan (2009). 'The Poetics of Devolution'. In: Matt McGuire and Colin Nicholson, eds, *The Edinburgh Companion to Contemporary Scottish Poetry*. Edinburgh: Edinburgh University Press, pp. 8–20.
Riach, Alan (2015). 'Mr and Mrs Scotland Are Taking a Vacation in the Autonomous Region'. In: Rachel Falconer, ed., *Kathleen Jamie: Essays and Poems on Her Work*. Edinburgh: Edinburgh University Press, pp. 21–31.
Rigby, Kate (2004a). 'Earth, World, Text: On the (Im)possibility of Ecopoiesis'. *New Literary History*, Critical Inquiries, Explorations, and Explanations, Summer, 35 (3): 427–42.
Rigby, Kate (2004b). *Topographies of the Sacred: The Poetics of Place in European Romanticism*. Charlottesville: University of Virginia Press.
Rigby, Kate (2014). 'Romanticism and Ecocriticism'. In: Greg Garrard, ed., *The Oxford Handbook of Ecocriticism*. Oxford: Oxford University Press, pp. 60–79.
Rilke, Rainer Maria (2009). *Duino Elegies and The Sonnets to Orpheus*. Ed. and trans. Stephen Mitchell. New York: Vintage.
Robertson, Robin (1997). *A Painted Field*. London: Picador.
Robertson, Robin (2002). *Slow Air*. London: Picador.
Robertson, Robin (2006). *Swithering*. London: Picador.
Robertson, Robin (2010). *The Wrecking Light*. London: Picador.
Robertson, Robin (2013). *Hill of Doors*. London: Picador.
Robertson, Robin (2014). 'Introduction. Eurypides.' *Bacchae*. Trans. Robin Robertson. London: Vintage, pp. xiii–xiv.
Robertson, Robin (2015). 'The SRB Interview: Robin Robertson'. *Scottish Review of Books*. 30 May, <https://www.scottishreviewofbooks.org/free-content/the-srb-interview-robin-robertson/> (last accessed 12 Feb. 2019).
Robertson, Robin (2018). *The Long Take*. London: Picador.
Roe, Nicholas (1992). *The Politics of Nature: Wordsworth and Some Contemporaries*. Basingstoke: Macmillan.
Rueckert, William (1978). 'Literature and Ecology: An Experiment in Ecocriticism'. *Iowa Review* 9 (1): 71–86.
Rybicka, Elżbieta (2014). *Geopoetyka: Przestrzeń i miejsce we współczesnych teoriach i praktykach literackich*. Cracow: Universitas.
Sampson, Fiona (2012). *Beyond the Lyric. A Map of Contemporary British Poetry*. London: Chatto and Windus.
Scigaj, Leonard M. (1999). *Sustainable Poetry: Four American Ecopoets*. Lexington: University of Kentucky Press.
Scott, Kirsty (2005). 'In the Nature of Things'. *The Guardian*, 18 June, <https://www.theguardian.com/books/2005/jun/18/featuresreviews.guardianreview15> (last accessed 20 Jan. 2018).
Serres, Michel (1995). *Natural Contract*. Trans. Elizabeth MacArthur and William Paulson. Ann Arbor: University of Michigan Press.
Severin, Laura (2011). 'A Scottish Ecopoetics: Feminism and Environmentalism in the Works of Kathleen Jamie and Valerie Gillies'. *Feminist Formations*, Summer, 23 (2): 98–110.
Shepard, Paul (1998). *Thinking Animals: Animals and the Development of Human Intelligence*. Athens and London: University of Georgia Press.

Shepherd, Nan (2011). *The Living Mountain*. Edinburgh: Canongate.
Simpson, Juliet (2015). '"Sweet-Wild Weeks": Birth, Being and Belonging in Jizzen'. In Rachel Falconer, ed., *Kathleen Jamie: Essays and Poems on Her Work*. Edinburgh: Edinburgh University Press, pp. 71–82.
Smith, Ben (2013). 'Beating the Bounds: Mapping the Borders of Self and Landscape in the Work of John Burnside and Tim Robinson'. *Green Letters: Studies in Ecocriticism* 17 (1): 67–76.
Smith, George Gregory (1919). *Scottish Literature, Character and Influence*. London: Macmillan.
Snyder, Gary (1990). *The Practice of the Wild*. Berkeley, CA: Counterpoint.
Solnit, Rebecca (2002). *Wanderlust: A History of Walking*. London: Verso.
Solnit, Rebecca (2005). *A Field Guide to Getting Lost*. Edinburgh and London: Canongate.
Stevenson, Robert Louis (1887). *Memories and Portraits*. London: T. Nelson and Sons.
Stilgoe, John (2015). *What Is Landscape?* Cambridge, MA: MIT Press.
Sultzbach, Kelly Elizabeth (2016). *Ecocriticism in the Modernist Imagination*. Cambridge: Cambridge University Press.
Szuba, Monika (2015). '"I think of them as guests": John Burnside's Encounters with Nature.' In: Philippe Laplace, ed., *Environmental and Ecological Readings: Nature, Human and Posthuman Dimensions in Scottish Literature & Arts (XVIII–XXI Century)*. Besançon: Presses Universitaires de Franche-Comté.
Szuba, Monika (2016). '"That Essentially Scottish Virtue of Openness": Literary and Philosophical References in John Burnside's Poetry'. In Aniela Korzeniowska and Izabela Szymańska, eds. *Scottish Culture: Dialogue and Self-Expression*. Warsaw: Semper, pp. 47–59.
Szuba, Monika (2017a). '"The *terra incognita* of the whole": John Burnside's Writing and the Entangled Bank of Culture'. *Litteraria Pragensia* 27 (53).
Szuba, Monika (2017b). '"Peering into the dark machinery": Modernity, Perception, and the Self in John Burnside's Poetry'. In: Julian Wolfreys, ed., *New Critical Thinking*. Edinburgh: Edinburgh University Press.
Szuba, Monika (2018a). '"Beyond our Illusory Homelands": Representability, Deception, and Epistemological Angst in John Burnside's *A Summer of Drowning*'. In: Stephen Butler and Agnieszka Sienkiewicz-Charlish, eds, *Crime Fiction: A Critical Casebook*. Frankfurt am Main: Peter Lang.
Szuba, Monika (2018b). 'Burnside's Bestiary: The Significance of Birds and Other Animals in John Burnside's Poetry'. In: Aniela Korzeniowska and Izabela Szymańska, eds, *Polish Scholars on Scottish Writers: An Interpretative Collage*. Warsaw: Semper
Szuba, Monika (2019a). '"The Wider Rootedness": John Burnside's Embodied Sense of Place'. In: Monika Szuba and Julian Wolfreys, eds, *The Poetics of Space and Place in Scottish Literature*. New York: Palgrave.
Szuba, Monika (2019b). '"A temporary, sometimes fleeting thing': Home and Dwelling in John Burnside's Poetry'. In: Ben Davies, ed., *John Burnside: Contemporary Critical Perspectives*. London: Bloomsbury Continuum.
Tymieniecka, Anna-Teresa, and Shoichi Matsuba (1998). *Immersing in the Concrete: Maurice Merleau-Ponty in the Japanese Perspective*. Analecta

Husserliana: The Yearbook of Phenomenological Research. Vol. LVIII. Dordrecht: Kluwer Academic.
Uexküll, Jacob von (2010). *A Foray into the Worlds of Animals and Humans, with a Theory of Meaning.* Trans. Joseph O'Neil. Int. Dorion Sagan. Afterword Geoffrey Winthrop-Young. Minneapolis: University of Minnesota Press.
Vasseleu, Cathryn (1998). *Textures of Light: Vision and Touch in Irigaray, Levinas and Merleau-Ponty.* London and New York: Routledge.
Vincenz, Marc (2010). 'A Celtic Mage's Muses'. Interview with Robin Robertson. 1 Jan., <https://www.openlettersmonthly.com/issue/interview-with-poet-robin-robertson/> (last accessed 26 Sep. 2018).
Westling, Louise (2013). *The Logos of the Living World: Merleau-Ponty, Animals, and Language.* New York: Fordham University Press.
Westphal, Bertrand (2011). *Geocriticism: Real and Fictional Places.* Trans. Robert T. Tally Jr. New York: Palgrave Macmillan.
Wheatley, David (2015). '"Proceeding Without a Map": Kathleen Jamie and the Lie of the Land'. In: Rachel Falconer, ed., *Kathleen Jamie: Essays and Poems on Her Work.* Edinburgh: Edinburgh University Press, pp. 52–61.
Wheeler, Michael (2011). 'Martin Heidegger'. In: Edward N. Zalta, ed., *The Stanford Encyclopedia of Philosophy*, 12 Oct., <https://plato.stanford.edu/entries/heidegger/> (last accessed 30 Jun. 2018).
White, Kenneth (1987). *L'Esprit nomade.* Paris: Grasset.
White, Kenneth (1989a). *The Bird Path: Collected Longer Poems.* London: Penguin.
White, Kenneth (1989b). *Travels in the Drifting Dawn.* London: Penguin.
White, Kenneth (1989c). 'What Is Geopoetics?', <http://www.geopoetics.org.uk/what-is-geopoetics/> (last accessed 31 Aug. 2018).
White, Kenneth (1990a). *The Blue Road.* Edinburgh: Mainstream.
White, Kenneth (1990b). *Handbook for the Diamond Country: Collected Shorter Poems 1960–1990.* Edinburgh: Mainstream.
White, Kenneth (1992). 'Elements of Geopoetics'. *Edinburgh Review* 88: 163–78.
White, Kenneth (1994). *Le Plateau de l'albatros: Introduction à la géopoétique.* Paris: Grasset.
White, Kenneth (1996). *Coast to Coast: Interviews and Conversations 1985–1995.* Glasgow: Mythic Horse Press.
White, Kenneth (1998). *On Scottish Ground.* Edinburgh: Polygon.
White, Kenneth (2003). *Open World: The Collected Poems 1960–2000.* Edinburgh: Polygon.
White, Kenneth (2004). *The Wanderer and His Charts: Exploring the Fields of Vagrant Thought and Vagabond Beauty. Essays on Cultural Renewal.* Edinburgh: Polygon.
White, Kenneth (2006). *On the Atlantic Edge.* Dingwall: Sandstone.
White, Kenneth (2007), *Dialogue avec Deleuze.* Paris: Grasset.
White, Kenneth (2013). *La Route bleue.* Trans. Marie-Claude White. Marseilles: Le mot et le reste.
White, Kenneth (2016). *La Mer des lumières.* Paris: Grasset.
Wilk, Mariusz (2012). *Lotem gęsi.* Warsaw: Noir sur Blanc.
Williams, Raymond (1975). *The Country and the City.* St Albans: Paladin.

Williams, Raymond (1980). 'Ideas of Nature'. In: *Problems in Materialism and Culture*. London: Verso, pp. 67–85.

Wills, David (2008). *Dorsality: Thinking Back through Technology and Politics*. Minneapolis: University of Minnesota Press.

Wiskus, Jessica (2015). *The Rhythm of Thought: Art, Literature, and Music after Merleau-Ponty*. Chicago: University of Chicago Press.

Wolfe, Cary (2003). *Animal Rites: American Culture, the Discourse of Species and Posthumanist Theory*. Chicago and London: University of Chicago Press.

Wolfe, Cary (2010). *What Is Posthumanism?* Minneapolis: University of Minnesota Press.

Wolfreys, Julian (2002). *Victorian Hauntings: Spectrality, Gothic, the Uncanny, and Literature*. Basingstoke and New York: Palgrave.

Wolfreys, Julian (2019). 'Take the Weather with You: Robin Robertson's Northeast Atmospheric of Landscape and Self'. In: Monika Szuba and Julian Wolfreys, eds, *The Poetics of Space and Place in Scottish Literature*. New York: Palgrave Macmillan, pp. 306–27.

Wroe, Nicholas (2008). 'Love and Loss'. Interview with Robin Robertson. *The Guardian*. 28 Mar., <https://www.theguardian.com/books/2008/mar/29/featuresreviews.guardianreview16> (last accessed 1 Jan. 2018).

Young, Julian, and Kenneth Haynes (2002). 'Translators' Preface'. In: Martin Heidegger, *Off the Beaten Track*. Cambridge: Cambridge University Press, pp. ix–x.

Ziarek, Krzysztof (2013). *Language after Heidegger*. Bloomington: Indiana University Press.

Index

Abram, David, 3, 16, 52, 88, 99, 107
Agamben, Giorgio, 64, 85, 151
Alaimo, Stacey, 47
aletheia, 12, 125
Ammons, A. R., 9
Anthropocene, 2, 3, 6, 60, 61, 62, 93
Apollinaire, Guillaume, 86
Arendt, Hannah, 108
Augustine (of Hippo), 62, 75

Baker, Timothy C., 92
Baldwin, Thomas, 100
Bashō, Matsuo, 21, 52
Bate, Jonathan, 5, 7, 93
Bateson, Gregory, 60
Baudelaire, Charles, 123
Being, 2–5, 11–16, 23, 25, 26–30, 32, 35–6, 40–2, 44, 46, 47, 52, 53, 58, 60, 62, 64, 71, 73, 74, 77, 78–80, 85, 86, 87–8, 93–6, 99, 100, 102, 105, 107, 109, 111–14, 118, 125, 128, 130, 136, 138, 139, 143–5, 146, 147, 149, 150, 152, 154, 155
Bennett, Charles, 68
Bennett, Jane, 10, 26, 73, 122, 123, 132, 139, 142, 145, 150
Bentham, Jeremy, 85
Berry, Wendell, 9
Bigwood, Carol, 112
Bingen, Hildegard von, 62, 71
Borthwick, David, 59, 92, 93, 123, 124
Brewster, Scott, 59
Bristow, Tom, 5–6, 59, 60, 70, 93

Brown, George Mackay, 59, 60, 105
Buell, Lawrence, 6, 7, 9, 10, 51
Burnside, John, 1–24, 58–90, 116, 152, 153, 155, 157

Cataldi, Suzanne L., 16
Chardin, Jean-Baptiste-Siméon, 123
chiasm, 1–2, 14, 39, 47, 53, 69, 74, 79, 84, 86, 87, 88, 94, 95, 101, 103, 107, 134, 137, 156
Clark, Timothy, 7, 9
Cohen, Jeffrey Jerome, 26, 31, 43, 52
Collins, Brigid, 118
Collins, Lucy, 92, 104, 108
Craig, Cairns, 28, 30, 31, 43
Crawford, Robert, 63, 65, 75, 92, 102

Dante Alighieri, 135, 137
Darwin, Charles, 17
Dasein, 32, 46, 144
Davidson, Lynn, 98
Davidson, Peter, 25, 105, 115
Deleuze, Gilles, 10, 26, 36–42, 54, 81, 85
Derrida, Jacques, 10, 76, 80–5, 87, 89, 128, 133, 148, 154
Descartes, René, 27
Dunn, Douglas, 25
Duns Scotus, 30, 35, 42

Écart, 13
ecopoetics, ecopoetry, 2, 3, 5, 6, 7, 10, 17, 19, 93, 157
Elder, John, 9

Eliot, T. S., 30, 145
Erigena, John Scotus, 30, 35

Falconer, Rachel, 92, 93, 95,
Fazzini, Marco, 28, 64, 65, 80, 84
Finlay, Ian Hamilton, 60
flesh, 14–15, 47, 49, 53, 58–90, 109, 111, 112, 128–9, 130, 137, 140, 149, 150, 154
Fra Angelico, 123, 145
Fromm, Harold, 9

Gairn, Louisa, 17, 29, 30, 60, 92, 96, 116
Garrard, Greg, 9
Geist, 69, 94
Gelassenheit, 40
geopoetics, 20, 21, 25, 30–4, 36, 37
Gibbon, Lewis Grassic, 60
Gifford, Terry, 9, 27
Glotfelty, Cheryll, 9
Goodbody, Axel, 16
Goya, Francisco, 123
Graham, Lesley, 27, 28, 29, 30
Gregory, Eric, 91
Guattari, Félix, 10, 36–7, 40, 42, 54, 81, 85
Gunn, Neil, 30, 31, 59

Hakuin, 38
Hall, Dewey W., 8
Heidegger, Martin, 2, 6, 10, 11, 12, 13, 21, 22, 26, 30, 32, 37, 40, 46, 51, 58, 62, 65–6, 85, 87, 92–3, 95–7, 104, 111, 113, 116, 118, 125, 135, 156
Heise, Ursula K., 8
Heraclitus, 30
Herrick, William S., 16
Highland Clearances, 17
Hölderlin, Friedrich, 34
Holzwege, 37, 97, 135
Hume, David, 30, 42
Husserl, Edmund, 2, 11–15, 42, 47, 49, 70, 99, 106, 115, 116, 148
Hutchings, Kevin, 8, 20
Hutton, James, 29, 30

Ingold, Tim, 99, 104
Irigaray, Luce, 10, 79–80, 129

Jamet, Pierre, 27–8, 36
Jamie, Kathleen, 1–24, 59, 60, 61, 67, 91–121, 153, 155
Jeffers, Robinson, 21

Kairos, 72
Kant, Immanuel, 10, 73, 111, 123, 132
Kerridge, Richard, 9, 103
Köhler, Wolfgang, 100
Kroeber, Karl, 7, 9

landscape, 5, 11, 16, 18, 19, 21–3, 26, 28, 30, 31, 32, 37, 41, 43, 45, 46, 48, 49, 51, 54, 72, 91–121, 122–4, 127, 129, 135, 151, 154–5, 156, 157
Latour, Bruno, 5
Lebenswelt, 14, 47, 109
Leopold, Aldo, 33, 51
Levinas, Emmanuel, 10, 93, 130, 147, 151, 152, 156
Lichtungstehend, 37
Lilley, Deborah, 92, 103
Logos, 6, 14, 31–9, 45, 47, 52, 96

McCaig, Norman, 40
MacDiarmid, Hugh, 17, 27, 30, 31, 35, 43, 59, 103
Macfarlane, Robert, 111
McGonigal, James, 59, 66
Mackay, Peter, 93, 104
McKusick, James C., 7
Malabou, Catherine, 10, 137–8, 141, 147, 154
Malpas, Jeff, 10, 11, 26, 39
Marratto, Scott, 71
Marx, Leo, 9
Matthews, Steven, 59
Meeker, Joseph, 9
Merleau-Ponty, Maurice, 1–3, 11, 13–16, 18, 26, 35, 39, 41–2, 45, 46–9, 52, 53, 58, 61, 67, 69, 71, 73–4, 78, 80, 83, 85, 86–7, 94, 97, 99, 100, 101, 106, 111, 113, 116, 117, 118, 125, 128–9, 130,

131, 134–5, 145, 147, 149, 152, 155
Merwin, W. S., 9
Michaelis, Amanda G., 94
Miller, J. Hillis, 37
Mitchell, Andrew, 56
Montale, Eugenio, 123
Morgan, Edwin, 17, 25
Morton, Timothy, 5, 8, 17, 60, 61

Neruda, Pablo, 123
Nietzsche, Friedrich, 21, 30, 36, 143, 146
Nonnus, 123
Novalis, 34

Oerlemans, Onno, 7
Offenheit, 15, 39
other, 18, 47, 60, 62, 64, 65, 70, 76, 77, 80, 81, 83, 84, 86, 87, 93, 110–11, 130, 132, 142, 143, 145, 147–8, 150, 152, 153
Ovid, 123

Palgrave, Francis T., 6
Paterson, Don, 59, 89
Patton, Charley, 70
Petrarch, Francesco, 144
Phainesthai, 128
phenomenology, 1–5, 9–16, 18, 19, 20, 21, 23, 26, 28, 29, 41, 47, 52, 58, 60, 63, 69, 70, 73, 88, 95, 96, 99, 101, 103, 106, 128, 133, 136, 138, 154, 157
Picabia, Francis, 151
Pick, Anat, 151
pleroma, 87, 88
Pliny, 124
Pneuma, 79
Poïesis, 1, 3, 6, 13, 34, 35, 125, 134
Potkay, Adam, 96
Pound, Ezra, 30

Quain, Richard, 108, 109

Riach, Alan, 92, 111, 123
Rigby, Kate, 8, 9, 16
Rilke, Rainer Maria, 13, 123
Rimbaud, Arthur, 36

Robertson, Robin, 1–24, 59, 61, 66, 67, 71, 75, 116, 122–59
Roe, Nicholas, 6
Romanticism, 1, 3–8, 11, 21, 33, 34, 46, 63, 93, 126, 152
Rueckert, William, 9

Sammells, Neil, 9
Sampson, Fiona, 69
Scigaj, Leonard M., 9
Scott, Kirsty, 91
Sehnsucht, 70
Serres, Michel, 27, 40
Severin, Laura, 92
Shelley, Percy Bysshe, 7
Shepard, Paul, 88
Shepherd, Nan, 121
Simpson, Juliet, 112
Slovic, Scott, 9
Smith, Ben, 80
Smith, George Gregory, 16–17
Smith, Iain Crichton, 60
Snyder, Gary, 4, 21, 28, 30, 111
Soper, Kate, 9
Stevenson, Robert Louis, 17, 19, 35
Stilgoe, John, 37, 102
Stimmung, 51
stravaiging, 37–40
Sultzbach, Kelly Elizabeth, 16

Thoreau, Henry David, 4, 21, 38
Tiepolo, Giovanni Battista, 123
topology, 32
Tranströmer, Thomas, 123

Uexküll, Jakob von, 85
Umgang, 156
Umwelt, 11
Unheimlich, 102

Vasseleu, Cathryn, 39, 44, 45, 47, 48, 138
Viriditas, 71–2, 77

Warner, Alan, 17, 92
Weltgeist, 34
Weltlichkeit, 69, 94
Westling, Louise, 2, 11, 16, 49, 94, 101–2

Westphal, Bertrand, 34
Wheatley, David, 92, 97, 103–4
White, Kenneth, 1–24, 25–57, 59, 60, 61, 66, 67, 97, 117, 153, 157
Whitman, Walt, 30
Wild Being, 11, 14, 41, 47, 48, 54, 77, 78, 105, 110
Williams, Raymond, 9, 18
Williams, William Carlos, 30

Wills, David, 10, 128–30, 144, 155, 156
Wiskus, Jessica, 51
Wolfe, Cary, 15, 85
Wolfreys, Julian, 133, 134, 137
Wordsworth, William, 7

Xenophantes, 38

Yeats, W. B., 30

EU representative:
Easy Access System Europe
Mustamäe tee 50, 10621 Tallinn, Estonia
Gpsr.requests@easproject.com